KANT AND MODE
POLITICAL PHILOS(

In this book Katrin Flikschuh examines the relevance of Kant's
political thought to major issues and problems in contemporary
political philosophy. She advances and defends two principal claims:
that Kant's philosophy of Right endorses the role of metaphysics in
political thinking, in contrast to its generally hostile reception in the
field today, and that his account of political obligation is cosmopolitan in its inception, assigning priority to the global rather than the
domestic context. She shows how Kant's metaphysics of freedom as
a shared idea of practical reason underlies the cosmopolitan scope of
his theory of justice, and she concludes that, despite the revival of
'Kantianism' in contemporary thinking, his account of justice is in
many respects very different from dominant approaches in contemporary liberal theory. Her study will be of interest to political
philosophers, political theorists, and historians of ideas.

Katrin Flikschuh is Lecturer in Philosophy at the University of
Essex. She has published articles in *European Journal of Philosophy*, *Res
Publica*, *History of Political Thought* and *Global Society*.

KANT AND MODERN
POLITICAL PHILOSOPHY

KATRIN FLIKSCHUH

University of Essex

CAMBRIDGE
UNIVERSITY PRESS

CAMBRIDGE UNIVERSITY PRESS
Cambridge, New York, Melbourne, Madrid, Cape Town, Singapore, São Paulo

Cambridge University Press
The Edinburgh Building, Cambridge CB2 8RU, UK

Published in the United States of America by Cambridge University Press, New York

www.cambridge.org
Information on this title: www.cambridge.org/9780521662376

First published 2000
This digitally printed version 2008

A catalogue record for this publication is available from the British Library

Library of Congress Cataloguing in Publication data
Flikschuh, Katrin.
Kant and modern political philosophy / Katrin Flikschuh.
p.   cm.
Includes bibliographical references and index.
ISBN 0 521 66237 0
1. Kant, Immanuel, 1724–1804 – Contributions in political science.
2. Political science – Philosophy.   I. Title.
JC181.K4F585   2000
320'.01 – dc21   99–088503

ISBN 978-0-521-66237-6 hardback
ISBN 978-0-521-07302-8 paperback

Contents

Acknowledgements

The project of this book has been with me during teaching positions held at three different departments: the Department of Government at the University of Manchester, the Department of Philosophy at the University of Bristol, and my present abode, the Department of Philosophy at the University of Essex. I would like to express my thanks and appreciation for the academic, intellectual, and other support given me by my colleagues in all these departments. Various people have read and offered valuable comments on drafts of individual chapters throughout. They include Nick Bunnin, Fiona Hughes, Onora O'Neill, Thomas Pogge, Tom Sorell, Hillel Steiner, Roger Sullivan, Christien van den Aanker, Ursula Vogel, Ken Westphal, and Howard Williams. My thanks to them all. My particular thanks go to Bob Goodin for his unceasing academic advice and support since my days as an undergraduate student of political philosophy, and to Onora O'Neill, whom I was privileged to have as supervisor of the doctoral thesis of which the present book is a successor, and from whom I have learned more about Kant's philosophy than I could have done from anyone else. Many thanks also to my editor, Hilary Gaskin, for her efficient and friendly assistance throughout. Finally, I would like to thank my parents, Winfried and Elizabeth Flikschuh, and especially my partner, Diarmuid Costello, without whom this book would almost certainly never have been completed. Last, but not least, my thanks go to our little son, Joschka, who kindly postponed his arrival in the world until after the completion of the manuscript.

As I mention in the Introduction, many of the ideas in this book were originally conceived during time spent in West Africa, especially in Burkina Faso and Ghana. Africa has long had a bad reputation for its political turbulence, humanitarian

vii

disasters, and chronic underdevelopment. At least on a personal level, my experience of Africa does not match this picture: despite the innumerable and seemingly never-ending hardships endured by the individuals and their families I met, their warmth, their grace, their hospitality, and their sheer perseverance have left me with an enduring impression of what we might mean when we speak of human dignity. This book is dedicated to them.

Kant's works and abbreviations

Major works:
The Critique of Pure Reason (CPR)
Groundwork of the Metaphysics of Morals (Groundwork)
The Critique of Practical Reason (CprR)
The Metaphysics of Morals (MM)
MM, Part 1: *The Metaphysical Elements of Justice (Rechtslehre)*
MM, Part 2: *The Metaphysical Elements of Virtue (Tugendlehre)*
Rechtslehre (RL)
Tugendlehre (TL)

Political and historical essays:
Idea for a Universal History with a Cosmopolitan Purpose (Universal History)
On the Conjectural Beginnings of Human History (Conjectural Beginnings)
An Answer to the Question: What is Enlightenment? (Enlightenment)
On the Common Saying: 'This may be true in theory but it does not apply in practice' (Theory and Practice)
Towards Perpetual Peace (Perpetual Peace)

Translations used:
The Critique of Pure Reason, trans. Norman Kemp Smith, London, Macmillan, 1933, second impression (1990 reprint).
Groundwork of the Metaphysics of Morals, trans. H. J. Paton, New York, Harper Torchbooks, 1964.
The Critique of Practical Reason, trans. Lewis White Beck, New York, Macmillan, 1956 (1993 reprint).
The Metaphysics of Morals (Parts 1 and 2), trans. Mary Gregor, Cambridge University Press, 1991.
Kant's Political Writings, trans. H. B. Nisbet, edited by Hans Reiss, Cambridge University Press, 1970.

Page references to Kant's works in the footnotes refer to the relevant volumes of the Prussian Academy edition, and are reprinted in the margins of all translations used, with the exception of Reiss, ed., *Kant's Political Writings*. References to the *Critique of Pure Reason* will be to the pagination of the first and second editions, indicated by the letters 'A' and 'B' respectively.

Unless stated otherwise, all translations from German of secondary literature are my own.

Introduction

The ideas behind this book initially emerged in 1987, when I was walking through the Sahel zone of Burkina Faso – though I did not then know that I was going to write a book on Kant's political philosophy. In fact, the Sahelian undertaking was rather fortuitous. When I arrived at Ouagadougou airport my luggage had been lost in transit. Although airport staff assured me that I would have it back within a week, it never showed up again. The loss turned out to be a good thing, however, in so far as it gave me the confidence to set out on the road bound northwards, towards Niger. The Sahel was not what I had expected. I had imagined something more like a 'proper' desert. The Sahel is a semi-arid transitional region between savannah and desert. It consists of stony ground and low-growing, thorny shrubs with a few stunted trees in-between and the odd enormous baobab-tree here and there. There is the occasional mount that rises abruptly from the ground, but for the most part the Sahel is flat, vast, hot, and silent. At first I was reluctant to ask people's help, but I quickly realised that in an environment like this everyone depends on the co-operation of everyone else. My memory of overnight stays is of an unquestioning hospitality that always followed the same basic pattern: first you were welcomed with a drink of water, then sat down and questioned about your 'mission', and eventually led outdoors to bathe over a bucket of water. Finally you were invited to your evening meal, usually alone, because others should not watch you eat. I was amazed by the grace and sophistication of the people, whose survival within the conditions around them seemed to me to depend on a delicate balancing act between themselves and nature.

It might seem inappropriate to begin a book on Kant's political philosophy by recounting travel anecdotes. However, there are three aspects about my experience of the Sahel that have shaped my reading of the *Rechtslehre*. The first concerns the importance of the constraints of nature in relation to human agency. The second revolves around the notion of human finitude and the unavoidable interdependence between individuals as agents. The third aspect is less tangible, and concerns the role of metaphysics in political thinking. All three themes – the constraints of nature, human finitude, and the role of metaphysics – form focal points of the ensuing interpretation of the *Rechtslehre*. To these, I should add a fourth, namely the idea of freedom. Unsurprisingly, the idea of freedom is central to Kant's political philosophy. Unsurprising, not only because Kant was an Enlightenment thinker for whom the idea of human freedom formed the 'keystone' of his entire critical philosophy, but also because the idea of freedom is given special emphasis in the current reception of Kant within liberal political philosophy. After years of neglect, Kant now ranks among – or even outranks – other great thinkers of the liberal tradition, such as Hobbes, Locke, Rousseau, and John Stuart Mill. Within the Anglo-American world, the assimilation of Kant into mainstream liberalism is due almost entirely to John Rawls' *Theory of Justice*.[1] In Germany, and perhaps within the continental tradition more generally, Kant's re-entry into the liberal political fold has been less dramatic because the neglect was never complete, if only for historical reasons. Kant has always had a place in the social and political writings of Jürgen Habermas, for example (though Habermas' assessment of Kant's political philosophy has arguably shifted over the years). Besides, the Kantian idea of the *Rechtsstaat* is well entrenched within the canons of liberal thinking in Germany.

It is a central claim of this book that the absorption of Kant's political thought into contemporary liberalism is partial at best. In many respects, Kant's departures from contemporary liberalism are more interesting philosophically and more instructive politically than are the points of convergence between them. The idea of freedom is a case in point. It is true that Rawls' Kantian conception of the free and equal moral person has had a major impact on the traditional liberal understanding of individual freedom, especially regarding its function in relation to political justification. If classical

---

[1] John Rawls, *A Theory of Justice* (Oxford University Press, 1973).

liberalism tended to view individual freedom as a natural right of each against each to unconstrained choice and action, Rawls' use of Kant affirms a strong connection between freedom, practical reasoning, and political justification (I shall clarify what I mean by 'classical liberalism' and its relation to contemporary liberalism in chapter 1). Liberals now think of individual freedom as a moral capacity rather than as a natural right; instead of construing it narrowly in terms of the rationality of individual choice, individual freedom is regarded as a prerequisite to possible social co-operation between individuals. This shift from a predominantly antagonistic, political conception of freedom to a predominantly co-operative, moral account is Kantian up to a point. Two qualifications are, however, in order. The first is that the current absorption of Kant into mainstream liberalism is based almost exclusively on Kant's *ethical* writings, i.e. on the *Groundwork* and, to a lesser extent, on *CprR*. Kant's political writings, especially the *Rechtslehre*, continue to be neglected by contemporary liberals. Secondly, current receptions of Kant are premised on an explicit rejection of Kant's practical metaphysics. The emphasis is on Kantian moral philosophy without Kantian metaphysics.

Although there is nothing wrong in principle with adopting or adapting aspects of Kant's philosophy while neglecting or rejecting others, doing so can encourage a distorted perception both of Kant's political thought and of contemporary liberalism's relation to it. One consequence of the focus on Kant's moral conception of freedom to the exclusion of his account of political freedom, is the resulting tension within current liberalism between what are, in effect, two incompatible theories of freedom. This can be illustrated with reference to Rawls' two principles of justice as fairness. Rawls' specifications of his first principle of justice, which is concerned with the equal standing of individuals as citizens, broadly coincide with what he characterises as his Kantian conception of the moral person. However, the second principle, which is concerned with distributive justice, is premised on an account of free agency and of the rationality of individual choice that is deeply un-Kantian. While the moral conception of the person as free and equal adopts a broadly Kantian view of reasonableness and public deliberation, at least within the confines of the individual state,[2] the account of

---

[2] For a critique of the limited scope of Rawls' Kantianism, see Onora O'Neill, 'Political

economic freedom that drives the difference principle accepts the motivational assumptions of standard economic theory, which are 'Hobbesian' in their basic orientation.[3] The tension between these two motivational aspects of Rawls theory – one moral the other self-interested – has often been noted. The question here is whether a Kantian conception of moral freedom can sustain Hobbesian assumptions about economic freedom. As will become evident in subsequent chapters, I believe that the answer to this has to be 'no'. In that case, much liberal theorising about social and distributive justice today might be less Kantian than it takes itself to be.

The consequences of neglecting Kant's political and economic conception of individual freedom of choice and action bring me to the second point mentioned, i.e. the rejection of Kantian metaphysics. Of course, this is nothing new. Admiration for Kant's moral theory has always been tempered by discomfort regarding its underlying metaphysical presuppositions. Again, it is the idea of freedom as an idea of pure practical reason which is responsible for the discomfort felt. Kant's distinction between the noumenal and the phenomenal standpoints of practical reasoning in his moral philosophy has met the same degree of resistance as his distinction between appearances and things-in-themselves in his theory of knowledge. Indeed, Kant's transcendental idealism has long had the effect on many philosophers that a red rag is said to have on a bull. But the current liberal rejection of metaphysics is more general and not directed at Kant's transcendental idealism exclusively. In contrast to the revival of interest in metaphysics within many other branches of contemporary philosophy, its rejection within political philosophy has, if anything, intensified. I believe this to be mistaken, not only with regard to Kant's political thought, but also with regard to the tasks of political philosophy more generally. One reason why I believe the hostility towards metaphysics mistaken is indicated in the noted tension within contemporary liberalism between two

Liberalism and Public Reason: A Critical Notice of John Rawls, *Political Liberalism*', *The Philosophical Review*, 106 (1997), 411–28.

[3] I use the term 'Hobbesian' hesitantly, meaning to refer to the current reception of Hobbes' political thought rather than to Hobbes himself. Like Kant, Hobbes' thought is often interpreted in a more one-sided manner than it arguably deserves to be. Although contemporary rational choice and decision-making theory takes itself to be departing from Hobbesian assumptions about individual agents' motivations, its psychologistic assumptions about agents' desire-pursuit and satisfaction are arguably just as much influenced by Benthamite utilitarianism as by Hobbes' materialist metaphysics.

incompatible conceptions of freedom. If Kantian moral freedom is incompatible with, say, Hobbesian assumptions about the individual rationality of political and economic choice, one should ask what makes it so. If aspects of two different theories cannot be combined at will, this suggests that each forms part of a wider theoretical framework which constrains it in certain respects such that it cannot, without distortion, be lifted from that framework. The incompatibility of Kantian moral freedom with Hobbesian political and economic freedom suggests that the former is constrained by underlying assumptions and presuppositions not recognised by the latter, which is therefore not constrained by them. This line of reasoning might amount to a negative defence of metaphysics as unavoidable. Anyone engaged in theory-building is constrained to depart from *some* assumptions and presuppositions about their object of inquiry without which theory-building could not get off the ground, and commitment to which unavoidably constrains what can coherently be included in the theory. To that extent, even those who disavow metaphysics cannot avoid helping themselves to some metaphysical assumptions, at least in the initial stages of theory-building. A positive formulation of essentially the same line of defence is to say not just that metaphysical assumptions are unavoidable, but that they are also indispensable. On this positive line of defence, metaphysics *facilitates* coherent theorising about, for example, the problem of justice. It does so by offering an underlying conceptual and normative framework within the constraints of which consistent practical theorising can proceed.

This book adopts the positive line of defence: one of the features that sets Kant's political philosophy apart from contemporary liberalism is his explicit endorsement of metaphysics. However, I shall avoid both the complexities of transcendental idealism as well as its contested status by adopting the more general, though recognisably Kantian, conception of metaphysics recently offered by Stephan Körner in terms of the notion of a 'categorial framework'.[4] Körner's notion of a categorial framework enables me to emphasise those aspects of Kant's metaphysics that are central to his political philosophy without committing me to an unqualified endorsement of transcendental idealism. In sum, chapter 1 introduces and develops Körner's notion of a categorial framework in relation to political

---

[4] Stephan Körner, *Metaphysics: Its Structure and Function* (Cambridge University Press, 1984).

thinking in general. Chapter 2 applies this notion to Kant's metaphysics of freedom as an idea of pure practical reason. Chapter 3
examines the implications of Kant's general metaphysics of freedom
for his account of political freedom. Here I shall do no more than
refer back to the constraints of nature and to the notion of human
finitude, which I mentioned above in recounting my Sahelian
experience. Kant's metaphysics of justice is based on the initial
juxtaposition between the claims to freedom and the constraints of
nature, and their eventual reconciliation by means of an act of
practical political judgement which reflects Kant's positive conception of human finitude. In other words, the idea of freedom, the
constraints of nature, and a particular conception of human finitude
in relation to practical political reasoning inform the underlying
categorial framework of Kant's *Rechtslehre*. It is the presence of this
underlying categorial or metaphysical framework which shapes
Kant's political thought and renders it, ultimately, very different
from that of contemporary liberalism.

2 THE 'RECHTSLEHRE'

The foregoing remarks should have given some indication of the
reasons behind the title of the present book, *Kant and Modern Political
Philosophy*. My engagement with Kant's *Rechtslehre* in the following
chapters is influenced by what strikes me as a central failing of
contemporary liberalism, namely its refusal to take seriously the
indispensable and positive role of metaphysics in political thinking. I
have indicated some of the negative practical implications of this
anti-metaphysical attitude with reference to Kant's conception of
freedom as an idea of pure practical reason, which is different from,
and arguably incompatible with, more traditional accounts of
individuals' natural right to freedom. In a sense, the line of argument
pursued in the first three chapters of the book is preparatory to the
central claims advanced and defended in the final three chapters
concerning the relation between freedom, individual property rights,
and political obligation. (More properly, chapters 1 and 2 are
preparatory: they deal with the current reception of Kantian
metaphysics in contemporary liberalism and with Kant's metaphysics of freedom in *CPR* respectively. They do not touch on the
Rechtslehre directly. Chapter 3 is transitional: it focuses on the contrast
between Kant's account of moral freedom in his ethical writings and

his conception of political freedom in the *Rechtslehre*.) That much 'stage-setting' may come as a disappointment to readers who might have expected a more comprehensive treatment of the many themes and topics to be found in Kant's late political work. My approach to the *Rechtslehre* is highly selective: I focus almost exclusively on divisions 1 and 2 of Section I, which is entitled 'On Private Right'. I bypass entirely the first division of Section II, which is entitled 'On Public Right', and which deals with the divisions of governmental authority within individual states. On the other hand, division 3 of Section II, which deals with 'cosmopolitan Right', is of great importance to the line of interpretation pursued in this book.

One obvious reason for this selective approach is space. The *Rechtslehre* is not a thick book – in fact, it is quite thin – but it is a rich and complex work. Its argument is also extremely obscure, a point I shall return to in a moment. In any case, reasons of space rule out a more inclusive treatment of the text. The second reason is choice: it actually seems to me preferable to cover less rather than more, but to cover it more thoroughly. This is partly because of my conviction that it is impossible to appreciate the distinctiveness of Kant's political thought without at least some awareness of the distinctiveness of his philosophical thinking in general – hence the necessity of a certain amount of preliminary stage-setting. There are a number of commentaries on the *Rechtslehre* that offer surveys of Kant's political thought. Many of these are highly informative as introductions to Kant's political writings, and as historical interpretations that locate Kant's thought within the traditions of Western political theory. However, many also tend to be quite state centred in their outlook; they tend to spend most of their time on Kant's account of the internal political organisation of the individual state. Part of the reason for this has to do with the obscurity of the argument in Section I, 'On Private Right', which has struck many readers over the last two hundred years as misguided and confused. The neglect of Kant's cosmopolitanism is more difficult to explain, though it may be due to historical reasons: the problem of global justice has never been, until recently, an important issue in Western political theory. This brings me to the third reason for my selective approach, which is significance. Although I focus on only a few sections in the *Rechtslehre*, I claim to be focusing on the most significant ones. The section on cosmopolitan Right is significant for obvious, political reasons – though again, contemporary mainstream liberalism often shows itself to be strangely myopic on that count. The section on Private Right, and especially Kant's property argument, is significant for exegetical reasons, and here I need to say a little more about the reasons for the general neglect, until recently, of the *Rechtslehre* as Kant's last major philosophical work.

I have mentioned twice now the obscurity of Kant's line of argument in the *Rechtslehre*, especially as regards Section I, 'On Private Right'. That obscurity expresses itself at several levels. Certainly the argument is obscure in part because of the complexity of the subject-matter it deals with – a complexity which is not helped by Kant's austere, almost clipped style of presentation that makes his better-known major works seem almost discursive by comparison. However, complexity of subject-matter forms the smaller part of possible explanations. In fact, the originally published text has struck generations of Kant scholars not only as obscure, but also as down-right confused. Particularly in the section pertaining to the so-called 'deduction' of the concept of rightful possession, confusion reigns, revealing a lack of logical sequence between individual paragraphs, the inclusion of material irrelevant to the subject-matter at hand, even the complete absence of any argument which might so much as approximate to a deduction. In short, Kant's manner of argument has struck many a patient reader as frustratingly undisciplined, confused – even as incoherent. The famous 'senility thesis', and the consequent virtually complete neglect of the *Rechtslehre*, have their origins in these textual distortions and resulting sense of frustration. The reason why the text was 'spoilt', so the growing general consensus, was because of Kant's waning intellectual powers and increasing senility. Unfortunately, the senility thesis not only gave an explanation for the state of the text; it also offered a reason for ignoring Kant's argument in it.

Despite individual attempts at rehabilitation,[5] the senility thesis stuck for a long time, gaining endorsement from specialists in Kant's political philosophy.[6] It is only during the last couple of decades, which have seen an astounding revival of interest in the *Rechtslehre*, that alternative explanations to the senility thesis began to be sought

---

[5] See especially Gerhard Buchda, 'Das Privatrecht Immanuel Kants. Ein Beitrag zur Geschichte und zum System des Naturrechts' (Unpublished dissertation, Jena, 1929).

[6] See, for example, Christian Ritter, *Der Rechtsgedanke Kants nach den frühen Quellen* (Frankfurt, 1971); also Hannah Arendt, *Lectures on Kant's Political Philosophy*, Ronald Beiner, ed. (University of Chicago Press, 1982), 7–8.

to explain the sorry state of the text. One influential if not uncontentious such alternative was advanced by Bernd Ludwig in his 1986 revised edition of the *Rechtslehre*.[7] According to Ludwig, the textual distortions are not a reflection of Kant's state of mental health at the time of writing, but are the product of editorial errors at the printing stage, over which Kant had no control. On Ludwig's thesis, it is the text's editor and its printers who bear principal responsibility for the work's poor textual organisation. There is no space to discuss the plausibility of Ludwig's (well-researched) historical claims.[8] The important point in the present context is that Ludwig combined his historical findings with his philosophical thesis that Kant's 'Postulate of Practical Reason with Regard to Right' in §2 of Section I constitutes the 'critical novum' of the *Rechtslehre*: it offers an entirely new approach to the problem of individual property rights. The result of this claim was to shift the section on property rights from near oblivion to centre stage. The interpretation of Kant's justification of individual property rights in chapter 4 of the present book is based on Ludwig's relocation of §2 (the original place of the postulate) into §6 (the place of the missing deduction) in his revised edition of Kant's *Rechtslehre*.[9] However, my interpretation goes beyond that of Ludwig in claiming a direct connection between Kant's justification of individual property rights and his cosmopolitan conception of individuals' ensuing obligations of justice. Thus, while chapter 4 focuses on the problem of individuals' claims to property rights as the ground of political obligation, chapter 5 argues that the obligations of justice themselves are cosmopolitan in scope, and that they are so as a direct consequence of Kant's particular approach to property rights. Chapter 6, finally, examines some of the implications of Kant's metaphysical and cosmopolitan conception of Right for contemporary thinking about global justice, focusing on global distributive justice in particular.

---

[7] Bernd Ludwig, ed., Immanuel Kant, *Metaphysische Anfangsgründe der Rechtslehre* (Hamburg, Felix Meiner Verlag, 1986).

[8] But see Bernd Ludwig, *Kants Rechtslehre*, especially the contribution on the history of Kant's text by Werner Stark (Hamburg, Felix Meiner Verlag, 1988), 7–28.

[9] In addition to the relocation of §2, subsections 4–8 of the original §6 are omitted in accordance with the findings of Buchda (see footnote 5). Interested readers may wish to compare Part I of Mary Gregor's 1991 translation of the *Metaphysics of Morals* (Cambridge University Press), which is based on the originally published text, with her 1996 translation of the *Metaphysical Elements of Justice* (Cambridge University Press), which follows Ludwig's revised edition.

3 KANTIAN TERMINOLOGY

Every book has an intended primary audience. Readers will probably suspect by now that in this regard the present book falls between two stools: political theorists and philosophers on the one hand, and Kant scholars on the other. This is indeed the case, and the danger of such an approach is that one manages to satisfy neither side. One side may feel that the book focuses too heavily on detailed textual exposition which, though perhaps of interest to Kant scholars, has no bearing on practical political problems. Those on the other side may find textual exposition insufficiently detailed to qualify as a convincing account of what Kant said and meant when and where. Again, those on one side may find themselves overburdened with unfamiliar Kantian terminology, while those on the other side may feel irritated by the fact that familiar Kantian terms and ideas are being laboured over at unnecessary length.

I am aware of these difficulties. If I could have written a different book, I might have done so. However, the present book is virtually designed to fall between two stools. As I said, my own reading of the *Rechtslehre* is influenced by issues in current political philosophy whose salience for political thinking seems to me ignored, but which yet do make Kant's work especially relevant today. Moreover, despite the breath-taking flurry of revived interest in the *Rechtslehre* among Kant scholars, Kant's political work continues to be passed over even by political philosophers who profess a version of Kantian liberalism. I think the latter has much to do with the apparent inaccessibility of the text, including its unusual approach to the question of political justification when compared with the more obviously classical texts in Western political theory. It is a principal aim of this book to reduce this feeling of the text's remoteness from contemporary concerns by relating the former explicitly to the latter, and by showing that the text does, in fact, speak to contemporary concerns.

I have tried, so far as possible, to avoid heavy use of technical Kantian terminology. Of course, this is not entirely avoidable, and I have helped myself without special explanation to widely familiar Kantian terms, such as his conception of the 'a priori validity' of principles of 'pure practical reason'. While the precise meaning of these terms is itself a subject of inquiry among Kant scholars, most readers will associate the a priori status of principles of pure practical reason with Kant's claim of their independence from contingently given empirical considerations, their groundedness in rational beings' capacity for reason, and hence their universal validity and authority for all finite rational beings as such. Other Kantian terms, such as 'intelligible possession', 'phenomenal possession', or 'the postulate of practical reason with regard to Right', are explained contextually with reference to the argument in the *Rechtslehre* rather than by way of cross-referencing with Kant's other works. My hope is that, in keeping special terminology to a necessary minimum, those less familiar with Kant's philosophy will not feel put off his political thought.

There is one terminological convention which I should clarify at the outset, namely the capitalisation of 'the concept of Right' instead of its replacement with the more familiar 'concept of justice'. The German term *Recht* is notoriously difficult to translate into English, not least because, in contrast to the Anglo-American tradition, the philosophy of law in Germany is shaped by Roman law rather than by common law. The term *Recht* has connotations of a mathematical exactitude missing from the common-law tradition, with its reliance on precedent and interpretation. *Recht* is that which gives each their due (which can be determined with exactitude) – it is fully captured neither by *Gesetz*, which in common parlance refers to positive law, nor by *Gerechtigkeit*, which is more or less synonymous with justice (and usually associated with social justice). In contrast to *Gesetz* or *Gerechtigkeit*, both of which are amenable to contextual modification, the exactitude of *Recht* gives it a claim to context-independent, a priori validity. Since the claim to a priori validity distinguishes Kant's *Rechtsbegriff* from current conceptions of justice, I follow Mary Gregor's convention of translating *Recht* as *Right* rather than as justice. Finally, while I use Right when referring to the 'concept of Right', or to 'principles of Right', 'right' and 'rights' refer to individuals' particular rights as derived from the concept of Right.

CHAPTER I

Kantian metaphysics in contemporary liberalism

Human reason has this peculiar fate that in one species of its knowledge it is burdened by questions which, as prescribed by the very nature of reason itself, it is not able to ignore, but which, as transcending all its powers, it is also not able to answer.

(*CPR*, Avii)

I INTRODUCTION

This chapter pursues two principal aims. The first is to assess the recent reception of metaphysics, especially of 'Kantian metaphysics', in contemporary liberalism. The second aim is to sketch a metaphysical framework for analysing Kant's account of political obligation in the *Rechtslehre*. As regards the first aim, I focus on the liberal theories of John Rawls[1] and Jürgen Habermas.[2] Not only are these two thinkers dominant figures in current liberal thinking – but their approaches to justice and political justification are also deeply influenced by Kant, albeit in very different ways. However, I do not offer a detailed discussion of their respective theories; my intention is merely to consider their views on the role of metaphysics in political thinking.

With regard to the second aim of this chapter, I draw on Stephan Körner's recent analysis of the structure and function of metaphysics in general.[3] In adapting Körner's analysis to the political context I first contrast his account of metaphysics in terms of a person's categorial framework with Rawls' most recent view of it as the expression of an individual's private beliefs about the world. I then

---

[1] Rawls, *A Theory of Justice*. See also, more recently, Rawls' *Political Liberalism* (New York, Columbia University Press, 1993).
[2] Jürgen Habermas, *Faktizität und Geltung* (Frankfurt, Suhrkamp, 1992).
[3] Körner, *Metaphysics: Its Structure and Function*.

consider the way in which metaphysics understood as a categorial framework avoids some of the difficulties that arise from the traditional juxtaposition between immanence and transcendence, which informs the recent exchange on metaphysics between Habermas and Dieter Henrich.[4]

In developing the notion of a categorial framework through an analysis of the two mentioned liberal perspectives, I hope to come away with a defensible outline of a possible approach to Kant's metaphysics. This will provide some unifying structure to the exegetical arguments advanced in subsequent chapters. Without being unduly anticipatory, the general idea is to structure the analysis of Kant's theory of justice around the relation between two central concepts or ideas that inform his philosophical thinking as a whole. These are the concept of nature, on the one hand, and the idea of freedom, on the other. According to Kant, the reconciliation between the causality of nature and the idea of human freedom forms the 'keystone' to his entire critical philosophy; it is therefore central also to an adequate understanding of his philosophy of Right. I say more about this towards the end of the chapter. However, the bulk of the present chapter is devoted not to Kant's metaphysics itself, but to liberal receptions of it. I begin with an overview of current views on the topic, including some remarks on the communitarian position, whose influence on Rawls has been considerable. I then offer more detailed analyses of Rawls' 'strategy of avoidance', and of Habermas' postmetaphysical critique respectively.

2 DIVERGENT CONCEPTIONS OF 'KANTIAN METAPHYSICS'

As I said in the introductory chapter, despite the renewed interest in metaphysics in other branches of philosophy, its rejection in political philosophy continues more or less unabated. Within liberal circles, scepticism towards metaphysics has been given renewed impetus through Rawls' thesis of the fact of pluralism. According to this thesis, the prevalence of divergent *individual* conceptions of the good in liberal societies renders unavailable a comprehensive conception of the *social* good, where comprehensiveness is taken to include public commitment to the particular metaphysical presuppositions

---

[4] Dieter Henrich, 'Was ist Metaphysik — was Moderne? Zwölf Thesen Gegen Habermas' in *Konzepte* (Frankfurt, Suhrkamp, 1987), 11–39; and Jürgen Habermas, *Nachmetaphysisches Denken* (Frankfurt, Suhrkamp, 1992), 11–60.

that support the account of the good in question. Since under conditions of pluralism not all individuals do or can endorse the same such presuppositions, metaphysics has lost its justificatory force in mature liberal societies.

The fact of pluralism has become a frequently cited reason for avoiding metaphysics in political thinking. At the same time, it is not evident whether, even accepting the fact of pluralism as a social thesis about current conditions in mature liberal societies, that fact taken by itself constitutes a sufficient reason for this avoidance. On the face of it, one might equally plausibly suggest that the fact of pluralism makes all the more urgent philosophical inquiry into metaphysical presuppositions sufficiently abstract in their conception to claim general validity. Arguably, therefore, liberal suspicions of metaphysics cut deeper, such that they would prevail even in the absence of the pluralism thesis. I here set aside the fact of pluralism to consider some of those deeper reasons for the general anti-metaphysical attitude that prevails in current liberal and communitarian thinking alike. For the purpose of discussion I draw a further distinction between 'classical liberals' and 'critical liberals'.

By classical liberalism I mean the political tradition as it was shaped initially by classical social contract theory, in particular by the theories of Hobbes, Locke, and Rousseau, as well as by British empiricism, including that of non-contractarian thinkers like Hume, and John Stuart Mill. Although the later Rawls has aligned himself closer to the tradition of American pragmatism, he remains the best-known representative of classical contractarian liberalism today. Of course, classical liberalism possesses its own internal division between a rights-based contractarianism and a teleologically or-iented utilitarianism. Despite Rawls' initial attempts to reconcile these two traditions of liberalism, the differences between them remain deep and often decisive. Since it is predominantly con-tractarians who claim a special affinity with Kant's practical phil-osophy, I here focus on the contractarian branch within classical liberalism.

The intellectual background of communitarianism is more diverse. Communitarian writers draw from the philosophies of Aristotle, Hegel, and the later Wittgenstein.[5] What unites them is a

---

[5] For a good overview of different communitarian perspectives, see Stephen Mulhall and Adam Swift, *Liberals and Communitarians* (Oxford, Basil Blackwell, 1992).

common aversion against philosophical abstraction and 'grand theorising'. Against this, communitarians emphasise attention to detail, contextual sensitivity, and appreciation of social and cultural diversity. By and large, communitarianism is a 'negative philosophy', united more by a general rejection of liberal thinking than by a positively formulated political project. Communitarians' philosophical convictions lie in the resolve to *resist* the temptations of abstract analyses and theory construction rather than in an endeavour to offer alternative schemes of social and political justice.[6]

Finally, there is critical liberalism. Although more influential in continental Europe, it offers an interesting counterpart to classical liberalism's reception of Kantian metaphysics. As its name suggests, critical liberalism developed out of Critical Theory, drawing from Karl Marx, Max Weber, Theodor Adorno, and Max Horkheimer, among others. To these, critical liberalism adds the idea of the *Rechtsstaat*, which links it back to the political philosophy of Kant. The most prominent proponent of critical liberalism is Habermas, who defends a postmetaphysical standpoint, and whose discourse ethical approach to political legitimation through democratic consensus is designed to meet the requirements of mature liberal postmetaphysical societies.

This rough classification of current perspectives within political philosophy is not exhaustive. Nor is it meant to suggest that crossfertilisation among them is non-existent: there are liberal communitarians,[7] communitarian liberals,[8] and classical liberals with sympathies for critical liberalism.[9] However, the three perspectives do share a common preoccupation with metaphysics, and they delimit their perceptions of themselves and of each other to a considerable extent in terms of their respective attitudes towards Kantian metaphysics. Of the three positions, the attitude of classical liberalism is perhaps the most ambivalent. Throughout the twentieth century, but especially since the end of the Second World War, classical liberalism has found itself attracted to Kant's universalistic moral theory, especially to terms and principles within that theory which resonate

---

[6] But see Michael Walzer, *Spheres of Justice. A Defence of Pluralism and Equality* (Oxford, Basil Blackwell, 1983).
[7] Joseph Raz, *The Morality of Freedom* (Oxford, Clarendon Press, 1986).
[8] Michael Walzer, *Thick and Thin. Moral Argument at Home and Abroad* (Notre Dame, Indiana, University of Notre Dame Press, 1994).
[9] Kenneth Baynes, *The Normative Grounds of Social Criticism: Kant, Rawls, and Habermas* (New York, State University of New York Press, 1992).

with classical liberalism's own moral vocabulary. Despite the frequently attested tension between supposedly authoritarian and liberal strands in Kant's political writings,[10] classical liberalism has also been keen to include Kant among the gallery of great contractarian thinkers who form part of its ancestry. However, the principal focus has been on Kant's *moral* philosophy, and on how it might enrich the conventional liberal–contractarian framework. Parallels have routinely been drawn between Lockean individual rights and Kantian respect for persons, for example, or between Millian autonomy as individual self-determination and Kantian autonomy as moral self-legislation. The more recent association between Kant and Hume may seem intuitively less obvious. Rawls' *Theory of Justice* combines a common sensible Hume with a common sensibilised Kant in the ideal conception of the person who possesses both a *sense* of justice and an *idea* of freedom. On the face of it, this is a precarious marriage between Hume as an anti-metaphysician *par excellence*, and Kant as a defender of a practically oriented metaphysics that grows in part from Kant's critical response to Humean epistemological scepticism. Yet the combination reflects a widely held assumption among proponents of classical liberalism, that the substantive content of Kant's moral theory can be divorced from its metaphysical underpinnings. Replacing Kant's metaphysical premises with more modest empiricist assumptions will yield, so the expectation, a more robust Kantianism which will constitute an improvement on Kant's theory.

Modesty and robustness characterise classical liberalism's empiricist commitments and its resulting attitude towards metaphysics. A moral theory is modest in so far as it does not aim to go beyond the bounds of common sense but takes as the basis of its moral prescriptions a generalised account of human nature gleaned from careful observation of actual human behaviour. Such a modest moral theory is robust in so far as its common-sense approach is likely to elicit wider public assent, ensuring a higher degree of practical success than metaphysically loaded alternatives. This makes

---

[10] See Hella Mandt, 'Historisch-politische Traditionselemente im politischen Denken Kants' in Zwi Batscha, ed., *Materialien zu Kants Rechtsphilosophie* (Frankfurt, Suhrkamp, 1976), 292–330; also Howard Williams, *Kant's Political Philosophy* (Oxford University Press, 1983). For a different view see Reinhardt Brandt, 'Die politische Institution bei Kant' in Gerhard Göhler, ed., *Politische Institutionen in Gesellschaftlichem Umbruch* (Opladen, Westdeutscher Verlag, 1990), 335–57.

metaphysical thinking immodest and outlandish by implication. Claims about the a priori status of moral principles, about their subject-independent validity, or about their deducibility from first principles, are rejected on the grounds that such claims, in going beyond what can be sensibly experienced, inevitably involve some appeal to a supersensible world of true ideas in which these purported moral truths are grounded. Since going beyond that which can be sensibly experienced is illicit, metaphysics is philosophically disreputable.[11]

Classical liberals often read Kant's distinction between the phenomenal and the noumenal standpoints of moral agency as an instance of such transcendent metaphysical impulses. Its presence in Kant's ethics is deemed the more objectionable given Kant's critique of rationalist metaphysics in his theory of knowledge. Kant's references in his moral writings to a noumenal perspective are regarded as an unfortunate lapse into a rationalist mode of inquiry he claims to have discredited.[12] For related reasons, replacing Kant's transcendent claims with the attribution to individuals of intuitively more plausible moral predicates is thought to constitute an improvement of Kant's theory. Predicating a sense of justice or an intuitive idea of freedom of individuals offers a sensible way of integrating the moral capacities of that elusive noumenal self with the physically embodied, psychologically motivated, altogether more tangible phenomenal self. Such modifications at the meta-ethical level leave unaltered Kant's universalistic commitments at the normative level, whilst rendering them intuitively more appealing and hence increasing their chances of practical success.

Communitarian critics of classical liberalism share the latter's suspicion of Kantian metaphysics. However, they do so against a different theoretical background and they are less optimistic about the possibility of separating Kant's metaphysics from his moral theory. According to communitarians, liberals cannot avoid embracing a Kantian metaphysics when they adopt a Kantian conception

---

[11] The best-known representatives of this influential line of thought are David Hume, *An Enquiry Concerning Human Understanding*, Part I, section IV, in L. A. Selby-Bigge, ed., *Hume's Enquiries*, 3rd edition (Oxford, Clarendon Press, 1987), 25–31; Rudolf Carnap, 'The Elimination of Metaphysics through Logical Analysis of Language' in A. J. Ayer, ed., *Logical Positivism* (New York, Free Press, 1959), 60–80; and A. J. Ayer, *Language, Truth and Logic* (Harmondsworth, Penguin Books, 1971), 13–29.
[12] Cf. P. F. Strawson, *The Bounds of Sense* (London, Routledge, 1966), 207–12.

of the person and affirm their allegiance to Kantian universal moral principles. For some communitarian writers, the liberal self is a direct descendant of Kant's noumenal self. This is the charge advanced by Michael Sandel in *Liberalism and the Limits of Justice*.[13] Sandel likens Rawls' account of rational choosers behind the veil of ignorance to Kant's transcendental unity of apperception in the *Critique of Pure Reason*. He detects in Kant's formal notion of the 'I think' as a necessary presupposition of unified, conscious experience the philosophical predecessor to Rawls' 'denuded' conception of the self as given 'prior to its ends'.[14] Kant's analytic distinction between the subject of experience and its experiences is said to provide the basis for Rawls' normative distinction between an individual's self-identity and the ends which define that self's identity.

Other communitarian thinkers do not draw as tight a connection between Kant's epistemology and Rawls' liberalism. Many explain what they perceive as the historical decline towards liberalism in terms of a general critique of the Enlightenment, of which Kant's philosophy constitutes the highest point.[15] From this perspective, Kantian metaphysics is an expression of Enlightenment rationalism, with its fondness for abstraction and generalisation, and with its pretensions towards a 'science of morality' that is inappropriately modelled on the successes of the newly established natural sciences. It is not clear whether communitarians detect in Kant's abstract universalism a pre-Enlightenment attachment to a supersensible world of true ideas. On the whole, communitarians are more worried about abstraction as such than about any particular philosophical expressions this might take. For similar reasons, not all communitarian writers are necessarily committed to the rejection of *all* metaphysical thinking. Neo-Aristotelians may accept a version of immanent metaphysics so long as the latter is interpreted as an articulation of the harmony of meanings implicit in the social practices that make up a particular society's form of life.

Finally, critical liberals reject Kantian metaphysics on the grounds that it is historically outdated. Habermas' postmetaphysical critique

---

[13] Michael Sandel, *Liberalism and the Limits of Justice* (Cambridge University Press, 1982).
[14] Ibid., 7–14.
[15] Cf. Alasdair MacIntyre, *After Virtue* (London, Duckworth, 1981); Charles Taylor, 'Atomism' in *Philosophy and the Human Sciences*. Philosophical Papers, volume 2 (Cambridge University Press, 1985), 187–210; also Charles Taylor, *Sources of the Self* (Cambridge, MA, Harvard University Press, 1989).

attributes a rationalist metaphysics to Kant, likening the noumenal realm to Plato's theory of forms, and condemning both for their non-democratic elitism.[16] However, in contrast to classical liberalism, critical liberalism does not advocate a modification so much as a transformation of Kant's moral theory. For Habermas, the need for such a transformation is due to specific developments in Western intellectual history. Like the communitarians, he locates the crucial changes in the Enlightenment, but, unlike them, he interprets these changes in progressive terms. The crucial philosophical juncture lies in the emergence of the natural sciences with their diversification into areas of special expertise and their shared methodological commitment to what Habermas refers to as 'the principle of fallibilism'. The natural sciences have displaced metaphysics from its traditional position as *prima philosophia*, undermining its claim of special access to the truth. A new type of 'procedural rationality' based on the scientific method of fallibilistic cognition characterises modern social reality. This historically distinctive, procedural conception of rationality provides the new paradigm for a discursively achieved and critically revisable consensus on principles of democratic political interaction. Habermas develops his conception of procedural rationality in analogy with what he regards as the non-dogmatic methods of scientific inquiry. He combines this with a form of transcendental argumentation which substitutes Kant's 'monological' account of the introspective noumenal self with the dialogical community of interlocutors whose implicit commitment to shared principles is instantiated in their very acts of discursive interaction with one another. This is the *tranzendental-pragmatische Wende*, or the linguistic turn within transcendental philosophy. It seeks to transform the elusive apriority of Kantian principles of pure practical reason into an account of the inescapable moral commitments which individuals enter into with each other in virtue of the fact that they are users of language.

As this brief overview shows, different political perspectives emphasise different aspects of Kant's metaphysics. Classical liberals' focus on the phenomenal/noumenal distinction lead them to interpret Kantian metaphysics as a version of transcendent rationalism; communitarians associate Kant's abstract universalism with

---

[16] The following sketch of Habermas' position is based on *Nachmetaphysisches Denken*, chapter 3. I consider Habermas' objections in more detail in section 5, below.

his form/content distinction; and critical liberals characterise transcendental idealism as a historically outdated *Bewußtseinsphilosophie*.
Despite these different emphases, all three positions associate Kant's
metaphysics with an appeal to a supersensible perspective that
comes uncomfortably close to a Platonic realm of true ideas. All of
them reject the permissibility of metaphysics in political thinking on
those grounds, even if not all of them disallow either an immanent,
socially interpreted metaphysics, or a metaphysics of personal reflection. This partial consensus among the three positions can be
summed up in the following general thesis:

In so far as it involves an appeal to a transcendent realm, metaphysical
reflection is permissible, if at all, only in the private sphere, never in the
public sphere.

The remainder of this chapter takes issue with this thesis. I argue,
first, that metaphysical thinking cannot be reduced to the level of
merely private reflection – this is my argument against Rawls.
Second, I suggest that, although a transcendent perspective is
indispensable to metaphysical thinking, this need not involve an
appeal to supersensible worlds – this is my argument against
Habermas. I do not, except in passing, engage any further with the
communitarian perspective.

3 THE PRIVATISATION OF METAPHYSICAL THINKING

The initial communitarian critique of Rawls, which focused on his
Kantian conception of the self and on his thin theory of the good,
had a profound influence on Rawls' subsequent reformulation of his
theory. As already mentioned, Rawls rebutted the communitarian
charge against him of an unexamined commitment to Kant's
metaphysics by pointing to the fact of pluralism. In a society
characterised by radical value pluralism among its individual
members, no resort to metaphysics is possible in connection with the
tasks of political justification. This is not to deny the importance to
individuals of their particular metaphysical commitments, nor is it to
reject out of hand the possible truth of any given metaphysical
system. Far from being dismissive or openly hostile, Rawls merely
advocates a strategy of avoidance: a liberal theory of justice and of
political justification must stay on the surface philosophically, 'not
because religious and metaphysical views are unimportant, but

because they are too important to be resolved politically through agreement'.[17] Citizens are not required to renounce their religious and metaphysical convictions, but are asked to set them aside when engaging in public political deliberation.

The ingenuity of Rawls' strategy of response lies in the fact that it allows him to avert the charge of metaphysics without committing him to the communitarian ideal of a comprehensive conception of the social good.[18] On the revised account, it simply does not form part of the brief of a defensible liberal theory either to advocate the adoption of any particular metaphysical worldview, or to adjudicate between such conflicting views. None the less, this strategy of avoidance comes at a cost. The contention is straightforward, that metaphysical beliefs are of no importance in the context of political justification. The converse claim is equally intelligible, that such beliefs are too important to be ignored. But there is something odd about saying that *because* of their importance such convictions *should* be discounted in the political context. This last claim makes sense only on the assumption that metaphysics can be relegated to the domain of persons' private beliefs. One indication that this is indeed Rawls' view is his tendency to equate metaphysical thinking with religious beliefs. He not only repeatedly mentions both in the same context, but he also routinely invokes the history of the Reformation, with its removal of religious beliefs from the public sphere to the private realm. Rawls thus conceives of religious beliefs in the 'protestant mode', i.e. as an intimate expression of faith concerning the relation between God and believer. This suggests that he has in mind a privatisation of metaphysics analogous to the privatisation of Christian denominations during the Reformation.[19] The question is whether such a view of metaphysics is sustainable. My answer in what follows is that it is not. I begin with an overview of Rawls' conception of metaphysics and of its development from his earlier work to his most recent writings.

Most striking about the development of Rawls' views on metaphysics

---

[17] John Rawls, 'Justice as Fairness: Political not Metaphysical', *Philosophy and Public Affairs*, 14 (1985), 230.

[18] This point is made by Jean Hampton in 'Should Political Philosophy be Done Without Metaphysics?', *Ethics*, 99 (1989), 794–814.

[19] Rawls' equation of metaphysics with religious beliefs, and his analogy between the fact of pluralism and the Reformation is stated most explicitly in 'The Idea of an Overlapping Consensus', *Oxford Journal of Legal Studies*, 7 (1987), 1–25; especially 1–5. But see also 'Justice as Fairness', 223 and 230; and *Political Liberalism*, 125–9, and 150–8.

in political thinking is the contrast between a relatively fixed, general conception of metaphysics and rather more shifting interpretations of Kant's moral theory in relation to that general conception. Rawls' general conception constitutes a version of the classical liberal view of metaphysics as a type of transcendent rationalism; Rawls' understanding of the rational intuitionisms of Henry Sidgwick, G. E. Moore, and W. D. Ross shapes his own formulation of that view. He tends to generalise from his account of the British intuitionists to the metaphysical systems of Plato, Aristotle, Spinoza, and Leibniz.[20] Hence it is fair to say that rational intuitionism constitutes Rawls' paradigm conception of metaphysics.[21] This is bound to render ambivalent his relation to Kant. While Rawls' deep sympathies with Kant's moral theory are evident, he concedes that Kant's practical philosophy is metaphysical. Since he views metaphysics by the lights of rational intuitionism, he must repudiate those aspects of Kant's moral theory that imply metaphysical commitments interpreted as a form of rational intuitionism. One immediate problem with this is that Kant's metaphysics is not adequately captured by rational intuitionism, as Rawls, in fact, recognises.[22] Hence neither critics nor supporters of Kant have found Rawls' modifications of Kant's theory particularly persuasive. While critics complain that the repudiation of rational intuitionism does not rid his theory of its Kantianism, Kantians reject Rawls' interpretation of Kant as a distortion of Kant's actual views. These criticisms from both sides of the divide help explain the shifting constellations in Rawls' account of the relation between rational intuitionism, Kantian metaphysics, and political liberalism. We can divide Rawls' interpretation of Kant into three broad phases:

(1) The assimilation of Kant's metaphysics under rational intuitionism in *A Theory of Justice*.

(2) The juxtaposition of rational intuitionism with Kantian constructivism in 'Kantian Constructivism'.

---

[20] John Rawls, 'Kantian Constructivism in Moral Theory', *Journal of Philosophy*, 77 (1980), 557.

[21] The influence of intuitionism on Rawls has often been noted, his criticisms of it notwithstanding. For discussions of Rawls and intuitionism, compare R. B. Brandt, *A Theory of the Right and the Good* (Oxford, Clarendon Press, 1979), chapter 1; Joel Feinberg, 'Rawls and Intuitionism' in Norman Daniels, ed., *Reading Rawls* (Oxford, Basil Blackwell, 1975), 108–23; Gerald Gaus, *Justificatory Liberalism* (Oxford University Press, 1996), chapter 7, 85–111. I say more about Rawls' account of rational intuitionism below.

[22] 'Kantian Constructivism', 557–9.

(3) The juxtaposition of rational intuitionism and Kantian constructivism with political constructivism in *Political Liberalism*.

(1) If the Kant of *A Theory of Justice* was more recognisable to his
communitarian critics than to Kantians, this is because Rawls'
modifications of Kant's metaphysics broadly accorded with classical
liberal orthodoxy. Rawls endeavoured to render Kant's moral theory
intuitively more plausible by replacing its metaphysical presuppositions with the intuitive ideas of everyday liberal morality. In keeping
with this aim, *A Theory of Justice* circumvents Kant's phenomenal/
noumenal distinction, in which Rawls detected an appeal to a
rationalist metaphysics, by reinterpreting his moral theory in terms
of the rational choice paradigm then dominant within the social
sciences. The section of the book entitled 'A Kantian Interpretation
of the Original Position' might equally have been headed 'An
Original Position Interpretation of Kant'. Rawls there summarises
Kant's moral philosophy as 'the study of the conception and
outcome of a suitably defined rational decision', which 'begin[s] with
the idea that moral principles are the object of rational choice'.[23] In
the course of elaborating this characterisation, Rawls glosses Kant's
concept of autonomy as 'an expression of individuals' nature as free
and equal rational beings', reformulates Kant's noumenal standpoint
in terms of his own 'veil of ignorance', and summarises his two
principles of justice as an 'intuitive articulation of the categorical
imperative'. These adjustments lead him to conclude that:

The original position may be viewed as a procedural interpretation of
Kant's . . . categorical imperative . . . The description of this situation
enables us to explain the sense in which acting from these principles [of
justice] expresses our nature as free and equal rational persons. *No longer are
these [Kantian] notions purely transcendent and lacking explicit connections with human
conduct*, for the procedural conception of the original position allows us to
make sense of these ties.[24]

In short, the pattern in *A Theory of Justice* follows that of classical
liberalism outlined above, which seeks to replace elements of
transcendental idealism from Kant's moral theory with common-
sense notions of morality.

(2) Rawls' initial attempt at metaphysical excision backfired
dramatically. While Kantians repudiated his decisionist reading of

---

[23] Rawls, *A Theory of Justice*, 251.
[24] Ibid., 255–7, emphasis added.

Kant's moral theory,[25] communitarians complained that the view of morality as a rational decision-making process was precisely what they found objectionable about Kant's metaphysics. In 'Kantian Constructivism', Rawls tried to delimit more carefully the extent of his Kantianism by contrasting it with rational intuitionism. The most significant change lay in an explicit emphasis on practical reason over theoretical reason: moral principles were not the product of a rational *choice* so much as the object of moral *deliberation* and *judgement*. At the same time, 'Kantian Constructivism' marked Rawls' move towards pragmatism: Rawls confessed himself indebted to John Dewey, who was, in turn, indebted to Hegel's socially immanent interpretation of morality as *Sittlichkeit*. Despite the explicitly Kantian focus on practical reasoning, the Dewey lectures thus signalled Rawls' abandonment of any reference even to a modified noumenal standpoint.

In 'Kantian Constructivism', Rawls characterises rational intuitionism as committed to two principal theses. According to the first, 'the basic moral concepts of the right and the good are not analysable in terms of non-moral concepts'.[26] According to the second, 'first principles of morals, when correctly stated, are self-evident propositions about the right and the good'.[27] These theses express a summary conception of metaphysics as the hypostatisation of an order of rationally intuited true ideas. The first thesis posits the existence of transcendent moral truths, and the second specifies our mode of rational access to them. In rational intuitionism,

> agreement in judgement is founded on the recognition of self-evident truths about good reasons. What these reasons are is fixed by a moral order that is prior to and independent of our conception of the person and the social role of morality. This is given by the nature of things and is known, not by sense, but by rational intuition.[28]

By contrast, Kantian constructivism does not treat ideas of the right and the good as a priori truths known independently of a conception of the person. Kantian constructivism assumes a 'relatively complex conception of the person'.[29] It derives principles of the right and the good from its conception of the person in

---

[25] See, for example, Onora O'Neill, 'Kantian Ethics and Kant's Ethics' in *Bounds of Justice* (Cambridge University Press, forthcoming); also O'Neill, 'Idealisation in Ethics' in *Constructions of Reason* (Cambridge University Press, 1989), 206–18.

[26] Rawls, 'Kantian Constructivism', 557.

[27] Ibid.   [28] Ibid.   [29] Ibid., 560.

combination with a conception of the well-ordered society. Instead of appeals to a supersensible world of true ideas, Kantian constructivism starts from values and beliefs latent in society and works these up into a shared conception of justice. Most importantly, Kantian constructivism claims no knowledge of moral truths. It accepts 'the inevitable limitations that constrain moral deliberations' and settles for 'acceptable and workable principles of justice'[30] in favour over transcendent truths. While the contrast between rational intuitionism and Kantian constructivism is marked and deliberate, the differences either between Kantian constructivism and Kant's ethics, or between Kant's ethics and rational intuitionism remain less sharply demarcated. On the one hand, Rawls' reading of Kant's ethics in the Dewey lectures is more nuanced, his engagement with Kant's ethics deeper and more explicit than in *A Theory of Justice*. The new emphasis on the primacy of practical reason and the references to human limitations represent a move towards Kant. Rawls also acknowledges that the apriority of Kant's moral principles is located not in an appeal to a transcendent realm, but in Kant's conception of practical reason itself. At the same time his own interpretation of the deliberative process in terms of a society's 'latent beliefs and values' signals a move away from Kant: like Dewey before him, Rawls finds it necessary to 'overcome the many dualisms which disfigure Kant's transcendental idealism'.[31] This continued attribution of remnants of a rationalist metaphysics to Kant's ethics distances the latter from Kantian constructivism, keeping it aligned with rational intuitionism.

(3) Rawls' third and most recent position is of principal interest to my contention that he privatises metaphysics. *Political Liberalism* contrasts rational intuitionism *and* Kantian constructivism with a third alternative, namely political constructivism. The reasons for this further realignment are motivated by the second wave of the communitarian critique, this time concerning the *comprehensiveness* of Rawls' liberalism. According to this criticism, even if Rawls' theory is not premised on Kantian metaphysics, it still presupposes a particular conception of the moral person and of the well-ordered society. Whatever the superficial differences between individuals' conceptions of the good, Rawlsian reasoners must share an underlying comprehensive scheme of values and beliefs as the basis of

---

[30] Ibid., 561.   [31] Ibid., 516.

their agreement on the two principles of justice. Rawls' realignment
of rational intuitionism and Kantian constructivism together with
his construction of a third alternative position represent an attempt
to emphasise the extent of value pluralism among individuals. As a
consequence, metaphysics enjoys a partial reinstatement. Both
rational intuitionism and Kantian constructivism are now characterised as metaphysical doctrines representing two divergent possible
comprehensive conceptions of the good. Neither is inadmissible so
long as they do not enter the realm of public debate. Both must
remain confined to a person's private view of the world. By contrast,
political constructivism possesses doctrinal autonomy: it does not
offer a comprehensive conception of the good. Political constructivism is strictly limited to the achievement of moral agreement on a
political conception of justice. As such, it represents an acknowledgement of the fact that, given value pluralism, moral agreement among
individuals can be partial at best. Thus, whereas *both* rational
intuitionism *and* Kantian constructivism now represent distinct
metaphysical positions, political constructivism occupies the non-
metaphysical position formerly reserved for Kantian constructivism.

Two questions arise from this realignment. The first concerns the
status of metaphysics in general. Does the fact that Rawls now thinks
of rational intuitionism and Kantian constructivism as two distinct
metaphysical doctrines mean that he has broadened his general
conception of metaphysics? Or does it mean that, in so far as both
represent metaphysical doctrines, Kantian constructivism (as distinct
from Kant's ethics) shares certain features with rational intuitionism,
which render both of them metaphysical? Either answer poses
problems for Rawls. If rational intuitionism and Kantian constructivism turn out to present two *distinct* metaphysical theories, much is
invalidated of Rawls' initial criticisms of metaphysics exclusively in
terms of a critique of rational intuitionism. But, if rational intuitionism and Kantian constructivism *share* certain features which
render them metaphysical, the thesis of radical pluralism is undermined by the extent of belief-convergence that must then obtain
between individuals.

The ambiguities in Rawls' revised conception of metaphysics
come to the fore in his discussion of the three positions. The
description of rational intuitionism has not changed much, except
that it is now characterised in terms of four features according to
which:

(i)   moral first principles are true statements about an independent order of values;

(ii) moral first principles are known by theoretical reason;

(iii) moral motivation is grounded in rational intuition of first principles;

(iv) moral judgements are true when they are both about and accurate to the independent order of moral values.[32]

These are contrasted with the four features of political constructivism according to which:

(i)   principles of political justice are the outcome of a reasoned procedure;

(ii) the procedure is based on practical reason;

(iii) moral deliberation presupposes a complex conception of the person;

(iv) political constructivism specifies a conception of the reasonable, not of truth.[33]

This contrast is reasonably clear – the question is where this leaves Kantian constructivism. After all, the four features now attributed to political constructivism previously served to characterise Kantian constructivism. So what distinguishes the latter from the former? Interestingly, Rawls now all but identifies Kantian constructivism with Kant's ethics: 'Kantian constructivism is a comprehensive moral view based on an ideal of individual autonomy.'[34] More specifically, 'constitutive autonomy is part of Kant's transcendental idealism', which is a metaphysical doctrine. But, if it is a metaphysical doctrine, does this make Kantian constructivism a version of rational intuitionism after all? This is what would seem to follow from Rawls' initial equation of metaphysics with rational intuitionism. But now things are no longer so clear. Rawls points out that 'the intuitionist's independently given order of values is part of the transcendent realism Kant takes his transcendental idealism to oppose'. Here we seem to have two possible conceptions of metaphysics – transcendent realism and transcendental idealism – implying a broader view of metaphysics than was suggested by its initial equation with the former. But does Rawls accept Kant's 'opposition' as genuine? Instead of a clear answer, Rawls remains ambiguous: Kant 'takes' transcendental idealism to oppose transcendent realism. If transcendent realism and transcendental idealism represent two distinct forms of metaphysical thinking, he might have to revise his initial conception and rejection of metaphysics, since the objections raised against transcendent rationalism may not equally apply to transcendental idealism. But if transcendental idealism is no more than a version of transcendent realism, value pluralism cannot be as radically divergent as political constructivism requires it to be.

If the relation between rational intuitionism and Kantian constructivism is no longer transparent, that between the latter two and political constructivism is even more obscure. As I said, the doctrinal autonomy of political constructivism is meant to ensure political agreement in the face of radical value pluralism. It is to enable individuals to reach agreement on political principles of justice despite the persistence of deep-reaching religious and metaphysical disagreements among them. The problem is that political constructivism is both larger than and smaller than comprehensive doctrines. Political constructivism is larger than any individual metaphysical doctrine because it is agnostic about the truth content of any of them. If a rational intuitionist were to claim that the two principles of justice as fairness reflect an independently given order of true ideas, political constructivism would neither deny nor affirm this.[35] Likewise, if a Kantian were to affirm the two principles as an expression of constitutive autonomy, political constructivism would remain silent. What matters is that each position can find some intra-doctrinal reasons for accepting the validity of the two principles of justice.[36] Here, political constructivism is depicted as larger than either of the two doctrinal positions because it can *contain* both (and many more besides).

On the other hand, political constructivism is also smaller than any metaphysical doctrine taken individually. As a partial, political conception, political constructivism can *fit into* any (reasonable) comprehensive doctrine.[37] It can be taken up and incorporated as part of the wider system of religious, moral, and philosophical beliefs

---

[35] Ibid., 95.

[36] Cf. Ibid., 126: 'Many if not most citizens may want to give the political conception of justice a metaphysical foundation as part of their comprehensive doctrine; and this includes a conception of the truth of moral judgements. Let us say, then, that when we speak of the moral truth of a political conception, we assess it from the point of view of our comprehensive doctrine.'

[37] Ibid., 140: 'It is left to citizens individually – as part of liberty of conscience – to settle how they think the values of the political domain are related to other values in their comprehensive doctrine.'

that comprise a metaphysical doctrine. So, on the one hand, political constructivism needs to be smaller because it needs to be endorsed from within particular comprehensive doctrines. On the other hand, it needs to be larger because it must be capable of bringing together, politically, a large number of divergent doctrines. Does political constructivism accommodate, or is it accommodated? Do comprehensive doctrines validate political constructivism, or does political constructivism validate comprehensive doctrines? Rawls' reply is riddled with ambiguity. He concedes that, 'in affirming a political conception of justice we may eventually have to assert at least aspects of our own comprehensive religious and philosophical doctrine'.[38] Here the suggestion is that political constructivism is smaller than comprehensive doctrines. The degree to which we *can* set aside religious and philosophical beliefs in political deliberation is ultimately limited: eventually those reasons may be the only ones left to us in defending our commitment to a political conception of justice. But Rawls' final answer turns out to be the reverse. Political constructivism is larger than individual comprehensive doctrines:

the political conception can be seen as part of a comprehensive doctrine *but it is not a consequence of that doctrine's non-political values. Its political values normally outweigh whatever other values oppose them*, at least under the reasonably favourable conditions that make constitutional democracy possible.[39]

Ultimately, then, a person's religious and metaphysical beliefs are legitimate so long as they support political constructivism. Where a person's religious and metaphysical beliefs exceed the limits of what is acceptable according to political constructivism, such beliefs are unreasonable. Publicly voicing one's opposition to political constructivism on the grounds that it does not accord with one's religious and metaphysical beliefs cannot be tolerated. As Rawls repeatedly reminds his readers, this line of reasoning constitutes a typical delimitation of the public/private distinction. It reflects what happened to Christianity as a consequence of the Reformation and in the course of political secularisation. It may not seem so far-fetched to suggest that, if privatisation worked for Christian denominations, it should work for metaphysics as well: we should 'apply the principle of toleration to [metaphysics] itself'.[40] In the next section I suggest

---

[38] Ibid., 152.   [39] Ibid., 155, emphasis added.
[40] Rawls, 'Justice as Fairness', 231.

that this expectation rests on a mistaken understanding of metaphysical thinking.

4 PRIVATE BELIEFS VERSUS CATEGORIAL FRAMEWORKS

One of the most confounding aspects of Rawls' enjoinder to remain on the philosophical surface and to 'apply the principle of toleration to philosophy itself' concerns the relation between political practice and political justification. Does the principle of toleration apply only at the level of liberal practice, or also at the level of liberal justification?[41] Presumably Rawls thinks toleration should be practised at both levels. Not only should we tolerate each other's private practices and beliefs, even if we disapprove, so long as they remain confined to the private realm; we should also set aside contentious philosophical differences when deliberating about principles of justice for a just social order. The latter requirement makes it difficult to see how professional metaphysicians could practise their vocation in Rawls' constitutional democracy. One would expect them to discuss, defend, and promulgate their conflicting metaphysical systems within the limits of the law, exercising toleration of each other's views as a matter of good liberal practice. But could one expect them to remain silent, or merely privately troubled, when it comes to questions of political justification and legitimation?[42] Does metaphysical thinking go thus far and no further? It may not be implausible to expect the privatisation of religious belief from a religious denomination whose founder himself advocated the separation of what is Caesar's from what belongs to God. The expectation that the same might work for metaphysical thinking is premised on the view of metaphysics as analogous to (Christian) religious belief. This view finds ready support in the depiction of metaphysics as the hypostatisation of a supersensible world of true ideas, the rational intuition of which is thought of as akin to religious revelation.[43]

---

[41] The idea of applying the principle of toleration to philosophical justification has fuelled debates about liberal neutrality. Compare Charles Larmore, *Patterns of Moral Complexity* (Cambridge University Press, 1987), chapter 3, 40–68; Thomas Nagel, 'Moral Conflict and Political Legitimacy', *Philosophy and Public Affairs*, 16 (1987), 215–40; Joseph Raz, 'Facing Diversity: The Case of Epistemic Abstinence', *Philosophy and Public Affairs*, 19 (1990), 3–46; Brian Barry, *Justice as Impartiality* (Oxford University Press, 1995), chapter 7, 160–90.

[42] Similar objections are raised by Hampton in 'Political Philosophy without Metaphysics?', 809–12.

[43] Cf. Barry, *Justice as Impartiality*, 169: 'The tradition of natural law thinking has as its core the idea that the contents of the natural law are in principle accessible to human reason. (It is

But it is not especially illuminating. It is the critics of metaphysics rather than its practitioners who tend to entertain such an undifferentiated conception of metaphysical truth. Within metaphysics as a discipline of philosophical reasoning, the possibility and status of metaphysical truths are much contested.[44] Even if references to 'the Absolute', to 'being *qua* being', or to 'the form of forms' invoke ideals of metaphysical truths, it is misleading to liken the route thereto to a leap of faith. Commitment to metaphysical truths differs from religious faith in that such commitment tends to remain provisional. Of course, religious believers, too, can come to have doubts, which might induce them to change their beliefs, or even cause them to lose faith altogether. None the less, such doubts are not intended: to make a leap of faith is to commit oneself beyond reason. When doubts arise, the believer suffers a crisis of faith. Commitment to metaphysical truths is precisely *not* commitment beyond reason.[45] Metaphysical thinking remains constrained by standards of rational consistency and publicly accessible reasoning. This means that the methods of metaphysics are essentially public: commitment to metaphysical truths is provisional because it remains open to public debate and critique.[46]

It is not only the methods and standards of metaphysical reasoning which make it a public undertaking. As T. L. S. Sprigge points out, metaphysicians believe that 'it makes a great difference to the character of the world which metaphysical system is true [because they] are inclined to expect a metaphysical theory to have bearings on matters of human interest'.[47] Its substantive commit-

held to be simply an odd coincidence that the only people who find this plausible happen to be Roman Catholics.)' The equation of metaphysical thinking with religious belief is criticised by Otfried Höffe in *Kategorische Rechtsprinzipien* (Frankfurt, Suhrkamp, 1994), 90–100.

[44] Cf., for example, Michael Loux's outline of the current debate between realists and nominalists in *Metaphysics. A Contemporary Introduction* (London, Routledge, 1998). See also Reinhardt Grossmann, *The Existence of the World* (London, Routledge, 1992).

[45] Again Rawls is careless when he asserts without argument in *Political Liberalism*, 153: 'For many the true, or the religiously and metaphysically well-grounded, goes beyond the reasonable.'

[46] The question of what constitute adequate standards of reasoning has itself become a matter of debate in metaphysics, especially since Kant. See, for example, W. H. Walsh, *Metaphysics* (New York, Harbinger Books, 1963); Rüdiger Bubner, 'Metaphysik und Erfahrung' in *Antike Themen und Ihre Verwandlung* (Frankfurt, Suhrkamp, 1992), 134–50; Dieter Henrich and Rolf-Peter Horstmann, eds., *Metaphysik nach Kant?* (Stuttgart, Klett, 1987); Kenneth Baynes, James Bohman, and Thomas McCarthy eds., *After Philosophy: End or Transformation?* (Chicago: MIT Press, 1987), Part II.

[47] Cf. T. L. S. Sprigge, 'Has Speculative Metaphysics a Future?', *The Monist*, 81 (1998), 525.

ments constitute the second reason why problems in metaphysics are not akin to crises of religious faith. They do not originate in introspective doubt, but result from flaws in philosophical reasoning, which are of a certain magnitude, and which are perceived to have repercussions on related areas of inquiry, such as the sciences, morality, and religion. Crises in metaphysical thinking do not simply affect the spiritual well-being of the individual metaphysician but are assumed to concern the interests of 'humanity at large'.

So far I have suggested that it is tempting but mistaken to model metaphysical thinking on religious beliefs. Commitment to a metaphysical system is not a private affair. Metaphysics as a discipline of philosophical reflection is constrained by standards of rational consistency and by requirements of public accessibility and critique. Secondly, given its normative concerns with matters of general human interests, metaphysical thinking addresses not only informed fellow metaphysicians but also, if less directly, the public at large. On neither count can one expect metaphysics to confine itself to the sphere of individuals' private concerns. In the remainder of this section I want to delineate a little more sharply the conception of metaphysics as a discipline of philosophical reflection about the world of public experience. Here I rely on Stephan Körner's notion of a categorial framework.

What renders Körner's account recognisably Kantian is his characterisation of human beings as cognitively experiencing subjects. According to this view, human beings' experience of the world is conceptually mediated – their experience of objects depends on their ability to conceptualise them *as* objects.[48] Hence, for Körner,

---

[48] Kant's metaphysics is sometimes described as a version of conceptualism, especially within analytic circles. Conceptualism differs from traditional metaphysics in terms of its greater proximity to epistemology than to ontology. Loux (in *Metaphysics*, 9) characterises the difference between Kant's metaphysics and traditional metaphysics by describing the former as 'an inquiry into the structure of human thought', while the latter presents 'an inquiry into the structure of the world thought is about'. The suggestion is that traditional metaphysics constitutes a more objective or more object-oriented form of metaphysical thinking. To some extent this may be true: conceptualism is often associated with claims about the possibility of radically different conceptual schemes. Critics accuse the latter of eliding the distinction between the way in which we think about the world and the way the world is independently of our thoughts. However, while Kant's 'Copernican turn' might have opened the door to conceptualism thus understood, its roots lie in post-Kantian absolute idealism rather than in Kant's transcendental idealism. Whatever the difficulties with the Kantian notion of 'things in themselves', his commitment to them suggests that the world as independent of our thought is not lost sight of in Kant's metaphysics. The sensibly given world, unknowable though it may be 'in itself', does impose a priori constraints on the structure of human thought. Similarly, Körner's notion of a categorial framework

our mode of access to empirical reality is cognitive, requiring cognitive ordering and stratification of otherwise discrete instances of sensible experience: 'The organisation of a person's beliefs about the public world, as a result of which the person accepts a more or less definite system of logically or non-logically "necessary" supreme principles, constitutes his "categorial framework".'[49] More specifically, subjects' cognitive ordering of empirical experience includes:

[A] differentiation of [a person's] experience into particulars and attributes; a deductive organization of the judgments by which he assigns or refuses attributes to particulars; a method of conferring intersubjectivity on what is subjectively given; a classification of intersubjective particulars into maximal kinds; a ranking or stratification of beliefs into classes of different epistemic strength.[50]

Körner's exposition of a person's categorial framework has an evident epistemological orientation, reflecting particular assumptions about the conditions of cognitive experience that I cannot discuss here. However, four general features of Körner's exposition are useful in the present context:

(i)   the claim that a person's metaphysics arises from their cognitive experience of the world;
(ii) the claim that a person's categorial framework refers to the *public* world of their experience;

should not be confused with a conceptual scheme. Körner does avoid appeal to a priori constraints and he does endorse a modest form of metaphysical relativism, which accepts the existence of different possible categorial frameworks. None the less, Körner's approach presupposes a mind-independent world of given objects, though the structure of the world may be differently interpreted. Moreover, his metaphysical relativism is limited by his insistence that all categorial frameworks 'as a matter of empirical fact' share some formal and substantive features (Körner, *Metaphysics*, 45–7). I mention this because the notion of the mind-independent constraints of nature will be of importance in the analysis of Kant's *Rechtslehre*. Kant's metaphysics should not be confused with conceptualism, nor should categorial frameworks be conflated with conceptual schemes, at least in so far as, in contrast to the latter, the former do maintain a distinction between mind and world, however differently they interpret the relation between them. Again, in contrast to Körner, Kant is not a relativist about different possible categorial frameworks, but considers his transcendental idealism to be the only defensible philosophical doctrine available. For a critique of the notion of radically different conceptual schemes, see Donald Davidson, 'On the very Idea of a Conceptual Scheme' in *Essays on Truth and Interpretation* (Oxford, Clarendon Press, 1984); 183–98. See also his 'The Method of Truth in Metaphysics' in the same volume, 199–213. For a defence, see Michael Forster, 'On the Very Idea of Denying the Existence of Radically Different Conceptual Schemes', *Inquiry*, 41 (1998), 133–86. For an overview of Kant's influence on contemporary analytic metaphysics see P. F. Strawson, 'Kant's New Foundations of Metaphysics' in Henrich and Horstmann, eds., *Metaphysik nach Kant?*

[49] Körner, *Metaphysics*, 2.
[50] Ibid.

(iii) the claim that a categorial framework must demonstrate (a reasoned claim to) intersubjective validity;

(iv) the claim that a categorial framework comprises the organisation of a person's theoretically and practically supreme principles alike.

The first feature expresses the requirement of reflective experiential relevance. Körner assumes not only that human beings are cognitively experiencing subjects, but also that they are conscious of themselves as such. A categorial framework constitutes a person's reflective reconstruction of what they take to be the structure of experience. In this sense, a person's articulation of a categorial framework arises *from* experience. In a different though complementary sense, a categorial framework articulates the necessary conditions *of* experience. It is only in virtue of their possessing such a framework that cognitively experiencing subjects can gain access to the world in a manner intelligible to them. On the basis of their particular experience of the world, cognitively experiencing subjects thus retrospectively reconstruct what they take to be the necessary structure of experience in general.

Secondly, the references to the public world of experience express a requirement of objectivity. They presuppose the subject's explicit recognition of their distinctness from the world as the object of their experience. A categorial framework aims to identify the general structure of a publicly accessible world, not that of the subject's imaginary world of private experiences. The world as object of experience must be acknowledged as distinct from the experiencing subject.

Related to this is, thirdly, the requirement of intersubjective validity, which demands communicability to others of a person's proposed categorial framework. If a categorial framework claims to identify the general structure of subjects' experience of the public world, it cannot simply amount to a person's private beliefs about that world. A person's categorial framework must be communicable to others who must be able, in principle, to understand the claims advanced in its behalf. By the same token, the categorial framework must be capable of eliciting general assent. It is not enough for a person to *claim* intersubjective validity for their proposed categorial framework; they must be able to demonstrate that the claim is warranted. If a categorial framework fails to be intelligible to relevant others, it cannot plausibly claim the status of intersubjective validity.

Finally, the fourth feature expresses requirements of internal coherence and consistency. Whereas the requirement of experiential relevance constitutes the most obvious counterpart to Rawls' description of rational intuitionism's transcendence of empirical experience, Körner's emphasis on the complementary character of theoretical and practical reason offers an important contrast to Rawls' assumption about their mutual exclusivity. While Rawls *contrasts* the focus on theoretical reason in rational intuitionism with the emphasis placed on practical reason by political constructivism,[51] Körner's account expressly requires a fit between a person's theoretically supreme principles and their practically supreme principles: a person's theoretical beliefs about the structure of the world constrain their practical beliefs about possible agency. What one takes to be the structure of empirical reality will affect one's judgements concerning constraints on human agency. In contrast to Rawls' constructivism, which thinks an account of theoretical reason irrelevant to the practical problems of political philosophy, Körner's outline of a categorial framework regards an account of theoretical reason as indispensable to an account of practical reason. This difference will be of considerable importance in subsequent chapters.

In sum, metaphysical thinking understood in terms of a categorial framework constitutes a person's reflective reconstruction of their cognitive experience of the publicly accessible world, the intersubjectively valid structure of which the categorial framework aims to identify and to elucidate for the purpose of guiding thought and action. The question is whether the notion of a categorial framework here sketched amounts to an adequate characterisation of metaphysical thinking.

5 IMMANENT METAPHYSICS VERSUS TRANSCENDENT METAPHYSICS

Critics may disagree that the above sketch of a person's categorial framework constitutes an adequate characterisation of metaphysical thinking. The principal difference between Körner's and Rawls' respective accounts lies in the fact that Körner eschews all reference to a transcendent perspective, while Rawls regards the appeal to

---

[51] See also Rawls' remarks on objectivity in *Political Liberalism*, 116–25, where he suggests that, as a theory of practical reason, political constructivism can do without an account of theoretical reason altogether.

such a perspective as a defining feature of metaphysics. Indeed, Körner explicitly states that a person's categorial framework defines their *immanent* metaphysics.[52] Critics might complain, therefore, that metaphysics understood as categorial framework thinking amounts itself to a 'strategy of avoidance'. Saying that a categorial framework denotes a person's organisation of their cognitively and practically supreme principles is not to say anything that is peculiar to metaphysics. A categorial framework thus understood simply describes the relation between a person's preferred epistemology and the moral theory implied by it. This hardly amounts to a metaphysical doctrine. A metaphysical doctrine is not content simply to *describe* the relation between epistemic structures and moral principles. It typically advances substantive claims about what it takes to be the nature of that relation.

It is true that metaphysics aims at more than the description of a person's theoretically and practically supreme principles, if only because it is concerned with the integration of these two perspectives. This search for integration is partly normative.[53] It is shaped by metaphysicians' conviction that their discipline has a bearing on matters of general human interest. In Körner's account, that conviction is given expression in the assumption that cognitively experiencing subjects are committed to these two perspectives because they require both perspectives in order to negotiate themselves through the world of public experience. However, such normative commitments need not be expressed as substantive claims that are extraneous to the process of metaphysical inquiry itself. Although the search for integration betrays a normative commitment which goes beyond the mere description of the structure of experience, that commitment is expressed in the search and identification of that structure: it need not be thought of as superimposed upon it.

But, even accepting that the normativity of a categorial framework *is* its structure, critics may object that claims about its general validity point beyond that structure. The claim that a categorial framework is valid for everyone must be made from outside that framework. It presupposes some additional vantage-point from which its general validity is affirmed. This is why it is misleading to speak of mere *intersubjective* validity in relation to metaphysical

---

[52] Körner, *Metaphysics*, 2.
[53] For a contrasting view see P. F. Strawson's distinction between 'descriptive metaphysics' and 'revisionary metaphysics' in *Individuals* (London, Routledge, 1959), 9–12.

doctrines. Intersubjective validity is usually taken to refer to consensual justification, where the validity of a particular principle or
proposition depends on everyone accepting it as such. But a
metaphysical doctrine typically claims general validity irrespective of
subjects' assent. This interpretation of 'valid for all irrespective of
the actual assent of each' really amounts to a claim of objective
validity in the sense of 'antecedently true', or 'true independently of
subjects' assent to its truth'. Even if one grants, therefore, that the
normativity of a proposed categorial framework is immanent to its
structure, the claim to objective validity on its behalf lies outside that
structure and presses into the transcendent realm.

Objections such as these raise doubts about whether the traditional distinction between immanent and transcendent metaphysics
can be upheld, or whether immanence does not inevitably shade
into transcendence. This question is not unimportant, since contemporary defenders of metaphysical thinking often base their
defence on that distinction. With the critics, they reject as indefen-
sible a transcendent metaphysics' hypostatisation of a realm of true
ideas; however they argue that immanent metaphysical reflection on
the structure of human experience remains a legitimate human
preoccupation. While Plato's transcendent metaphysics is widely
repudiated, Aristotelian immanent metaphysics is often defended on
the grounds that it does not venture beyond the realm of empirical
experience. At this point I should make it clear that Körner himself
does not treat immanent and transcendent perspectives as alternative ways of metaphysical thinking. Much of the interest in
Körner's approach lies in his contention that *every* metaphysical
system comprises both an immanent and a transcendent perspective.
Körner would agree, therefore, that the exposition of a person's
immanent metaphysics amounts to only half the story: anyone who
holds an immanent metaphysics is committed thereby to a transcendent metaphysics.[54] I shall return to Körner's view of the relation
between immanence and transcendence in the next section. Here I
want to consider aspects of a recent debate between Dieter Henrich
and Jürgen Habermas that touch upon the issue, if only indirectly.[55]
My intention is to make a case for the indispensability of a
transcendent perspective within metaphysical thinking.

---

[54] Körner, *Metaphysics*, chapters 10–12, 114–48.
[55] Henrich, 'Zwölf Thesen'; and Habermas, *Nachmetaphysisches Denken*.

I mentioned at the beginning of this chapter that, as the predominant proponent of what I call critical liberalism, Habermas' rejection of metaphysics is premised on his view of modernity as a distinct historical and philosophical era. Quite where in historical time modernity begins according to Habermas is somewhat unclear – indeed, the historical as well as the philosophical delimitation of modernity is itself a bone of contention between Henrich and Habermas. Whereas, for Henrich, the *Bewußtseinsphilosophie* of German Idealism marks the philosophical beginnings of modernity, Habermas regards the shedding of philosophical preoccupations with 'the subject' an essential prerequisite to the achievement of modernity. According to Habermas, this requires a philosophical paradigm shift that paves the way for a specifically postmetaphysical form of philosophical thinking. The status of *Bewußtseinsphilosophie* in relation to the 'project of modernity' thus forms the focal point of the exchange between them.[56] I shall touch on this issue only in so far as it has a bearing on the status of the immanence/transcendence distinction, which is of principal interest in the present context.

In 'Metaphysics and Modernity: Twelve Theses against Habermas',[57] Henrich mounts two principal complaints against his opponent. The first is the historical–philosophical complaint that Habermas has betrayed the 'unfinished project of modernity' by abandoning *Bewußtseinsphilosophie* for analytic philosophy of language.[58] The second objection focuses on Henrich's more general disquiet about Habermas' rejection of metaphysics as philosophically outdated. Henrich detects in Habermas' call for a philosophical paradigm shift the emergence of a 'new naturalism' which threatens to sideline the metaphysical problems Henrich considers to be specific to modernity. All the same, Henrich treads cautiously in his defence of a metaphysics of modernity. Adamant that modern metaphysics need not rely on the hypostatisation of a supersensible

---

[56] See Peter Dews, 'Modernity, Self-Consciousness and the Scope of Philosophy: Jürgen Habermas and Dieter Henrich in Debate' in *The Limits of Disenchantment* (London, Verso, 1996), 169–93.

[57] Henrich's piece on Habermas has recently been translated by Peter Dews in Peter Dews, ed., *Habermas, A Critical Reader* (Oxford, Basil Blackwell, 1999). I am grateful to Peter Dews for allowing me to use his translation for the purpose of quotation. The relevant page references refer to the original publication in German.

[58] See also Dieter Henrich, 'The Origins of the Theory of the Subject' in Axel Honneth, ed., *Philosophical Interventions in the Unfinished Project of Modernity* (Cambridge, MA, MIT Press, 1992), and Dieter Henrich, 'Die Grundstruktur der Modernen Philosophie' in *Selbstverhältnisse* (Stuttgart, Reclam, 1982).

world, he defines metaphysical thinking by appealing to the notion of *Abschlußgedanken* – 'thoughts of a resolving closure' – regarding the relation between self and world. The central concepts of modern metaphysics are 'freedom', 'life', and 'spirit'. This somewhat idiosyncratic combination of Kant, Aristotle, and Hegel places the emphasis firmly on immanent metaphysical reflection. Henrich shares Kant's contention that metaphysics has its source in human reason, though he is keen to dissociate it from a *philosophical* conception of the discipline of reason.[59] His account is meditative rather than critical: 'metaphysics takes shape in the spontaneous thinking of every human being, long before its eventual formulation in the language of theory'.[60] Nor does he subscribe to Kant's view that human reason 'poses itself questions *which it cannot answer*'.[61] For Henrich, the end of metaphysical reflection – reconciliation between self and world – is known. However, the insights that answer to this end may not be expressible in the form of statements with clear propositional content, but may be more akin in their nature to spiritual insight.

While the source of metaphysics is Kantian, its task is Hegelian. Metaphysics has the subject meditate on lived experience: 'whoever reflects has already understood that he is not at home only in one world, and that he cannot merge seamlessly with the world'.[62] Subjects' alienation from the world is grounded in their consciousness of themselves as subjects and can only be overcome through introspective reflection on the conditions of consciousness which produce that experience of alienation. Self-reflective understanding of those conditions issues in enhanced self-understanding. This results, in turn, in the subject's reconciliation with the world of experience. The perceived chasm between self and world dissolves in the subject's enlarged understanding of itself as an integral part of that world after all. The task of modern metaphysics is to 'develop ultimate, and thus reconciling, conceptions [*sic*], in which conscious life can come to understand itself'.[63]

When Henrich turns to assess the comparative failings of Habermas' non-metaphysical approach to modernity, his most

---

[59] On the 'Discipline of Reason', see *CPR*, A707–794/B735–822. For an illuminating discussion of the relevant passages see Onora O'Neill, 'Vindicating Reason' in Paul Guyer, ed., *The Cambridge Companion to Kant* (Cambridge University Press, 1992), 280–308.
[60] Henrich, 'Zwölf Thesen', 14.
[61] *CPR*, Avii, emphasis added.
[62] Henrich, 'Zwölf Thesen', 19.   [63] Ibid., 26.

important charge is what one might call the charge of metaphysical deflation. The target is the 'new naturalism' of Habermas' discourse–theoretical approach. As already mentioned, Habermas' postmetaphysical paradigm shift combines a proceduralist conception of rationality derived from the natural sciences with linguistics and aspects of analytic philosophy of language. However, according to Henrich, Habermas' theory of communicative action reduces complex philosophical questions to a matter of seeking intersubjective clarification by means of a rule-governed *Sprachverständigung*, or rules of communication. This approach assumes the answerability, in principle, of all meaningful questions by fixing the terms of debate in advance. It denies legitimate philosophical reflection on precisely those questions that do not by their very nature admit of a clear (i.e. easily and publicly verifiable) answer. Habermas' 'refusal to think philosophically'[64] – his refusal to accord philosophical reflection a status distinct both from scientific discourse and from everyday speech – leads to an impoverished understanding of the irreducibly spiritual dimension of human experience and self-understanding.

It is important to note that Henrich is not advocating the privatisation of metaphysics. Despite his introspectivist leanings, Henrich perceives the tasks of metaphysical reflection to be public in nature. The idea is not that those among us who have the urge should feel free to indulge in a search of the self: coming to understand the nature of subjectivity is the historical, philosophical, and political task of modernity. In contrast to Rawls, Henrich does not seek to set aside contentious metaphysical issues in political discussion: he thinks they should be moved centre-stage. This is appreciated by Habermas, who worries about 'the political implications' of Henrich's proposal.[65] What worries Habermas is the quietism implicit in Henrich's search for reflective closure. The desired reconciliation between self and world amounts to a loss, according to Habermas, of a critical perspective on to the world as distinct from the self. Of interest in the present context is the manner of Habermas' defence of a critical perspective against Henrich's quietism. At least on one possible interpretation, the defence amounts to an argument for a transcendent perspective against immanent closure.

I should point out that Habermas would balk at such a suggestion.

---

[64] Ibid., 40.   [65] Habermas, *Nachmetaphysisches Denken*, 20.

In what follows I am interpreting rather than representing his position. It is none the less not implausible to interpret his response to Henrich in the manner proposed. This is so for two related reasons. The first is that Habermas' general arguments against metaphysics entirely fail to engage with Henrich's specific conception of the metaphysics of modernity. The second is that, when he does directly engage with Henrich's account, Habermas' objections betray a Platonic streak in their emphasis on philosophical critique over meditative reflection, which arguably conflicts with his avowedly postmetaphysical stance. Turning to the first point, Habermas' general conception of metaphysics is not unlike that of Rawls, though the historical reference points differ. Habermas conceives of metaphysics as a crude Platonism that involves the hypostatisation of a transcendent realm of true ideas: 'ignoring the Aristotelian line of thinking, I define "metaphysics" as a type of philosophical idealism which reaches from Plato, Descartes, Spinoza, to Kant, Fichte, Schelling, and Hegel'.[66] Philosophical idealism is summarised in terms of three trans-historical categories:

(i) 'identity thinking', which reduces philosophical truths to 'the unity of one' by declaring seemingly diverse empirical phenomena to be reducible to a single abstract idea such as 'being as such';

(ii) 'idealism', which turns that single idea into the source of everything that exists, so that 'the true nature of the world is conceptual';

(iii) 'a strong concept of theory', which privileges the contemplative life over the active life, 'demanding the rejection of a natural attitude towards the world in return for its promise of contact with the extraordinary'.[67]

As with Rawls' account of rational intuitionism, this general conception of metaphysics is tailor-made for rejection. Indeed, Habermas' reasons for its dismissal largely overlap with those given by Rawls, albeit with differing points of emphases.[68] The pertinent

---

[66] Ibid., 35.   [67] Ibid., 36–40.

[68] Whereas Rawls emphasises rational intuitionism's greater emphasis on theoretical reason over practical reason, Habermas charges metaphysics with 'elitism' in its claim to 'special access to the truth'. Again, while Rawls tends to conflate metaphysics with religious belief, Habermas views it as an outdated form of philosophical thinking. A more systematic difference lies in Rawls' attitude of toleration towards privately held 'metaphysical beliefs', against Habermas' insistence on the need of a paradigm shift and of individuals' shared commitment to postmetaphysical thinking.

point here is that this characterisation of metaphysics and the considerations Habermas advances against it fail even to touch on Henrich's immanent metaphysics. By ignoring 'the Aristotelian line of thinking', Habermas ignores the fact that it is precisely his concern to avoid Habermas' standard charges against transcendent metaphysics that lead Henrich to develop the immanent Aristotelian alternative. Habermas' general objections to transcendent metaphysics are therefore of no help in assessing his qualms about Henrich's metaphysics of reflective closure. These qualms become evident in Habermas' attempts to defend himself against Henrich's charge of naturalistic reductivism. Despite the polemical tone of his charge, Henrich is not entirely mistaken when he identifies elements of naturalism in Habermas' discourse ethics. He is equally correct in pointing to the deep ambiguities in some of Habermas' central concepts, such as the concept of a 'lifeworld'. When Habermas describes the lifeworld as 'the non-objectified, non-theorised unity which we encounter intuitively and unproblematically as the ever present sphere of common sense',[69] this is hardly the language of a hardened naturalist. Henrich finds in remarks like these support for his own contention of the inescapably metaphysical dimension of philosophical thinking. Yet Henrich is, at best, partially vindicated in unearthing such Habermasian remarks. Even if the description of a lifeworld reverberates with normative and possibly with metaphysical commitments that sit uneasily with the avowedly modest function Habermas assigns to philosophical thinking, the metaphysical outlook implicit in these descriptions is not of a meditative kind. To the contrary, it is the universalistic commitments of Habermas' normative orientation that ultimately fuel his resistance to Henrich's immanent reflections. Henrich's political quietism is based on his search for reconciliation between self and world. At least on one possible reading such reconciliation demands the self's adapting itself to the ways of the world by means of ascribing to the latter a subject transcending spiritual significance. Coming to understand one's place in the world is to acquiesce in the ways of the world. It is this demand for (and guarantee of) *spiritual* reconciliation which Habermas finds politically unpalatable.

While Habermas' objections to Henrich's meditative metaphysics of reflection are normative in the first instance, they thereby mobilise

---

[69] Habermas, *Nachmetaphysisches Denken*, 46.

his own metaphysical impulses. Confronted with Henrich's imma-
nentist challenge, Habermas all but abandons his usual admonitions
that philosophy must give up its role as *prima philosophia*, that it must
cede pride of place to the sciences, and that it must adopt the
proceduralist and fallibilistic standards of scientific reasoning. When
pushed, Habermas passionately defends what he perceives to be the
critical function of philosophical thinking: philosophical inquiry is
'at its best' when it 'stubbornly persists in its engagement with
questions of universal significance'[70] – questions that exceed the
competencies of the natural sciences and that resist pressures for
reflective closure. Such stubborn, normative and universalistic persistence presses against the naturalistic thrust of Habermas' faith in
the sciences *and* expresses his rejection of immanent metaphysical
thinking. Habermas is not unaware of these tensions in his postmetaphysical thinking:

Philosophy continues to maintain its connection with pre-theoretical
knowledge and with the non-objectified totality of meanings underlying the
lifeworld. From there, transcending the boundaries of scientific methodology, philosophical thinking is in a position to review critically the
pronouncements of the natural sciences. In contrast to metaphysical claims
of access to 'ultimate truths', such philosophical reflection seeks to explicate
the sensory bases [*Sinnesfundamente*] of scientific theories as they obtain in
pre-scientific praxis.[71]

Remarks like these pull in opposite directions. Intimations of
philosophy's 'special access' to pre-theoretical knowledge, and references to its ability to 'transcend' the boundaries of science lean
towards a transcendent perspective. At the same time, the rejection
of 'ultimate truths', followed by an appeal to the 'sensory bases' of
knowledge keenly disavow such transcendent leanings. None the
less, and without dwelling on Habermas' own ambivalence, the
exchange between the two thinkers puts into question the accepted
distinction between immanence and transcendence as alternative
ways of doing metaphysics. This is so not just if one feels uncomfor-
table about the quietism implicit in many immanent perspectives,
for one might not. The point is a more general one: if a metaphysical
system's claim to general intelligibility must be grounded in experience, intelligibility also demands that these claims do in some sense
go beyond experience. Even the claim that the aim of metaphysical

[70] Ibid.   [71] Ibid., 57.

reflection lies in reconciling self and world takes one beyond the immanent perspective. It asserts something about the purported end of the immanent perspective that cannot be asserted from within that perspective itself. Questions regarding the grounds and ends of immanent reflection take one beyond that perspective to a higher level of metaphysical thinking. This higher level is the transcendent perspective. The question is whether its unavoidable commitment to a transcendent perspective renders illegitimate (or at least inappropriate) metaphysics in political thinking.

6 RECASTING IMMANENCE AND TRANSCENDENCE

I have suggested that commitment to the general validity of a proposed immanent metaphysics or categorial framework implies commitment to a transcendent metaphysics. Claims about a categorial framework's validity and purpose must be made from outside that framework, requiring an immanence-transcending perspective. Körner's position on the relation between immanence and transcendence is similar in that he, too, contends that every immanent perspective carries implicit transcendent commitments. However, he is more permissive about what can legitimately be included within the perspective of transcendent metaphysics. According to Körner, 'immanent philosophy refers to inquiries into the supreme principles governing one's own and other people's beliefs about the world of intersubjectively interpreted experience'.[72] Transcendent philosophy 'refers to attempts at *grasping the nature of this reality* and at answering questions which cannot be answered without a grasp of it'.[73] A person's transcendent philosophy must not be *inconsistent* with their immanent philosophy: 'A philosopher who holds that his insights into transcendent reality logically implies the logical inconsistency of his or anybody's beliefs about the world of his intersubjective experience contradicts or deceives himself'.[74] However, a person's transcendent metaphysics can be *independent* of their immanent metaphysics: it can belong to 'religious or mystical experience, [which] is not expressible in propositional judgements'.[75]

Körner's view that religious and mystical experiences do qualify as *metaphysical* beliefs seems to me too inclusive. If it is to offer

---

[72] Körner, *Metaphysics*, 48, emphasis added.
[73] Ibid., emphasis added.   [74] Ibid., 49.   [75] Ibid.

warrant for the general validity of the claims made on behalf of a given immanent metaphysics, the transcendent perspective must remain constrained by requirements of rational consistency and intersubjective accessibility. Of course, in one sense Körner is right in saying that the transcendent perspective of a proposed metaphysical system lies 'beyond cognition' – i.e. that it refers to a level of metaphysical insight that lies beyond subjects' *cognitive* powers. There has to be a qualitative difference between immanent and transcendent metaphysical thinking. If transcendent metaphysical thinking were simply a matter of advancing further knowledge claims about the structure of experience, the immanent/transcendent distinction would be spurious. Hence Körner's reference to grasping the nature of reality rather than cognising it: *grasping* the nature of reality instead of cognising it indicates the ineliminably elusive quality of what it is that is being grasped about the structure of experience. None the less, the admission of religious or mystical experiences as possible candidates of transcendent metaphysical insight, hence as warrants for the validity or justifiability of such knowledge claims, drives too great a wedge between the immanent and the transcendent perspectives by putting in jeopardy the demand for intersubjective validity. Even if transcendent metaphysical insight lies beyond *cognition*, it ought not therefore lie beyond intersubjectively accessible and criticisable standards of reasoning. Here Collingwood's distinction between 'ultimate truths' and 'ultimate presuppositions' may be useful.[76] In contrast to ultimate truth claims, arguments about the ultimate presuppositions of immanent knowledge claims fall short of cognition. But they do satisfy the requirements of reason so long as they only affirm what we must presuppose at the level of transcendent metaphysical reflection in order for our knowledge at the immanent level to have rational warrant. So long as they remain intersubjectively accessible and criticisable, transcendent claims, though they lie beyond cognition, do not lie beyond reason. The difference between ontological proofs of the existence of God and revelatory religious experience may serve as an example of the distinction between a reasoned transcendent perspective and religious or mystical insight. Rationalist metaphysicians' ontological proofs are based on rational arguments, which usually seek to demonstrate what has to be the case (i.e. God's existence) for

---

[76] See R. G. Collingwood, *An Essay on Metaphysics* (Oxford, 1940).

something else to be the case (e.g. the existence of the world). In offering argument, such rationalist metaphysical claims explicitly seek reasoned assent and endorsement from others, and thus leave themselves open to criticism and correction. By contrast, the belief that Holy Communion transforms bread into the body of Christ denies the need for any such argument or proof in its behalf: to ask for proof is to miss the point of religious faith. Critics of (transcendent) metaphysics often conflate ontological proofs with professions of religious faith, though they ought not to. Confessions of faith are sufficient unto themselves: to confess one's belief in God is simply to say that one believes in God. Ontological proofs are not sufficient unto themselves in this way: in so far as something else (e.g. the existence of the world) is said to follow from (or be secured through) proof of the necessary existence of God, the proof affords us insight into something which goes beyond the content of the proof itself – it is intended to afford us a grasp of the ultimate, if elusive, nature of reality.

Kant famously rejected the possibility of ontological proofs of the existence of God. According to him, such proofs amount to illicit knowledge claims that involve an inferential leap from the logical possibility of God's existence to His actual existence. Since such inferences violate the conditions of possible human knowledge, they are rejected as illegitimate. In Kant's terminology, rationalist metaphysics entertains a 'positive conception' of transcendent metaphysics: it advances positive knowledge claims regarding the purported content of the transcendent realm to which it is in no way entitled. Whether this is an entirely fair assessment of rationalist metaphysics is a moot point.[77] The important consideration in the present context is that, despite his rejection of the transcendent perspective in its 'positive conception', Kant acknowledges its legitimacy understood as a 'negative idea' or as a 'limiting concept'.[78] This endorsement of the transcendent perspective as a limiting concept is related to Kant's treatment of human finitude. The conception of human beings as cognitively experiencing subjects implies their consciousness of the fact that they are constrained to order sensibly given experience in accordance with their cognitive capacities. Consciousness of themselves as systematisers of sensibly given experience constitutes an awareness of a cognitive limitation, i.e. it constitutes an

---

[77] Cf. Karl Ameriks, 'The Critique of Metaphysics: Kant and Traditional Ontology' in Paul Guyer, ed., *The Cambridge Companion to Kant* (Cambridge University Press, 1992), 249–79.
[78] *CPR*, A235/260, B295/315.

awareness of the fact that our access to the world of sensible experience is not direct, but mediated by our particular cognitive capacities. Questions then arise concerning the adequacy of our categorial framework.

But if the transcendent perspective does arise from recognised limitations of the immanent perspective, how does the former undercut the tendencies towards reflective closure at the immanent level? For Kant, it can do so only if transcendent reflection desists from advancing *knowledge* claims about the ultimate nature of reality. This, arguably, is the substance of his complaint against rationalist metaphysics: the quest for positive truths at the transcendent level replaces the dangers of immanent closure with those of transcendent closure. By contrast, where the transcendent perspective desists from advancing knowledge claims, it functions as a negative, limiting perspective. The transcendent perspective then limits the pretensions of the immanent perspective by showing the truth content of the latter's cognitive claims to remain ultimately provisional and revisable.

7 METAPHYSICS IN KANT'S 'RECHTSLEHRE'

The foregoing sketch of metaphysics in terms of the notion of a categorial framework remains exploratory and incomplete. Apart from defending the public function of metaphysics in political thinking, I have suggested that the immanent/transcendent distinction is best understood in terms of two complementary perspectives within any given metaphysical system, rather than as two alternative ways of doing metaphysics. While the immanent perspective enables us to structure our experience of empirical reality, the transcendent perspective fulfils a critical function in reminding us of the provisional, and hence revisable, status of truth claims made at the immanent level. Admittedly, there is a danger that immanent closure is avoided only at the price of transcendent closure. Hence the importance of Kant's conception of the transcendent perspective as a mere negative idea or limiting concept: the transcendent perspective exerts critical constraint on the truth claims advanced at the immanent level only to the extent to which it desists from advancing ultimate truth claims of its own. I shall close this chapter with some remarks on the bearing of the preceding argument on the interpretation of the *Rechtslehre* in subsequent chapters.

Kant's immanent metaphysics – the organisation and integration of his theoretically and practically supreme principles – is articulated in terms of his philosophical doctrine of transcendental idealism. According to this doctrine, our knowledge of the sensibly given world is mediated by determinate epistemic conditions. Since the latter attach to the experiencing subject rather than to the objects of experience, we can have knowledge of the sensibly given world only as it appears to us, not as it is in itself. Transcendental idealism is a hotly contested philosophical doctrine, and this book will bypass questions about its defensibility. Within the framework of transcendental idealism two broad themes are, however, of importance. The first is Kant's concept of causality; the second is his idea of freedom. In the following chapters, the concept of causality represents what Körner would refer to as Kant's theoretically supreme principle, while the idea of freedom constitutes his practically supreme principle. The *Rechtslehre* aims to reconcile, from the perspective of political agency, the concept of causality with the idea of freedom by specifying the necessary conditions for the possibility of the lawful freedom of each within the constraints of empirical reality.

If the reconciliation between the constraints of empirical reality and the claims to freedom defines the task of the immanent perspective, the transcendent perspective evokes Kant's conception of humans as finite rational beings. On the one hand, Kant treats the notion of human finitude as a limiting concept: he says nothing about the source of human finitude. On the other hand, human finitude is not depicted as a privation. To the contrary, the thesis of the limits of human understanding has as its corollary the thesis of the primacy of practical reason. Although the extent of our knowledge of the world may be limited, this, in effect, increases the scope of practical reasoning: certain questions which are not answerable from a theoretical perspective do admit of a practical answer. The concept of Right in the *Rechtslehre* is a case in point: although its 'theoretical principles lose themselves in intelligible grounds',[79] the problem of Right does admit of a practical answer. With regard to the relation between the immanent and the transcendent perspectives, the guiding thought thus is that the reconciliation between causality and freedom in the *Rechtslehre* can be achieved only in

---

[79] *RL*, 6: 252.

practical terms, and this presupposes an acknowledgement of the finitude of human knowledge.

I appreciate the sketchy character of these closing remarks, but I hope that they will become clearer in the next chapter, which exam ines the conflict between causality and freedom within the context of Kant's metaphysics of freedom. For the moment the most important point to bear in mind is that the following chapters treat the concept of causality, the idea of freedom, and the notion of human finitude as the three central metaphysical categories that shape Kant's approach to the problem of Right in the *Rechtslehre*.

CHAPTER 2

The metaphysics of freedom as an idea of reason

Is it truly a disjunctive proposition to say that every effect in the world must arise *either* from nature *or* from freedom; or must we not rather say that, in one and the same event, in different relations, both can be found? *(CPR, A536/B564)*

I INTRODUCTION

This chapter offers an interpretation of Kant's metaphysics of freedom as initially set out in the third antinomy of the *Critique of Pure Reason*. Kant's characterisation of freedom as an idea of reason constitutes the most contentious aspect of his moral philosophy. His distinction between the negative and the positive conceptions of freedom is well known. While the negative conception defines freedom as a rational being's independence from determination by the causality of nature, the positive conception refers to its capacity to act from principles of pure practical reason alone. Kant often refers to the negative conception as the transcendental idea of freedom, and to the positive conception as practical or moral freedom. This chapter is primarily concerned with the negative conception, or transcendental freedom; chapter 3 deals with moral freedom, especially in relation to the *Rechtslehre*.

Despite the distinction between them, negative and positive freedom are not unrelated. Although we can have no *knowledge* of transcendental freedom, we must assume its reality for practical purposes. The possibility of practical freedom thus depends on the idea of transcendental freedom. In his moral writings, Kant frequently articulates the negative/positive distinction with reference to the noumenal standpoint from which agents assess and determine the actions of their phenomenal selves. Since the noumenal self stands outside the conditions of space and time, it is not subject to the laws of causality. Transcendental freedom thus appears to confront us with a classic case of metaphysical dualism.[1] It is hardly surprising if, the many sophisticated recent commentaries on Kant's ethics notwithstanding, moral philosophers continue to give the conception of negative freedom a wide berth.[2] Nor, until more recently, has the third antinomy been considered crucial to Kant's epistemology, especially not among those who think his transcendental idealism problematic at best.[3] This is not to say that the problem of freedom in Kant has been ignored altogether: it has tended to occupy a separate place from where it has been broached as a version of the classic debate between free will and determinism. This tendency is especially noticeable within Anglo-American Kant exegesis. On the whole, the continental tradition is more prepared to accept the problem of freedom as a live metaphysical issue, distinct from (though a successor to) the classic free will debate.[4] Moreover, the division between Kant's theoretical writings and his practical philosophy is drawn less rigorously within this tradition, possibly

---

[1] Note, however, that Kant does not usually refer to the noumenal *self*. The latter does evoke the image of a 'homunculus' – i.e. of a miniature self inside the embodied, phenomenal self that steers the phenomenal self's actions in the manner it sees fit. The image of such a 'homunculus' is a popular caricature of Kant's conception of the noumenal standpoint (see, for example, Ted Honderich, *How Free Are You?* (Oxford University Press, 1993)). This dualist interpretation of the phenomenal/noumenal distinction is criticised in Onora O'Neill, 'Action, Anthropology and Autonomy' in *Constructions of Reason* (Cambridge University Press, 1989), 66–80. See also Thomas Hill, 'Kant's Argument for the Rationality of Moral Conduct', *Pacific Philosophical Quarterly*, 66 (1985), 3–23.

[2] See, for example, the recent collections of essays by Barbara Herman, *The Practice of Moral Judgment* (Cambridge, MA, Harvard University Press, 1993); Thomas Hill, *Dignity and Practical Reason in Kant's Moral Theory* (Ithaca, Cornell University Press, 1992); Christine Korsgaard, *Creating the Kingdom of Ends* (Cambridge University Press, 1996). Although most of these essays discuss aspects of Kant's ethics in great detail and with much philosophical ingenuity, the idea of freedom is generally avoided by these authors. When the concept of moral freedom is discussed, commentators often strain to play down the metaphysical dimension of Kant's account. See, for example, Korsgaard's 'Morality as Freedom', in *The Kingdom of Ends*, 159–87.

[3] See especially Jonathan Bennett, *Kant's Dialectic* (Cambridge University Press, 1974), chapter 10, 184–227; Paul Guyer, *Kant and the Claims of Knowledge* (Cambridge University Press, 1987), chapter 18, 385–428; Strawson, *The Bounds of Sense*, Part III, 155–234. For a different view, see Henry Allison, *Kant's Transcendental Idealism* (New Haven, Yale University Press, 1983), chapter 15, 310–29; and W. H. Walsh, *Kant's Criticism of Metaphysics* (Edinburgh University Press, 1975), chapter 5, 169–255.

[4] See, for example, Heinrich Böckerstette, *Aporien der Freiheit und ihre Aufklärung durch Kant* (Stuttgart, Frommann-Holzboog, 1984); Heinz Heimsoeth, 'Zum Kosmologischen Ursprung der Kantischen Freiheitsantinomie', *Kantstudien*, 57 (1966), 206–29; Wilhelm Vossenkuhl, 'Von der äußersten Grenze aller praktischen Philosophie' in Otfried Höffe, ed., *Grundlegung zur Metaphysik der Sitten. Ein Kooperativer Kommentar* (Frankfurt, Vittorio Klostermann, 1993), 299–313.

because of the greater abiding interest in systems of philosophical thought. Of course, the differences are not as clear-cut as these remarks suggest. The most insightful approaches to Kant's theory of freedom are often those that draw from both traditions without feeling beholden to either. The limitations of the compatibilist/incompatibilist distinction routinely drawn within the free will debate have been pointed out by Allen Wood, for example, who emphasises Kant's concern to *reconcile* freedom and causality; Wood thus questions the widespread characterisation of Kant as an incompatibilist.[5] Similarly, Lewis White Beck's treatment of Kant's 'fact of reason' and his 'Wille/Willkür' distinction do not refer to the traditional free will debate at all, and remain among the most searching analyses of Kant on the problem of freedom.[6]

None the less, an excessively sharp division between theoretical and practical philosophy can hamper the understanding of central arguments in the *Rechtslehre*. As mentioned in chapter 1, within the English-speaking world, Kant's political philosophy continues to be assessed predominantly from the perspective of his ethical writings. Often the distinction between moral freedom and political freedom is explained by contrasting action from duty in Kant's ethics with freedom of choice in the *Rechtslehre*. While not entirely mistaken, the implied contrast between obligation and choice encourages the attribution to Kant of a conception of political freedom defined as non-interference by others with a person's pursuit of their desire-based choices. This is a familiar liberal view: the problem is that it conflicts with Kant's non-compatibilist metaphysics of freedom as a shared idea of pure practical reason. Some of the difficulties that arise from attributing to Kant a compatibilist conception of political freedom as desire-based choice will be addressed in the next chapter. The present chapter focuses on the relation between freedom and nature in the third antinomy. The initial tension, which Kant seeks to resolve, between the constraints of nature and the claims of freedom has important implications for his subsequent account of political obligation in the *Rechtslehre*, not least because it puts in question the view that theoretical or epistemological issues have no

---

[5] Allen Wood, 'Kant's Compatibilism', in Wood, ed., *Self and Nature in the Philosophy of Kant* (Ithaca, Cornell University Press, 1984), 73–101.

[6] Lewis White Beck, 'The Fact of Reason: An Essay on Justification in Ethics', and 'Kant's Two Conceptions of the Will in their Political Context', both in *Studies in the Philosophy of Kant* (New York, Bobbs Merrill, 1965), 200–14, and 215–29.

bearing on practical or political concerns. Of course, for Kant, the resolution of the conflict between freedom and nature presupposes the doctrine of transcendental idealism. In the present context, this is problematic both for reasons of space (a detailed defence of transcendental idealism is not possible), and in light of the strong reactions which transcendental idealism tends to provoke. Here Körner's exposition of a categorial framework may offer an acceptable alternative to those either unfamiliar with or suspicious of transcendental idealism. Recall that, according to Körner, metaphysical questions do not supersede experience but arise from it – at least in the first instance. Moreover, a systematic organisation of the structure of experience imposes consistency requirements on a framework's practically supreme principles relative to its theoretically supreme principles. Finally, immanent metaphysical questions, though they do arise from experience, ultimately point beyond experience towards a transcendent perspective. I suggested in the previous chapter that the transcendent perspective exerts a constraining influence on the truth claims advanced at the immanent level. In Kant's case, this constraining influence is expressed in terms of a conception of human finitude that has as its corollary his thesis of the primacy of practical reason. The contention that certain metaphysical questions admit of no speculative answer, but that they can be resolved only at the level of practical reason, gives the transcendent perspective an explicitly normative dimension.

Modelling the third antinomy on Körner's general framework, we find that the problem of human freedom arises from experience: it concerns questions about the conditions of human agency which we cannot avoid addressing. None the less, a solution to the problem is conceivable only in so far as it does not violate the general conditions of experience. The solution thus requires the reconciliation between the idea of freedom as the supreme principle of practical reason and the concept of causality as a theoretically supreme principle. Finally, Kant denies any possible knowledge of the reality of freedom. Although, as agents, we are constrained to think of ourselves as free, we can have no knowledge of the 'intelligible grounds of freedom'. Kant acknowledges the indispensability of a transcendent perspective but denies that we can affirm anything positive about it: transcendence functions as a negative idea or as a limiting concept.

Apart from the distinctiveness of Kant's metaphysical starting-point and of its implications for his political conception of freedom, there is a further reason for beginning with the third antinomy. This is the fact that a version of the antinomical dispute recurs in the *Rechtslehre*, albeit in highly condensed form. The antinomy of Right forms a central element in the reconstruction of Kant's account of political obligation in chapter 4. Given the obscurity of its treatment in the later work, Kant's detailed analysis and discussion of the third antinomy in *CPR* provide important clues to the function of the antinomy of Right in the *Rechtslehre*. There are thus three good reasons for approaching the problem of political freedom in the *Rechtslehre* against the background of the third antinomy. First, there is the metaphysical status of freedom, i.e. the relation between freedom and causality and, more generally, that between practical and theoretical reason, modelled, as far as possible, on Körner's notion of a categorial framework. Second, there are the different substantive implications regarding political freedom that follow from Kant's non-compatibilist solution compared to liberal compatibilist solutions. Third, there are the structural similarities between the third antinomy of *CPR* and the antinomy of Right in the *Rechtslehre*. In what follows, I begin with some general remarks on Kant's notion of an 'antinomy of reason'. I then provide a sketch of the conflicting positions of thesis and antithesis in the third antinomy. The ensuing discussion of Kant's solution to the conflict focuses on the substantive issues at stake. Finally, I argue the importance of taking seriously Kant's analogy between the 'lawlike-ness' of freedom and the causality of nature.

2 SOME PRELIMINARY REMARKS ON CAUSALITY AND FREEDOM

I just suggested that the traditional compatibilist/incompatibilist distinction is not the most appropriate for broaching the conflict between freedom and nature in the third antinomy. Kant's theory of freedom is neither incompatibilist nor compatibilist. Allen Wood offers a crisp delimitation of the two standard positions:

Compatibilists hold that our actions may be determined by natural causes and yet also be free in the sense necessary for moral agency and responsibility. Freedom and determinism are compatible. Incompatibilists hold that if our actions are determined to take place by natural causes, then free agency and moral responsibility are illusions. Freedom and determinism are incompatible.[7]

[7] Wood, 'Kant's Compatibilism', 73.

Wood expresses the incompatibilist position in conditional terms: *if* determinism is true, *then* there is no freedom. It is often assumed that Kant does hold determinism to be true with regard to the causality of events in nature, but that he excludes human actions from the class of natural events. This allows him to argue that, in contrast to natural events, human actions are freely determined. The price for this incompatibilism is a glaring dualism. Wood rightly points out, however, that Kant's concern to *reconcile* freedom and causality should caution against the ascription to him of an incompatibilist dualism. At the same time, it would be a mistake to conclude that Kant is a compatibilist. The perceived need for reconciliation implies a tension between freedom and causality, which compatibilists are usually keen to deny. For compatibilists, the distinction between free agency and causally determined events is psychological rather than metaphysical – any perceived tension is illusory rather than real. According to the compatibilisms of both Hobbes and Hume, for example, what we mean by freedom is perfectly intelligible in the terms of everyday language when correctly defined and requires no resort to metaphysical speculation. An action is free when no external impediments interfere with or prevent its occurrence, and when the action is done voluntarily in the sense of according with the agent's desires rather than with those imposed on the agent by third parties. Absence of external impediments and capacity for desire-based choice constitute the two defining elements of compatibilist free agency. However, since, for Kant, an agent's desires form part of their phenomenal nature, actions determined by the causality of desire amount to no more than a 'relative freedom'.[8]

If Kant is not an incompatibilist, neither is he a compatibilist. As Wood puts it, Kant's search for a third alternative makes him an 'incompatibilist compatibilist',[9] or what I call a non-compatibilist. The question is whether this third position offers a plausible or even a coherent alternative. As I said, in the past commentators have usually responded in the negative, and, for most, their conclusions have been based on an overwhelming preference for a version of Hume's psychological compatibilism. More recently, the Kantian

---

[8] In *CprR*, Kant dismisses such a 'relative' freedom of choice as 'the freedom of the turnspit'. None the less, as already indicated, Kant's unqualified assignment of desires to agents' phenomenal nature presents problems for his treatment of external freedom in the *Rechtslehre*. These are discussed in chapter 3.

[9] Wood, 'Kant's Compatibilism', 74.

alternative has received more serious attention, partly as a result of a growing interest in Kant's distinctive conception of causal determination.[10] The compatibilist/incompatibilist distinction assumes a view according to which causal laws express determinate relations between objects and events in nature, where these relations obtain irrespective of whether or not they are perceived by human observers. This view of causality as specifying an objective relation in nature was famously criticised by Hume. However, it is Kant's answer to Hume which undermines the compatibilist/incompatibilist distinction. Although there is no space for a detailed discussion of Kantian causality, a general reminder of his account is in order, given its importance for the argument of the third antinomy.

As is well known, according to Hume we have no rational warrant for attaching the notion of necessity to the concept of causality. No necessary relations connecting successive objects and events are observable in nature as a matter of empirical fact. Hence, all we are entitled to conclude on the basis of our repeated observation of instances of such successive orders is a relation of constant conjunction between their constituent elements. If we do have a tendency to infer the presence of a *necessary relation* from the observation of a mere constant conjunction, this tells us more about ourselves than it tells us about nature. We have a psychological propensity to attribute necessity where all that is rationally warranted is regularity in succession: necessary connection is not something which the human mind observes in nature. Instead, it reads it into nature.[11]

Kant agrees with Hume in one crucial respect. This is Hume's contention that we bring the concept of causality to nature rather than drawing it from nature. However, in contrast to Hume, Kant insists that our attaching the notion of necessity to the concept of causality does have rational warrant. For Kant, the concept of causality does not refer to a psychological propensity but is a category of cognition supplied to nature in the act of human cognition. As Beck has shown, Kant's answer to Hume consists in a small but

[10] See, for example, Ralf Meerbote, 'Kant on the Nondeterminate Character of Human Actions' in William Harper and Ralf Meerbote, eds., *Kant on Causality, Freedom, and Objectivity* (Minnesota University Press, 1984), 138–63; Michael Rosen, 'Kant's Anti-Determinism', *Proceedings of the Aristotelian Society*, 89 (1989), 125–41; Pirmin Stekeler-Weithofer, 'Wille und Willkür bei Kant', *Kantstudien*, 81 (1990), 304–19; Gideon Yaffe, 'Freedom, Natural Necessity and the Categorical Imperative, *Kantstudien*, 86 (1995), 446–58.

[11] David Hume, *A Treatise of Human Nature*, Part III, ed. L. A. Selby-Bigge, second edition (Oxford University Press, 1978), 69–83.

crucial correction.[12] Whereas Hume maintains that we apply the concept of causality *to* experience, Kant argues that it is a necessary condition *of* experience. Without the concept of causality we would not be able to distinguish an 'objective succession' (an event) from a merely 'subjective succession' (a random happening).[13] Hence, while, for Hume, the concept of causality is a posteriori, Kant assigns it a priori status. Hume holds that we attribute a relation of necessary connection between objects and events on the basis of our repeated observation of their successive occurrence. By contrast, Kant argues that our very capacity to discriminate between the occurrence of an event and a random succession of happenings presupposes our application of the concept of causality to sensible experience. How else could we judge there to be a necessary connection between the first billiard-ball setting the second in motion upon impact, but deny a necessary connection between the apple falling off the tree and the man walking past the tree a moment earlier? According to Kant, Hume helps himself to the concept of causal necessity even while rejecting it as rationally unwarranted. Unless Hume could assume a necessary relation in the observed succession of events, he would not even be able to report their successive occurrence *as* events. In short, Kant and Hume both agree that the concept of causality is supplied to nature by the human mind, but in contrast to Hume, Kant attaches epistemic necessity to the concept. In Körner's terms, the concept of causality constitutes one of Kant's theoretically supreme principles with reference to which cognitively experiencing subjects structure their experience of empirical reality, and without which they could have no cognitive grasp of empirical reality as they experience it. When turning to the conflict between causality and nature in the third antinomy, it is important to keep in mind the epistemic necessity that attaches to Kant's use of the concept of causality.

Before concluding this section I want to offer one last set of

---

[12] See especially Lewis White Beck, 'Kant's Answer to Hume', in *Essays on Kant and Hume* (New Haven, Yale University Press, 1978). For discussions of Kant's concept of causality see the contributions in Harper and Meerbote, eds., *Kant on Causality, Freedom, and Objectivity*. For assessments of the reception of Kantian causality in the philosophy of science, compare Michael Friedman, 'Causal Laws and the Foundations of Natural Science' in Paul Guyer, ed., *The Cambridge Companion to Kant* (Cambridge University Press, 1992), 161–99; and Gerd Buchdahl, 'The Kantian "Dynamic of Reason" with Special Reference to the Place of Causality in Kant's System' in Lewis White Beck, ed., *Kant Studies Today* (Illinois, La Salle, 1969).

[13] Cf. *CPR*, A189–196/B234–42.

preliminary remarks. They concern the notion of an antinomy itself.
Kant defines an antinomy as a 'conflict of reason'. More specifically,
it is 'a conflict of reason with itself'.[14] He discusses the antinomies of
reason, of which he identifies four, in the section of *CPR* entitled the
'Transcendental Dialectic'.[15] This relatively neglected section contains both a critique of rationalist metaphysics and a defence of the
legitimate demands of reason. Kant pursues two aims with this dual
strategy of critique and defence. On the one hand, there is the claim
that metaphysical questions arise from the structure of human
reason itself:

Human reason has this peculiar fate that in one species of its knowledge it
is burdened by questions which, as prescribed by the very nature of reason
itself, it is not able to ignore, but which, as transcending all its powers, it is
also not able to answer.[16]

This characterisation of the source of metaphysics already implies
reason's conflict with itself: reason is constitutionally incapable of
answering questions which it is constitutionally unable to ignore. On
the other hand, Kant also contends that the two dominant philosophical traditions to date – rationalism and empiricism – have
failed adequately to address these metaphysical questions. They
have failed to appreciate that metaphysical questions originate in the
structure of human reason rather than pertaining to the ultimate
reality of nature as such, i.e. to reality considered independently of
human cognition. Kant's purpose is thus not just to explore peren-
nial metaphysical problems; he is using the antinomies in order to
advocate his philosophical doctrine of transcendental idealism as the
only possible solution to these otherwise intractable conflicts of
reason. This is why the discussion of the antinomies is highly stylised.
Kant refers to them as cosmological disputes, which concern 'reason's
search for an absolute totality of conditions for any conditioned'. This
search arises from the theoretical principle according to which 'if the
conditioned is given, the entire sum of conditions, and consequently
the absolutely unconditioned . . . is also given'.[17] In plain language,
empirical experience, in giving us conditional knowledge of the
succession of events in nature, raises questions about the ultimate

---

[14] *CPR*, A423/B451.
[15] See *CPR*, A405–567/B432–595. The third antinomy and Kant's discussion of its solution
can be found at A444–52/B472–81, and at A532–58/B560–86.
[16] *CPR*, Avii.   [17] *CPR*, A409/B436.

grounds of such knowledge, thereby taking us beyond empirical experience to its 'absolutely unconditioned' condition.

The discussion of the antinomies in *CPR* proceeds in pairs. The first two raise claims about the totality of conditions of the world understood as an 'aggregate whole' – Kant refers to them as 'mathematical antinomies'. The last two are concerned with the totality of conditions of the world understood as an 'explanatory whole' – these Kant calls 'dynamical antinomies'. Kant's treatment of the mathematical antinomies is often considered the more successful among interpreters of the first critique, largely because of their evident epistemological orientation. The dynamical antinomies are often repudiated for their preoccupation with the normative implications of epistemological questions, which are deemed out of place within the framework of *CPR*. In the following, I shall be concerned only with the third antinomy, where the possibility of human freedom is raised in the course of the dispute concerning the supposed necessity of assuming an uncaused first cause in relation to the laws of causality. However, since all of the antinomies share certain methodological features, I here summarise the most important of them for ease of the subsequent expositions both of the third antinomy in this chapter and of the antinomy of Right in chapter 4.

First, the antinomies take the form of a dispute between a thesis and an antithesis, where the thesis always represents a generalised rationalist position, while the antithesis always defends a generalised empiricist position. A second feature is that theses and antitheses alike employ strategies of indirect proof. Thus, each infers the validity of its own position from a supposed demonstration of the falsity of its opponent's position. Presumably, this is meant to emphasise the intractable nature of the conflict between them: each side can prove the other side wrong. As a result, neither side can sustain its position against the onslaught of its opponent. In his solution to the disputes, Kant claims that the conclusions of theses and antitheses in the two mathematical antinomies are both false. He also avers, however, that the conclusions of the parties to the two dynamical antinomies 'may both be true'.[18] This latter claim has met with widespread incomprehension. A third and related feature is Kant's contention that, despite their conflicting conclusions, thesis and antithesis in each antinomy share the same underlying premise.

[18] *CPR*, A532/B560.

They each treat the world as an 'existing whole', i.e. as a thing-in-itself. The solution to the conflict depends on a rejection of this premise and on the advocacy of a change of philosophical perspective. Since neither rationalism nor empiricism is capable of offering a way out of the antinomical stalemate, the only remaining alternative is transcendental idealism. As I am not directly addressing the issue of transcendental idealism, I shall rephrase Kant's solution as advocating a shift from a cosmological to an anthropocentric perspective. Considered from the cosmological perspective, i.e. as claims about the ultimate nature of reality, these conflicts remain irresolvable. But when considered from an anthropological perspective, i.e. in terms of their normative import for human beings, their resolution leads not to a growth of knowledge so much as to a deepened understanding of the conditions of human knowledge and agency.

It is evident from Kant's systematic if stylised treatment of the antinomies that he perceives them to possess a certain unity. Not only does he suggest that the four antinomies summarise the central cosmological questions that preoccupy mankind, he also believes that the proposed change of perspective will lead to an entirely new way of thinking. Unsurprisingly, this expectation has met with much criticism. To many, the whole purpose of Kant's discussion of the antinomies is shrouded in obscurity.[19] Others perceive Kant's strategy of analysis as unashamedly rigged to fit his desired conclusions in favour of transcendental idealism.[20] Even those who do find merit in Kant's exposition of these cosmological disputes remain sceptical about the success of particular steps in Kant's arguments in any of the four antinomies. Although the following section offers a brief outline of the proof strategies of thesis and antithesis in the third antinomy, the principal concern here is not with the details of Kant's strategy of argumentation so much as with its normative implications. Two themes are of particular relevance to the subsequent analysis of the *Rechtslehre*. The first theme centres around what Kant refers to as the 'interests of reason' in the dispute; the second concerns the analogy he draws between lawlike causal determination

---

[19] This is the conclusion reached by both Bennett in *Kant's Dialectic*, 226–31, and Strawson in *The Bounds of Sense*, 215.
[20] This objection is emphasised by Heinz Röttges in 'Kant's Auflösung der Freiheitsanti-nomie', *Kantstudien*, 65 (1974), 33–49.

on the one hand and the 'lawlikeness' of freedom as an idea of reason on the other.

3 THE THIRD ANTINOMY OUTLINED

As Henry Allison has noted, 'one of the most perplexing aspects of Kant's treatment of the problem of freedom is the radical gulf separating the cosmological context of the third antinomy, in which the problem is initially posed, from the moral context in which the significance of freedom is fully realized'.[21] The cosmological dispute is over the necessity or otherwise of positing an uncaused first cause, or a spontaneous first beginning of the chain of causally determined events in space and time. As this formulation of the problem indicates, thesis and antithesis accept as their common premise the principle of causality. According to this principle, 'all alterations [in nature] take place in conformity with the law of the connection of cause and effect'.[22] However, the two positions draw conflicting conclusions from this shared premise. While the thesis affirms the necessity of positing an initiating first cause of the causal chain, the antithesis denies the legitimacy of so doing. Since a first cause must itself be unconditioned, it cannot be subject to the conditions of causal determination it initiates. If everything in nature is subject to the laws of causal determination, an uncaused first cause must operate outside the conditions of space and time. With the thesis' appeal to a transcendent perspective and the antithesis' denial of the legitimacy of such an appeal, Kant models the conflict as one between rationalism and empiricism concerning the presuppositions of the law of causality.

Allison's problem of a gulf arises from the nature of Kant's critical solution to the conflict. In suggesting that the claims of thesis and antithesis may both be true, Kant argues that, although everything that happens in time and space must indeed be subject to the laws of thoroughgoing causality, it may still be plausible to think of human actions as initiated spontaneously. Kant thus shifts from an 'absolute beginning in time' to a 'spontaneous beginning in causality'. The latter refers to the spontaneity of human agency in space and time, and the puzzle is why Kant should think himself entitled to

---

[21] Allison, *Kant's Transcendental Idealism*, 310.　　[22] *CPR*, B232.

reformulate the cosmological problem about an uncaused first cause as the moral problem of human freedom.

As we shall see, part of the answer to this puzzle lies in Kant's conception of causality as a category of cognition which human subjects bring *to* nature rather than discovering causal relations *in* nature. In fact, for Kant, the idea of freedom is a corollary of our epistemological commitment to the concept of causality. Whatever one thinks of this strategy, Kant clearly approaches the problem of human freedom from an unusual angle, and one should expect his general conception of practical freedom, including freedom of choice and action, to differ from more conventional accounts. In what follows I begin with an outline of the formal arguments of thesis and antithesis respectively. I then briefly consider the bearing of Kant's epistemic conception of causality on his formulation of the dispute. However, it is only when he considers 'the interests of reason' in the dispute that Kant approaches his own solution to the antinomy. The latter is the theme of the next section.

Remember that thesis and antithesis both accept the law of thoroughgoing causality. The thesis none the less claims that:

Causality in accordance with the laws of nature is not the only causality from which the appearances of the world can one and all be derived. To explain these appearances it is necessary to assume that there is also another causality, that of freedom.[23]

According to the thesis, an uncaused first cause is necessary to provide a sufficiently complete explanation of the causal series as we encounter it in empirical reality. For:

(i)   Suppose that there is no such freedom, and assume that there is a causal law in accordance with which every event in nature is preceded by a cause as the condition for its occurrence.

(ii) Then every cause must in turn be an event that is preceded by a cause.

(iii) This means that there is an infinite regress of cause and event.

(iv) But this is 'contrary to the law of nature, which is just this, that nothing takes place without a cause sufficiently determined a priori'.

(v)   Since an infinite regress can never yield an explanation sufficiently determined a priori, it is contrary to the law of causality.

(vi) Hence the assumption of freedom as absolute beginning is

23 *CPR*, A444/B472.

necessary to avoid such self-contradiction regarding the law of causality.

In direct opposition to the thesis, the antithesis asserts that:

There is no freedom; everything in the world takes place solely in accordance with the laws of nature.[24]

According to the antithesis, there can be no uncaused first cause that operates outside the conditions of space and time. Nothing is conceivable beyond the world of empirical experience. For:

(i)   Assume that there is such freedom as spontaneous beginning, and that the chain of causality has a first cause which is not itself caused.

(ii)   Then freedom initiates a causal chain without itself being subject to causality.

(iii)   There is then 'no antecedent through which [this uncaused cause], in taking place, is determined in accordance with fixed laws'.[25]

(v)   But this is contrary to the conditions of experience according to which there can be no event without a preceding cause.

(vi)   Therefore the assumption of freedom as a first beginning destroys the unity of experience, and this is illicit.

There are several difficulties with Kant's presentation of the antinomy. These range from the much-noted asymmetry between the proof strategies of thesis and antithesis, to worries about the merits of the adopted strategy of indirect proof itself, to complaints about Kant's use of his own critical terminology in the exposition of what is supposedly a pre-critical dispute. The latter complaint has given rise to the suspicion that Kant's critical solution is presupposed all along, casting doubts on the genuineness of the dispute itself. The issue I want to focus on in the present context refers to Allison's worries about the 'gulf' between the dispute's cosmological origins and its anthropocentric solution. It is a standard criticism of the third antinomy that this gulf cannot be bridged – i.e. that there is no intuitively obvious way in which to understand the supposed connection between the cosmological idea of an uncaused first cause, on the one hand, and the idea of human freedom, on the other. To many commentators, the third antinomy is an artificially constructed dispute whose place in *CPR* is of dubious legitimacy at best. Jonathan Bennet, for example, advises his readers to ignore the cosmological

---

[24] *CPR*, A445/B473.   [25] *CPR*, A445/B473.

origin of the dispute altogether: 'we should turn our attention solely to the problem of human freedom, forgetting the cosmological route to the question . . . This is because the sections whose main content is cosmological, are irrelevant to the problem of human freedom'.[26] Bennet's advice represents a widespread view, according to which Kant's concern in the third antinomy is to make room for freedom within an otherwise deterministic view of the world. 'Making room for freedom' is perceived as fuelled by a concern to rescue familiar notions of moral responsibility and moral culpability from encroach-ments upon them by Newtonian science. On this view, there is no intrinsic connection between the (scientific) concept of causality and the (moral) idea of freedom – hence the third antinomy's supposedly dubious standing in a work largely on epistemology.

A similar conclusion is reached by P. F. Strawson, who likewise casts doubt on the genuineness of the dispute when he concludes that 'the conventional critical solution would be to say that the antithesis is true and the thesis is false'.[27] Given his commitment to the principle of causality, so the intimation, Kant cannot coherently entertain the possibility that thesis and antithesis both make valid claims. The fact that he does entertain this possibility betrays a lack of philosophical nerve on Kant's part. Once one has decided that the law of thoroughgoing causality applies uniformly across all events in nature, one cannot suddenly exempt human actions, as events in nature, from the constraints of causal determination. It is only because of his quite independent moral concerns that Kant falls into the dualist trap of incompatibilism according to which human actions *are* miraculously exempt from causal constraints.

The problem with objections such as the above is that they neglect the importance of Kant's understanding of causality as an episte-mological concept or category which we bring to nature. On this understanding, it is not just the case that we decide that, or realise that, or discover that the laws of causality apply to nature. In a sense, we produce ourselves the causally ordered sequence of events that make up our conception of empirical reality as a causally connected unity. Michael Rosen's proposed inversion of the standard view is helpful here. Rosen suggests that, instead of thinking of Kant as a (Newtonian) determinist who tries to make room for freedom, we should think of him as a libertarian trying to make room for

---

[26] Bennett, *Kant's Dialectic*, 189.   [27] Strawson, *The Bounds of Sense*, 209.

determinism.[28] This is perhaps a rather dramatic way in which to oppose the standard reading. However, Rosen's underlying thought is sound, that we are unlikely to make much headway with the third antinomy unless we take seriously Kant's conception of causality as a contribution of human cognition to nature, rather than as already given in nature. Rosen puts the difference between Kant's conception of causality and more traditional views in terms of a contrast between a 'mechanical' and a 'systematic' order:

Transcendental idealism about the causal relations of objects argues that, in order for an event to be perceivable as an *event* at all, it must be possible to fit it into a systematic context of antecedent determination according to rules – bluntly, it must have a cause. What transcendental idealism does in this case is to vindicate a realistic attitude which we spontaneously take up with regard to causal processes: we naturally think that for everything which we see happen there was some mechanism because of which it had to happen. But in fact, transcendental idealism does not tell us this. What it says is that unless we could fit appearances into a systematic context of explanation we would not be able to determine our perceptions as perceptions of events at all. And this, it is clear, amounts to something less than the thesis that whatever happens happens because there is a mechanism necessitating it to happen.[29]

Rosen's point here is that it is both easy and tempting to equate Kant's epistemic conception of causality with our standard view of it as referring to a 'mechanistically' ordered universe. The price of that equation is that one loses sight of the connection Kant perceives between the epistemic conception of causality on the one hand and the idea of freedom on the other. However, in contrast to a mechanical order, in a systematic order it is we who do the fitting, i.e. it is we who order events in the world. This does not mean that we are free to order events in the world any which way we like. As I said earlier, Kant assigns the concept of causality a priori status. Given our mode of cognitive access to the world, it is not so much up to us as incumbent upon us to order events in the world *according to rules* – meaning here, in accordance with the concept of causality. Once it is appreciated that when Kants' talks about a causal order he has in mind a systematically constructed order rather than a mechanically given order, it may be easier to see how the problem of human freedom arises for Kant from the (epistemic) concept of causality. If it is we who bring (the concept of) causality to the succession of events in the world, then even if we are *constrained* to do so (given our cognitive capacities), we may in a certain sense think of ourselves as the 'first causes' of that causal order. This should, of course, be understood in no more than a metaphorical sense: we are not literally originating causes of the causal chain of events in the world.[30] None the less, in so far as we are aware of the fact that we are constrained to order events in the world in accordance with rules, questions arise for us not only with respect to these ordering activities (how are we capable of ordering natural events the way we do? Why is it necessary that we do? etc.), but also in regard of types of events which we might not immediately class as natural events. Are human actions of a kind with natural events such that they, too, are subject to being ordered in accordance with the rules of antecedent determination? On the view of causality presently under consideration, there is something peculiar about considering human actions in this way. If we do order natural events in accordance with the causal law, then if human actions were of a kind with natural events this would mean that we impose causal determination upon our actions even as we initiate them. The oddity of this thought lies in the fact that this makes us the authors of our action's dependence on causal determination.[31]

A principal reason, then, why, for Kant, the concept of causality gives rise to the problem of freedom is because we supply causality to nature. For the same reason, Kant must reject the formulation of the problem of freedom in terms of the cosmological problem of a first cause. The fact that thesis and antithesis both construe the problem in this way (the thesis positively so and the antithesis negatively so),

---

[30] Thus, to suggest that we might consider ourselves 'first causes' with respect to our cognitive employment of the *concept* of causality is not to say that we cause the existence of those objects and events to which we apply the causal concept. It is only as systematisers of our sensible experience in accordance with the concept of causality that we may be entitled to think of ourselves as originators of the causal order which we (are constrained to) impose on sensible experience. Even then, the extent to which we can think of ourselves as the 'first causes' of causality in the epistemic sense is severely limited. Unlike the cosmological first cause of the thesis, being the first cause in an epistemic sense does not elevate us above the conditions of time and space. Even on a sympathetic interpretation, therefore, it remains difficult to see Kant's implied analogy between an 'absolute' first cause, and an 'epistemic' first cause. I shall return to this difficulty in the next section.

[31] Of course our actions, once enacted, must conform to the laws of causality in space and time. The issue here is whether we initiate our actions independently of causal determination, or whether they are the result of causally determined antecedents. I elaborate on the difference between the initiation and the enactment of actions in the sections below.

suggests that both interpret the causal law as given in nature rather than as supplied by the mind. Hence Kant's objection that thesis and antithesis treat the world as an existing whole, or, in his more usual terminology, as a thing-in-itself. Both think that the causal law and what it implies about the necessity or otherwise of an uncaused first cause have to do with the nature of ultimate reality rather than with the structure of empirical reality as we are constrained to conceive it. A brief sketch of the ways in which thesis and antithesis draw conflicting conclusions from what Kant regards as their same faulty premise concerning the law of thoroughgoing causality may help to elucidate the nature of Kant's proposed solution.

Starting with the thesis, the crucial phrase is obviously its reference to 'the appearances of the world' in the statement of its position. I mentioned that Kant's reference to appearances here is often taken to evoke his own transcendental distinction between appearances and things-in-themselves, reference to which is re-garded as illicit at this stage in the argument. Alternatively, however, we can interpret the reference to appearances in pre-critical, i.e. rationalist terms. On this reading, appearances *of* the world refer to the rationalist conception of empirically perceived phenomena as imperfect copies or impressions of a supersensible, absolute reality. They are appearances of a world beyond appearances. In conjunc-tion with the law of causality, the thesis then asserts that the causal regress of the order of appearances points beyond the realm of appearances towards the supersensible realm, which constitutes the originating cause of the chain of appearances. In other words, the law of causality provides us with access to ultimate reality: we can deduce the necessity of an uncaused first beginning from the causal regress itself, thereby gaining rational knowledge of appearances' spontaneous beginning in the supersensible world beyond appear-ances.

Against this, the antithesis denies the existence of a 'world beyond appearances': 'everything . . . takes place solely in accordance with the laws of nature'. Given the antithesis' commitment to the principle of infinite regress together with its categorical rejection of an uncaused first cause, no commitment to knowledge of the world as an existing *whole* seems to be implied. Why does Kant insist that the antithesis, too, treats the world as such a 'thing-in-itself'? Here the antithesis' conception of causality as *a law of nature* becomes important. The antithesis claims that we experience the causal order of objects and events in the world incrementally and in passive receptivity: nature's laws divulge themselves to us. Through experience we gradually gain more and more knowledge of nature's mechanically determined processes: the growth of knowledge is potentially never-ending. However, whatever knowledge we do gain in this fashion is knowledge of the world directly, i.e. as it is in itself. The occurrence of one empirically given event explains that of another, and all the events taken together constitute the facts of the world as a whole. There is nothing left to explain.

Since Kant holds that our access to the world is conceptually mediated, and since he regards the concept of causality as constitutive of the way in which we structure empirical reality, he cannot accept the position of either thesis or antithesis. While the thesis affirms too much in claiming rational access to a supersensible reality as the first cause of the world of appearances, the antithesis denies too much in asserting that nothing exists beyond empirical reality. It looks as though we can neither affirm nor deny the existence of a first cause or absolute beginning. But what does this have to do with the problem of *human* freedom? To answer this question we must turn to Kant's consideration of 'the interests of reason in this dispute'.

4 FREEDOM AND THE INTERESTS OF REASON: FROM COSMOLOGY TO PRACTICAL REASON

A principal reason why Kant cannot accept the position of either thesis or antithesis lies in the fact that he has a conception of causality which is different from theirs. But why, then, does he conclude that thesis and antithesis may both be true? In approaching his own solution, Kant discusses 'the interests of reason in the dispute', thus implying the possibility of disinterested adjudication between the two positions. In the position of the thesis, he detects a 'certain practical interest', i.e. a concern with morality and religion, 'in which every well-disposed man, if he has understanding of what truly concerns him heartily shares'.[32] The thesis also displays a 'speculative interest' in its attempt to 'grasp the derivation of the unconditioned completely a priori'.[33] This combination of practical *and* speculative interests betrays the thesis' search for a comprehen-

---

[32] *CPR*, A466/B494.   [33] *CPR*, A467/B495.

sive account of the human condition and explains its popularity, not least because 'the common understanding finds not the least difficulty in the idea of [an] unconditioned beginning'.[34] Against this, the antithesis displays no 'practical interest' in morals and religion. But in compensation its speculative interests 'are very attractive and far surpass those which dogmatic [i.e. rationalist] teaching can offer'. The antithesis refuses to issue knowledge claims that go beyond the conditions of sensible experience: 'according to the principle of empiricism the understanding is always on its proper ground, namely the field of genuinely possible experiences, investigating their laws, and by means of these laws affording indefinite extension to the sure and comprehensible knowledge which it supplies'.[35] At the same time, its commitment to an infinite causal regress explains its lack of popularity, for 'in the restless ascent from the conditioned to the condition, always with one foot in the air, there can be no satisfaction'.[36]

This brief summary of the 'interests of reason' could be taken as confirmation of Bennet's conjecture that the third antinomy is concerned solely with the question of morality. While Kant endorses the antithesis' position regarding the limits of human knowledge, he commends the thesis for its interest in 'morality and religion'. He may indeed appear to be trying to fit morality into an otherwise causally determined conception of nature. But Kant's references to the 'unity of reason' are of greater immediate interest. In assessing the two positions, Kant asserts abruptly, that 'human reason is by nature architectonic'[37] – it strives for unity or completion. While the antithesis 'fails to satisfy the demands of the architectonic interest of reason', the thesis' misguided efforts in this direction open the doors, ultimately, to scepticism about human reason's illegitimate flights of fancy into the supersensible world. Kant's defence of the unity of reason suggests that, rather than the one making room for the other, causality and freedom must accommodate one another in a unified account of theoretical and practical reason. I have already mentioned this demand for reconciliation when referring to the gulf that separates Kant's shift from a cosmological first cause characterised

[34] *CPR*, A467/B495. This remark betrays Kant's own jaded view of the philosophical credentials of common sense and of much rationalist metaphysics alike. The very fact that common folk have no problems in taking on board the idea of an uncaused first cause should caution a philosopher *against* all too ready an acceptance of it.
[35] *CPR*, A468/B497.   [36] *CPR*, A467/B495.   [37] *CPR*, A474/B502.

as an absolute beginning in time, to the idea of human freedom understood as a spontaneous beginning in causality. As I said, Kant's epistemic conception of causality offers a possible starting-point for narrowing that gulf in so far as it allows us to view ourselves, if only in a metaphorical sense, as the first causes of the causally determined order in terms of which we structure sensible experience. A similar line of interpretation is developed by Henry Allison, who challenges the conventional reading of the third antinomy as focused exclusively on questions of morality. Indeed, Allison follows Gerald Prauss[38] in rejecting the conventional equation of practical freedom with moral freedom, and in arguing that, at least in the third antinomy, Kant does not conceive of free human agency in exclusively moral terms:

> If one were to limit oneself to the *Critique of Pure Reason*, assuming by way of a thought experiment that the subsequent ethical works were never written, a considerably different picture of Kant's conception of freedom would emerge. The conception would, of course, still be linked to the cosmological dispute of the third antinomy, but it would also be connected to a view of human agency in general, rather than merely to moral agency.[39]

I shall query Allison's contention that the third antinomy affords a non-moral conception of free agency in the final section of this chapter. However, his proposal to close the gulf between first cause and freedom is insightful in so far as it leads him to focus on Kant's notion of the 'spontaneity of reason'. In so doing, Allison explicitly takes issue with the view according to which Kant introduces the spontaneity of reason for specifically moral reasons and quite independently of his epistemological concerns.[40] Against this view, Allison shows that the spontaneity of (theoretical) reason is essential to Kant's epistemology. It fulfils an indispensable function in Kant's deduction of the pure concepts or categories of the understanding, including the concept of causality, with reference to which we structure our experience of empirical reality:

> Kant's claim that the understanding is spontaneous can best be understood in terms of his identification of its fundamental activity with judgement . . . Knowledge of objects requires the active taking up of sensible data by the mind, its unification in a concept or synthesis, and its reference to an

---

[38] Gerald Prauss, *Kant über Freiheit als Autonomie* (Frankfurt, Vittorio Klostermann, 1983).

[39] Allison, *Kant's Transcendental Idealism*, 310.

[40] Henry Allison, *Kant's Theory of Freedom* (Cambridge University Press, 1990), 36: 'In order to understand Kant's seemingly gratuitous insistence on a merely intelligible moment in the conception of rational agency we must look not to his moral theory . . . but rather to his views on the spontaneity of understanding and reason in their epistemic functions.'

object. All this is the work of judgement, which is simply the spontaneity of the understanding in action.[41]

This is, however, only the first step. Allison's emphasis on the spontaneity of the understanding goes some way in showing that the respective concerns of theoretical and practical reason are not as unrelated as some readings assume. It also indicates a family resemblance between the capacity of a first cause to initiate a spontaneous beginning in time, and the understanding's capacity for spontaneous judgement in relation to sensibly given experience. None the less, a crucial difference remains between a spontaneous power that operates *outside* the conditions of space and time, and a spontaneous power that functions *within* these conditions.[42] As long as this gap remains, it is difficult to see how Kant can justify the shift from the one perspective to the other. It is in his second step that Allison tackles this crucial difference by invoking the notion of reflective self-awareness: 'Kant's account of the understanding commits him not only to the doctrine of the spontaneity of thinking, but also to the assumption of a consciousness of this spontaneity as merely intellectual or intelligible.'[43] This is a reference to Kant's famous notion of the 'I think, which must be able to accompany all my representations'.[44] In 'accompanying' all my representations of empirical reality, the 'I think' expresses my consciousness of myself as a cognitively experiencing subject. Not only do I spontaneously structure my experience of empirical reality in accordance with the rules of the understanding, but I am also conscious of my being cognitively active in this way. I am aware of myself as a thinking and judging being. In the present context, the important point is that, although consciousness of myself as a cognitively experiencing subject must *accompany* all my experiences (how else could I think of them as mine?), the 'I think' is not itself capable of being represented empirically. The 'I think' is merely intellectual or intelligible. As Kant says:

Man, who knows all the rest of nature solely through the senses, knows himself also through pure apperception; and this, indeed, *in acts and inner determinations, which he cannot regard as impressions of the senses.*[45]

---

[41] Ibid.
[42] Cf. Meerbote, 'Kant on the Nondeterminate Character of Human Actions', 151–7.
[43] Allison, *Kant's Theory of Freedom*, 37.   [44] *CPR*, B131.
[45] *CPR*, A546/B574, emphasis added.

Here a more decisive parallel emerges between an uncaused first cause and consciousness of ourselves as cognitively experiencing and rationally deliberating subjects. As 'pure intelligence', consciousness of self is independent of causal determination in space and time: 'in willing and in thinking, we have an activity of which we can become conscious, but which . . . cannot be [sensibly] experienced in the strict Kantian sense of the term'.[46] This is a plausible reconstruction of the possible analogy between a spontaneous beginning in time and the spontaneity of reason in subjects who are aware of themselves as thinking and judging beings. Even though the latter, as 'pure intelligences', are not strictly timeless, it is not implausible to regard a thinking being's awareness of itself as thinking as non-empirical, and therefore as independent of the laws of causality in time and space.

It is Allison's third step which is problematic. He contends that, if we can draw an analogy between the spontaneity of a first cause and the spontaneity of a thinking subject, we can draw a further analogy between the spontaneity of a thinking subject and the spontaneity of an acting subject. Just as Kant posits an 'I think' which spontaneously 'takes up' sensibly given data in the act of cognitive judgement, so we can posit an 'I act' whose function as 'pure intelligence' in the sphere of practical reason is analogous to the 'I think' in the sphere of theoretical reason. The shift here is from the spontaneity of cognitive judgement to the spontaneity of practical deliberation:

To conceive of oneself as a rational agent is to adopt a model of deliberative rationality in terms of which choice involves a taking as and a framing or positing. Since these activities, as expressions of spontaneity, are themselves merely intelligible (they can be thought but not [sensibly] experienced), it is necessary to attribute an intelligible character to the acting subject.[47]

On this account, the capacity for freedom as a spontaneous beginning in causality consists in agents' capacity to 'frame for themselves' projects and goals of their choice, which they may subsequently decide to pursue. Allison is not suggesting that in its empirical manifestations 'the causality of freedom' runs alongside or competes with the causality of nature. Once a freely decided course of action is *enacted*, it is subject to the constraints of the causal law just like any other causally determined sequence in time and space.

---

[46] Allison, *Kant's Transcendental Idealism*, 322.
[47] Allison, *Kant's Theory of Freedom*, 38.

What qualifies human actions as free is not a parallel causality of freedom in time and space, but the empirically unobservable, spontaneous moment of deliberative rationality expressed in the consciousness of oneself as a framer of projects and goals which precedes the subsequent causality of action in time and space:

> Agency includes, but involves more than, a capacity to think. It also includes a capacity to set goals, to adopt a course of action on the basis of these goals, and to resist the pull of inclinations which lure us in directions opposed to these goals. In short, it involves not merely reason, but a 'causality of reason'.[48]

What is wrong with this picture of practical freedom as deliberative agent spontaneity? There are two worries about Allison's analysis that I want to take up in the final section of this chapter. The first worry is methodological and concerns the way in which Allison reconstructs the shift from the cosmological perspective to the anthropocentric perspective. Although insightful, Allison's series of analogies between a spontaneous first cause, a spontaneously judging thinker, and a spontaneously deliberating agent, fails to overcome the apparent gulf between the two perspectives. Indeed, in so far as Allison succeeds in showing that the spontaneity of reason is as crucial to Kant's epistemology as it is to his practical philosophy, he might have derived the spontaneity of practical freedom from that of theoretical reason without referring to the cosmological dispute at all. It should have sufficed to draw attention to the analogy between Kant's 'I think' and Allison's 'I act'. With Allison's analysis we have moved so far from the cosmological origin of the problem of freedom that it is difficult to see why Kant ever began with it in the first place. The second worry relates to Allison's aim to develop a non-moral account of practical freedom from the argument of the third antinomy that is independent of Kant's subsequent elaboration of the laws of freedom in terms of the categorical imperative as the supreme principle of practical reason. Allison's analysis takes a markedly individualistic turn when he locates freedom in agents' 'moment of deliberative spontaneity', and when he relates the causality of reason to agents' capacity to frame for themselves projects and goals of their choosing. It is questionable whether Kant's conception of freedom as an idea of reason can be reduced to agents' capacity for deliberative rationality. The methodological and

---

[48] Allison, *Kant's Transcendental Idealism*, 323–4.

the normative worries are related: Allison's individualistic turn is partly a consequence of his neglect of the cosmological connection. To see this we must turn to Kant's conception of the lawlikeness of freedom as an idea of reason.

5 LAWS OF FREEDOM AND LAWS OF NATURE

I suggested above that Allison's lack of interest in Kant's cosmological route to the problem of human freedom is not unrelated to his attempt to derive a non-moral account of free agency from the third antinomy. This is borne out by his own characterisation of the reconstruction he offers. Although he defends a non-compatibilist reading of free agency, Allison makes it plain that this is not to be understood as a metaphysical defence. Kant's contention that free agency includes a non-reducible, purely intelligible 'moment' in the idea of self-conscious willing is not to be read as a reference to a substantive 'noumenal self'. Instead, the thought of the 'I act' as merely intelligible, i.e. as non-empirical and as independent of the causality of time and space, is said to be contained in the concept of freedom itself. It is how we are committed to viewing ourselves when we think of ourselves as free. Allison is adamant that Kant's point is conceptual rather than metaphysical.[49] (Note, however, that Kant usually refers to the *idea* of freedom rather than to the concept of freedom.) Although Allison is not explicit about what he means by a metaphysical conception of freedom, his repudiation, on Kant's behalf, of a *substantive* conception of the noumenal self suggests that he has in mind a variant of rationalist metaphysics. Given his rejection of the thesis, this is in any case hardly a metaphysic Kant himself would endorse. The question is whether Kant's conception of freedom as an idea of reason can be thought of as metaphysical without equating it with a rationalist metaphysics.

Here it is important to emphasise not only the analogy between a spontaneous first cause and a spontaneous 'I act', but equally the analogy between the causality of nature and the causality of free-

---

[49] See especially his 'Kant on Freedom: A Reply to my Critics', in *Idealism and Freedom* (Cambridge University Press, 1996); 109–28. The critics in question are Stephen Engstrom, 'Allison on Rational Agency', Andrews Reath, 'Intelligible Character and the Reciprocity Thesis', and Marcia Baron, 'Freedom, Frailty, and Impurity', all contributors to the symposium on *Kant's Theory of Freedom* in *Inquiry*, 36 (1993), 405–41.

dom. Since Kant's talk of a causality of freedom in relation to human actions is often thought to entail the problem of parallel causation in time and space,[50] Allison's point is well taken, that the causality at issue only refers to agents' 'inner determinations', i.e. to their reflective deliberation about a proposed course of action. The enactment of a freely determined course of action must respect the causal constraints of empirical reality. None the less, on Allison's account, the intelligible causality of reason is indexed to agents' capacity to frame goals and projects *for themselves*. In the third antinomy, Kant does talk of a framing capacity in relation to the causality of freedom. But this framing capacity does not refer to individuals' particular goals and projects. It is *reason* that is credited with the capacity to 'frame for itself with perfect spontaneity an order of ideas of its own'.[51] Kant juxtaposes causality understood as the laws of nature (or the laws of empirical cognition) with freedom understood as the laws of practical reason. Now a law always indicates, for Kant, objective validity and universal authority. But this means that Allison's description of the spontaneity of reason in terms of individuals' capacity to frame their own goals and projects is misleading at best. At issue is not *individuals'* capacity for deliberative rationality, so much as *humanity's* capacity to create a lawlike order within the sphere of practical reason and agency, i.e. within the sphere of morality broadly understood. Hence, just as the laws of causality govern our systematic ordering of events in nature, so the laws of reason, in their practical capacity, regulate human subjects' freely determined actions. Allison is right to insist that Kant does not, in the third antinomy, possess a fully worked out conception of positive freedom as action in accordance with the categorical imperative. But this does not mean that the conception of freedom there developed diverges sharply from that of Kant's practical philosophy. Kant's references to the causality of reason and to reason's capacity to frame an order of ideas of its own are pointers towards the positive conception of freedom which finds its full expression in his later moral writings. It is Allison's independent advocacy of a non-moral conception of practical freedom that leads him to ignore the analogy between the lawlikeness of nature and the lawlikeness of freedom.

---

[50] Meerbote, 'Kant on the Nondeterminate Character of Human Actions', 153.
[51] *CPR*, A548/B576.

The importance which Kant attaches to the lawlike character of freedom stems from the *problematic* status which he assigns freedom as an idea of reason. The antinomies address the peculiarity of human reason, which is fated to ask itself questions that it can neither answer nor ignore. Clearly, this is a metaphysical proposition, not a conceptual point about what we mean by 'reason'. It attributes to human subjects a reasonable suspicion that there may be more to the nature of ultimate reality than the powers of human reason and cognition are able to fathom – a suspicion which provides the cue to the rationalist endeavours of the thesis. It is also a normative proposition, in that it expresses Kant's appreciation of the deeply unsettling effects the recognition of their cognitive limitations have on human beings. In moving confidently from the conditioned to its condition in accordance with the laws of causality, we eventually confront the realisation that the causal regress, whilst giving us conditional knowledge of the structure of empirical reality, fails to yield ultimate certainty with respect to such conditional knowledge. It is at this point that Kant proposes a shift from a speculative metaphysics to a practical metaphysics of freedom. Whereas the antithesis refuses even to acknowledge the problem of freedom, the thesis' proposed solution remains unsatisfactory in so far as it violates the condition of human knowledge. I want to emphasise that Kant's practical solution remains a metaphysical conception of freedom none the less. To see this, consider the way in which the notion of human finitude mediates between the causality of nature and the idea of freedom. When, in the preface to *CPR*, Kant tells his readers that he has 'found it necessary to limit knowledge in order to make room for faith',[52] he has in mind the antinomies of reason and the crises in metaphysical thinking they have produced. It is possible to give Kant's self-imposed task in *CPR* a negative interpretation in the spirit of the antithesis: human knowledge is limited to knowledge of an infinite regress, and beyond these limits lie nothing but faith and superstition. However, faith, in the sense employed by Kant, is practical and refers to practical reason and agency. On the one hand, it may well be disappointing that human knowledge is limited to conditional knowledge of empirical reality, and that it cannot ascend from the conditioned to the unconditioned. On the other hand, the non-availability of

---

[52] *CPR*, bxxx.

ultimate knowledge or absolute certainty creates a space for the idea of freedom in its practical capacity. Kant's thesis of the primacy of practical reason constitutes a constructive response to the recognition of the limits of the understanding. It is only in so far as human knowledge is finite that the future, considered from the human standpoint, is open; and it is only because the future is open, that reason *can* frame an order of ideas of its own with regard to human agency. In Kant's philosophy, the conception of humans as finite rational beings, the idea of freedom as an idea of practical reason, and the possibility of a human history are thus intimately related. This is one reason why one should guard against an excessively individualistic reading of Kantian freedom, and why one should take seriously Kant's characterisation of human freedom as a task set humanity at large rather than merely a capacity possessed by each individual considered separately.

To suggest that the idea of practical freedom makes possible the idea of the future, more specifically of human history, is not to say that freedom and nature are opposed after all. The possibilities of the future do not open up where nature stops and freedom begins, so to speak. The aim of the third antinomy is not to juxtapose freedom and nature, or to pitch them against one another, but to reconcile them. In fact, throughout his subsequent moral writings Kant maintains what he perceives as the intimate relation between freedom and nature, or causality. Again, it is the notion of law-likeness which both distinguishes freedom and nature from one another and which maintains the relation between them. Thus, in the *Groundwork*, Kant refers to the laws of nature as a 'typic', or model, for the laws or principles of pure practical reason.[53] As we have seen, Kant thinks of causality as a law-governed order which the understanding imposes upon nature: the cognition of objects and events must follow a systematic order to be intelligible to us. Analogously, freely determined actions are intelligible only in so far as they are distinguishable from arbitrary movements or actions, that is, in so far as they are law-governed. This can be rendered more intuitive through the distinction between retrospective causal

---

[53] This point is emphasised by Yaffe in 'Freedom, Natural Necessity and the Categorical Imperative'. Yaffe argues against both H. J. Paton and Allison that Kant's conception of the causality of nature is crucial to his conception of freedom as the causality of reason. The former provides a 'typic' or model for the efficacy of the latter as disciplined reasoning in accordance with principles (or laws) of reason.

explanation and prospective action evaluation. The law of causality enables us to offer a retrospective, causal explanation of the inevitable occurrence of natural events or even of individuals' actions. It also enables us to predict the (likely) occurrence of particular natural events under certain conditions. On the other hand, we cannot predict the causality of actions in the same way. This applies especially with regard to our own actions. We may (think that we can) predict the actions of others by way of applying causal laws; but with regard to our own actions we are constrained to adopt a deliberative stance. Yet to be intelligible, deliberation about action must follow certain rules or principles. Here the causality of nature provides a model or 'typic' for the causality of reason. Just as the occurrence of particular natural events would seem unintelligible to us in the absence of causal laws which render their occurrence explicable, so individuals' actions would seem unintelligible in the absence of reasons for action which can be proffered in justification of these actions and which render them intelligible to ourselves and to others. (Of course, Kant also emphasises an important *disanalogy* here: while causal laws *determine* the order of natural events, principles of practical reason can *guide* but they cannot determine agents' deliberations about actions. While the laws of causality are constitutive principles of empirical cognition, the laws of freedom are regulative principles of practical reason, i.e. they are action guiding without being action determining.)

There is a second, more extended sense in which the laws of nature provide a 'typic' for the laws of freedom. It is of particular importance to the *Rechtslehre*. The idea of freedom and of free agency presupposes an explicit acknowledgement of the constraints of nature. It does so not just in the sense that the causality of freedom, in referring to an agent's inner determinations, must not contradict the causal laws that govern the action's external execution. Additionally, acknowledgement of the constraints of nature must form an integral part of agents' deliberation about action. If, in acting on the idea of freedom, agents failed to be cognisant of the causal constraints of nature, their actions would again seem arbitrary or at least misguided, and the efficacy of their practical reasoning would be jeopardised. Not everything one wants to do is feasible or even possible. An adequate understanding of what actions are possible presupposes an acknowledgement of the constraints of nature on action. This does not mean that free actions are *determined* by the causality of nature after all: to be cognisant of the constraints of nature in relation to one's actions is simply to take those constraints into account in one's practical deliberations. None the less, disciplined practical reasoning presupposes an understanding of cognitive and causal constraints, and cannot for that reason orient itself solely in accordance with agents' particular projects, goals, and desires.

These two aspects of lawlike practical freedom – human beings' capacity to frame a conception of a possible law-governed future which is cognisant of the constraints of nature on human agency without being determined by them – are crucial to Kant's conception of political freedom in the *Rechtslehre*. More generally, the idea of freedom as a shared idea of reason and as a task of humanity at large is crucial to Kant's cosmopolitan conception of Right, or of political justice according to which the freedom of none is wholly achieved until the freedom of each has been secured at the global level. It is partly because of the very different implications, at the level of political practice, of Kant's metaphysical conception of freedom as an idea of reason that one should guard against its all too ready assimilation under the more individualistic model of conventional liberal theory.

CHAPTER 3

The morality of external freedom

> The *capacity for desire* is the capacity to be by means of one's representations the cause of the objects of these representations. The capacity of a being to act in accordance with its representations is called *life*. (*MM*, 211)

I INTRODUCTION

The previous chapter emphasised the lawlikeness of Kant's metaphysics of freedom as an idea of pure practical reason, focusing on two aspects of lawlikeness.[1] The first concerned the analogy between the laws of causality, on the one hand, and the laws of freedom, on the other, and, in a more extended sense, the relation between human finitude and the idea of freedom, as indicated in the shift from a cosmological to an anthropocentric perspective. In the third antinomy, the idea of practical freedom arises in connection with human beings' recognition of their limited claims to knowledge. Given their epistemic dependence on the concept of causality, and given the morally unsettling implications of the latter's infinite regress in its empirical application, it is both natural and futile for finite reasoners to inquire into the causal law's ultimate grounds. It is natural in so far as the prospects of an infinite regress are themselves barely intelligible to finite rational beings (hence the thesis' claim that the causal law implies an unconditioned first cause). But the search for such an uncaused first cause is also futile in so far as questions concerning it arise for finite rational beings precisely because they are incapable of answering them. No such question would arise for a perfectly rational, omniscient being, for whom a

---

[1] This chapter is based on my paper, 'Kantian Desires: Freedom of Choice and Action in the *Rechtslehre*' in Mark Timmons, ed., *New Essays on Kant's Metaphysics of Morals* (Oxford University Press, forthcoming).

first cause would be as transparent as everything that followed from it. For finite rational beings, by contrast, knowledge of a first cause remains constitutionally inaccessible. This is why the question of freedom can be answered only from a practical perspective, not from a speculative, transcendent perspective: pure practical reason must give itself an order of ideas of its own.

From this conclusion, it does not follow that Kant offers an exclusively immanent conception of freedom. In many ways, the most interesting feature of his account is the contention that the immanent perspective of practical freedom presupposes a transcendent perspective, if only as a 'negative idea'.[2] As we have seen, Kant not only distinguishes between transcendental freedom and practical freedom; he also insists that the intelligibility of practical freedom depends on the possibility of transcendental freedom. Although we cannot *know* that the will is independent of the causality of nature, we must assume the possibility of such independence for practical purposes.[3] My claim is that, because practical freedom presupposes the transcendental idea of freedom, a free will cannot be an arbitrary or lawless will. To entertain the idea of the will's possible freedom from causal determination is to entertain the idea of a causality of reason. In so far as knowledge of negative freedom is not possible for finite rational beings, *knowledge* of the laws of pure practical reason is also not possible. Hence the laws of nature provide a *typic* or model of lawlikeness in analogy with which finite rational beings form a conception of the action-guiding laws of practical freedom, as

---

[2] Strictly speaking, I should be referring to the 'transcendental perspective', given Kant's distinction between the transcendent metaphysics of rationalism and his own transcendental philosophy. However, I here use 'transcendent' in Körner's general sense of the term, i.e. by way of distinguishing it from the immanent perspective.

[3] It is essentially this contention which rules out either a compatibilist or an incompatibilist interpretation of Kant's idea of freedom. If he were a compatibilist, he would reject the negative or transcendental idea of freedom as illusory. If he were an incompatibilist, he would claim knowledge of negative or transcendental freedom. But, although Kant denies the possibility of such knowledge, his position should not be confused with the superficially similar argument of contemporary compatibilists that the thesis of determinism is immaterial to the morality of freedom. According to the latter, the truth or falsity of determinism is irrelevant to the issue of moral freedom because the former pertains to matters of fact, whereas the latter is the preserve of human feelings and psychology. Given the fact/value distinction, we can concede the moral importance of freedom without settling the issue of determinism. For the classic statement of this position, see P. F. Strawson, 'Freedom and Resentment' in *Freedom and Resentment and Other Essays* (London, Methuen Publishers, 1974), 1–25. For Kant, the problem of determinism is not irrelevant to the idea of freedom, since, in the absence of the former, the latter could not arise as a problematic idea of reason.

articulated in the categorical imperative as the supreme principle of practical reason.

I shall come back to the connection between Kant's metaphysics of freedom and his conception of human finitude in chapter 6. The present chapter focuses on the second aspect of lawlike freedom. This is Kant's treatment of freedom as a *shared* idea of reason. As already mentioned, for Kant, a law always implies universal validity and general authority: something's being a law makes it valid for all cases which fall under its authority. His allusions to the laws of freedom then suggest a conception of free agency whereby a particular action qualifies as free only in so far as it accords with relevantly authoritative principles of action. This emphasis on law-likeness differs from classical liberal, compatibilist conceptions of free agency. The latter usually view freedom as an attribute or property possessed by each individual considered separately, where that property is defined with reference to individuals' capacity for desire-based choice. Although this view does not deny the necessity of instituting lawful constraints with respect to individuals' dealings with one another, it does not regard lawlikeness as constitutive of the concept of freedom. To the contrary, the concept of freedom is usually taken to denote the *absence* of constraint by laws. Whether or not a particular action qualifies as free can be settled independently of whether the action accords with generally valid principles of action. What decides the question of freedom on this account is whether the agent acted voluntarily, i.e. in accordance with their choices.

As we have seen, despite acknowledging the importance of lawlike freedom to Kant's *ethics*, Allison makes a case for a general, non-moral conception of Kantian freedom that is based on a particular reading of the third antinomy. Allison accepts that in his moral philosophy Kant focuses on the mutually entailing relation between morality and freedom.[4] However he claims that, at least in *CPR*, Kant possesses the theoretical resources on the basis of which he *could have* developed the more general, non-moral conception of free agency that Allison himself advocates. In advancing his alternative interpretation, Allison emphasises the rationality of free agency over its morality, locating the spontaneity of reason in individuals'

---

[4] Allison calls this Kant's 'reciprocity thesis'. See Allison, *Kant's Theory of Freedom*, chapter 11, 201–13.

capacity to frame projects and goals of their own. Although Allison does not himself engage with Kant's political philosophy, his advocacy of a non-moral conception of freedom lends indirect support to the often more casual attributions to Kant of a classical liberal conception of political freedom.[5] In other words, Allison's individualistic treatment of the spontaneity of reason in the third antinomy helps to underwrite the view of those who detect in Kant's references to freedom of choice and action in the *Rechtslehre* a straightforward appeal to liberal individualism.

There are a number of problems with such a move. First of all, it requires repudiating or at least ignoring the metaphysical dimension of Kantian practical freedom along the lines sketched under the heading of 'classical liberalism' in chapter 1. Second, such a move appears to land Kant with two conceptions of freedom – one ethical the other political – threatening the overall coherence of Kant's conception of human agency.[6] Third, the subsumption of Kantian political freedom under the classical liberal, individualistic account deprives one of much of what is distinctive about Kant's political philosophy, especially in relation to his cosmopolitanism. The principal aim of the present chapter is to argue against the view according to which Kant's conception of political freedom falls outside the bounds of his general account of moral agency. Law (politics) and ethics – designated by Kant as the spheres of external freedom and internal freedom respectively – form two distinct but equal branches of morality.[7] This means that the notion of law-likeness is as indispensable to Kant's conception of external freedom as it is to his account of internal freedom.

None the less, there is one complicating factor that may be

---

[5] A recent example is Allen Rosen, *Kant's Theory of Justice* (Ithaca, Cornell University Press, 1993).

[6] Henry Sidgwick accused Kant of advocating two such mutually exclusive conceptions of freedom. Sidgwick, 'The Kantian Conception of Free Will', *Mind*, 13 (1888), 405–13. For a repudiation of Sidgwick's argument see Nelson Potter, 'Does Kant have two Concepts of Freedom?' in G. Funke and I. Kopper, eds., *Akten des Vierten Internationalen Kant Kongresses* (Berlin, de Gruyter, 1974), 590–6. See also, Lewis White Beck, 'Kant's Two Conceptions of the Will in their Political Context' in *Studies in the Philosophy of Kant*, 215–29.

[7] The distinct but complementary spheres of law and ethics within Kant's division of morality is well explained by Wolfgang Kersting in *Wohlgeordnete Freiheit* (Frankfurt, Suhrkamp, 1993), 175–81. According to Kersting, the categorical imperative fulfils a 'dual legislative function' (*doppelte Gesetzgebung*), which neither subsumes law under ethics nor renders law independent of the requirements of morality. Kersting's interpretation is supported by Kant's formulation of the universal principle of Right, which is evidently a version of the categorical imperative as it applies to law. I say more about this in sections 2 and 3, below.

thought to lend support to the opposing view, according to which Kant's conception of political freedom must needs be non-moral. It concerns the function of individuals' desires in relation to external freedom. In the *Rechtslehre*, Kant explicitly acknowledges the legitimate role of individuals' desires in relation to external freedom. He does so for good reason. The concept of external freedom plays a pivotal role in Kant's justification of individual property rights and in his deduction of the obligations of justice incurred by individuals as a consequence of their claims to property. Property claims refer to individuals' desires for material objects of their choice. Yet Kant's acknowledgement of the legitimacy of such desire-based claims to external freedom is in apparent conflict with his insistence in the *Groundwork* that only autonomous actions, i.e. actions determined independently of agents' inclinations and desires, qualify as freely determined actions. Given the equation of practical freedom with autonomous willing in the *Groundwork*, how can an act of materially determined choice qualify as an act of (external) freedom? Is Kant not here subscribing to a conception of heteronomously determined choice and action, thereby endorsing an account of external freedom that is consonant with liberal, compatibilist views?

Much depends on how one construes the function of desires and of desiring in the *Rechtslehre*. My defence of external freedom as lawlike freedom in the sense of autonomous choosing takes an indirect route, focusing on Kant's understanding of individuals' capacity for desire as a rational capacity. I attribute to Kant the view that it is only in so far as they have the capacity to reason that finite rational beings have a capacity for desire-formation. In so far as the capacity for desire presupposes a being's ability to reason, a rational being's desires are susceptible to the constraints of reason in general.[8] They are then also susceptible, at least by implication, to the constraints of pure practical reason, i.e. to the laws of freedom.

---

[8] A 'reasoned desire' is not the same as a 'rational desire'. The concept of the latter, which is quite prevalent in current political decision-making theory, refers to a desire which it is rational for individuals to have – either because it is important to their general well-being, or because it satisfies some valued aspiration of theirs. The rationality of the desire is not intrinsic to the formation of the desire, but is indexed to the end served by the desire as a means. By contrast, a 'reasoned desire' refers to desire-formation as the product of a reasoning process. Hence, a reasoned desire is justified in terms of the reasoning process of which it is the product, not with reference to the putatively rational end served by having that desire. I hope to make the notion of a reasoned desire clearer in section 4 below.

Admittedly, the view of desiring as presupposing a being's capacity to reason contrasts with much of what Kant says about the pathology of desires and inclinations in his earlier writings. None the less, I believe that a plausible case for the alternative interpretation can be made, at least for the *Rechtslehre*, on the basis of Kant's remarks on the 'capacity for desire' in the general introduction to the *Metaphysics of Morals*.[9] What is more, Kant *requires* a conception of reasoned desiring if he wants to maintain, as he must, that acts of external freedom, though distinct from acts of internal freedom, nevertheless qualify as freely determined acts in virtue of their conformity with the categorical imperative as the supreme 'law of freedom'. In what follows, I begin with a brief exposition of the differences between internal and external freedom. Section 3 contrasts two opposing attempts to resolve the apparent tension between external freedom and the categorical imperative as a principle of moral self-legislation. If neither succeeds in offering a persuasive account of external freedom as the freedom of choice and action in accordance with the categorical imperative, this is because both ignore the specific function of desiring in relation to external freedom. Sections 4 and 5 offer an interpretation of Kant's conception of rational beings' capacity for desire that accords with the requirements of self-legislation under the categorical imperative as the supreme law of freedom. Hence a conception of external freedom is possible which both endorses individuals' legitimate desire for material objects of their choice, and regards the formation and pursuit of such desires as subject to the constraints of the laws of freedom.

2 INTERNAL FREEDOM AND EXTERNAL FREEDOM

Kant does not formally introduce the distinction between external freedom and internal freedom until the *Metaphysics of Morals* itself, where it tracks the division of that work into the *Rechtslehre* and the *Tugendlehre* respectively. Even then, he says little explicitly about the distinguishing criteria between internal and external freedom. This is surprising, since the new distinction introduces additional complexity into Kant's already demanding theory of freedom. More specifically, it is not evident that the conception of external freedom

---

[9] Cf. *MM*, 6: 211.

can be accommodated within the account of practical freedom developed in the *Groundwork* and the *CprR*. Despite occasional references in those works to subjects' juridical duties, especially in connection with his account of perfect obligations, Kant there expounds a general theory of freedom very much in keeping with what he later speaks of in more restrictive terms as internal freedom. Although the present chapter is concerned with the concept of external freedom, a reminder of some of Kant's fundamental moves relating to internal freedom in the *Groundwork* will shed light on the contrast between them.

The *Groundwork* takes up the distinction between the negative and the positive conceptions of freedom familiar from the third antinomy. Negative (transcendental) freedom defines the independence of a subject's will from causal determination; positive (practical) freedom refers to the will's capacity to determine itself in accordance with principles of pure practical reason. Positive freedom presupposes negative freedom in that only a being which can be assumed to have the capacity to will independently of the causality of nature can be assumed to have the further capacity for self-legislated willing in accordance with the laws of freedom. In the *Groundwork*, Kant notoriously defines subjects' inclinations and desires as belonging to their 'phenomenal nature' and as subject to the causality of nature. The clear implication of this is that a will determined by the causality of a subject's desires cannot be free. Since such a will does not fulfil the necessary condition of negative freedom, it cannot fulfil the requirements of positive freedom. This claim is further elaborated with the distinction between heteronomous willing and autonomous willing. Kant points out that the will of a finite rational being is inevitably affected by the sensuous impulses that form part of its phenomenal nature. However, a heteronomous will is not only affected by, but is also determined by, the subject's sensuous impulses and inclinations. *CprR* characterises a heteronomous will as determined by 'material practical principles':[10] although the will is guided by principles of practical reason, those principles are, in turn, responsive to the agent's desires and inclinations, hence to their phenomenal nature. This characterisation of heteronomous willing as materially determined willing has led some commentators to regard Kant's conception of heteronomous willing as of a piece,

---

[10] *CprR*, 5: 22.

essentially, with the Humean conception of instrumental reasoning where desires, not reason, determine the course of action. Whether this is entirely accurate is difficult to say. On the whole, it is the subjectively determined nature of material practical principles rather than their instrumental character which, for Kant, disqualifies them from being *laws* of reason in the strict sense. Since material practical principles are responsive to agents' subjectively given desires, they cannot be valid for all irrespective of the particular desires of each.[11]

In contrast to a heteronomously determined will, an autonomous will abstracts from all subjectively given desires and inclinations as the ground of its determination and acts on its conception of an objectively valid formal practical law alone. In disregarding subjective desires, an autonomous will fulfils the condition of negative freedom: it wills independently of the causality of the subject's phenomenal nature. In acting on its conception of the form of a practical law as such (i.e. an objectively valid principle), an autonomous will fulfils the requirements of positive freedom. Strictly speaking, only a perfectly rational being acts directly from its conception of the form of a practical law as such. A finite rational being, whose will is inevitably affected by, though not inevitably determined by, sensuous impulses, experiences objectively valid principles as imperatives or commands of reason. Hence the autonomous will of a finite rational being is a will whose maxim it is to act *from duty* and in accordance with principles of pure practical reason.

Even from this brief summary of freedom as autonomous willing in his earlier writings, we can identify two central problems for Kant's subsequent account of external freedom. The first is the already mentioned difficulty concerning subjects' legitimate desires for external objects of their choice – desires which suggest a view of will determination closer to material practical principles than to formal practical principles. The second difficulty concerns the close association between autonomous willing and the maxim of duty. Since in his ethical writings Kant usually associates acting from duty with the agents' idea of an ethically good will, the implication is that autonomous willing requires an ethically good will. But being 'good-willing' is a distinguishing feature of internal freedom; the concept of

---

[11] *CprR*, 5: 21: 'All practical principles which presuppose an object (material) of the faculty of desire as the determining ground of the will are without exception empirical and can hand down no practical laws.'

external freedom explicitly abstracts from this ethical requirement. If, therefore, an ethically good will is indeed a prerequisite to autonomous willing, external freedom cannot be conceived in terms of autonomous willing. It then becomes questionable whether external freedom can be thought of as a Kantian conception of freedom at all. In order to see the force of these difficulties more clearly, let us turn to the exposition of external freedom in the *Rechtslehre* itself.

Since the *Rechtslehre* does not concern itself with internal freedom, we can assume that Kant's view of the latter remains essentially that expounded in the *Groundwork* and *CprR*. Internal freedom denotes an agent's purity of will and their ethically good intentions, or maxims of action. That agent is ethically good, and internally free, who acts independently of the causality of their desires and from the maxim of duty, hence in accordance with the requirements of principles of pure practical reason. The novel conception of external freedom is derived from Kant's references to the 'innate right to freedom of each' in the introduction of the *Rechtslehre*. The innate right to freedom, which each individual possesses merely in virtue of their humanity,[12] comprises subjects' innate equality, their independence from the arbitrary will of another, and their right to free interaction with others on an equal footing. Independence from the will of another and the right to free interaction with others imply subjects' capacity for freedom of choice and action. This preliminary definition of external freedom as affirming individuals' right to freedom of choice and action is substantiated in Kant's subsequent definition of the concept of Right, which regulates the *form of external relations between agents with regard to their choices*:

The concept of Right . . . has to do, *first*, only with the external and indeed practical relation of one person to another, in so far as their actions, as facts, can have (direct or indirect) influence on each other. But, *second*, it does not signify the relation of one's choice to the mere wish of the other . . . but only a relation to the other's choice. *Third*, in this reciprocal

---

[12] I here follow Bernd Ludwig's interpretation in *Kants Rechtslehre. Kant Forschungen, Bd.2*, Reinhard Brandt and Werner Stark, eds. (Hamburg, Felix Meiner Verlag, 1988), 103. According to Ludwig, Kant's reference to subjects' humanity suggests that he takes himself to have vindicated the innate right of each in his justification of human freedom in the *Groundwork* and *CprR*. The *Rechtslehre* thus presupposes this right as already established. Kant himself notes that, since the *Rechtslehre* is not directly concerned with the innate right of each, 'it can be put in the prolegomena and the division of the doctrine of Right can refer only to what is externally mine or yours' (*RL*, 6: 239).

relation of choice, no account is taken of the matter of choice, that is, of the end each has in mind with the object he wants.[13]

The concept of Right thus abstracts both from the content of agents' choices and from the maxims of their actions – agents' internal dispositions towards others are of no consequence in judging the rightfulness of their external relations with one another. The same emphasis on the form of external relations between agents is repeated in the formulation of the universal principle of Right, which follows as a corollary of the innate right to freedom of each and the general concept of Right:

Any action is right if it can coexist with everyone's freedom in accordance with a universal law, or if on its maxim the freedom of choice of each can coexist with everyone's freedom in accordance with a universal law.[14]

The reference to subjects' maxims in this formulation should not mislead one into thinking that internal dispositions matter after all. All the universal principle of Right requires is that the *execution in action* of an agent's maxim not violate the external conditions of choice of another. In a business transaction between two agents, for example, the maxim of the one may well be to profit from the relative disadvantage of the other. Though such a maxim may be ethically unworthy, it is not 'contrary to Right' so long as in acting on that maxim the agent does not violate the external conditions of choice of the other.[15] Rightful action need not be ethical. But this brings us to the crucial difference between internal freedom and external freedom, simultaneously raising questions about the status of autonomous willing in relation to external freedom. In contrast to internal freedom, external freedom is externally enforceable. While one cannot be compelled to adopt an ethically good disposition towards others, one can be compelled to act externally in accordance with the universal principle of Right. The universal principle of

---

[13] *RL*, 6: 230.   [14] *RL*, 6: 230.

[15] It is notoriously difficult to judge under what circumstances someone's conditions of choice have been violated or compromised. As Onora O'Neill has shown, much coercion is implicit rather than explicit, especially in the context of political and economic agency, relying on forms of deceit and manipulation of people's wills and circumstances of choice. See O'Neill, *Towards Justice and Virtue* (Cambridge University Press, 1996), chapters 5 and 6. Kant's standard example of a person who acts non-ethically but justly is of a creditor who insists on the repayment of a loan in full knowledge of the fact that this will ruin his debtor. The example assumes that the initial transaction was freely undertaken by both parties, in the sense that both could have chosen not to enter into the arrangement. In many choice situations this assumption is arguably unwarranted, even when the formal conditions of choice suggest otherwise.

Right ensures protection from violation by others of one's right to external freedom, if necessary by coercive means: 'if a certain use of freedom is itself a hindrance to freedom in accordance with universal law, coercion that is opposed to this hindrance is consistent with freedom in accordance with universal laws'.[16] The question is whether the universal principle of Right functions *exclusively* as an externally imposed constraint on action or whether, its coercive character notwithstanding, the principle's normative grounds derive from Kant's general conception of the self-legislative character of practical freedom as autonomous willing. On this point, different passages in the text give rise to conflicting possible interpretations. It is possible to interpret the universal principle of Right as an exclusively external principle of legislation which ensures agents' outward conformity with its requirements by appealing to their prudential self-interest, relegating external freedom to a form of heteronomous willing as a result. Alternatively, the text also supports a view according to which the universal principle of Right functions primarily as a principle of self-legislation, with coercive enforcement stepping in only in cases of failed self-legislation. On this interpretation external freedom might yet be found to be consistent with the requirements of autonomous willing.

Principal support for what one might call the prudential interpretation comes from Kant's distinction in the general introduction to the *Metaphysics of Morals* between different possible action incentives:

All lawgiving can be distinguished with respect to incentives. That lawgiving which makes an action a duty and also makes this duty an incentive is ethical. But that lawgiving which does not include the incentive of duty in the law and so admits of an incentive other than the idea of duty itself is juridical. It is clear that in the latter case this incentive that is something other than the Idea of duty must be drawn from sensibly dependent determining grounds of choice, inclinations and aversions, and among these from aversions, since it is a lawgiving which constrains, not an allurement which invites.[17]

Kant's claim that rightful action admits of an incentive other than duty, and that this must be a sensibly based incentive which appeals to an aversion, invites the conclusion that subjects' outward conformity with the universal principle of Right rests on enlightened self-interest – i.e. on a disinclination to suffer the sanctions of an

---

[16] *RL*, 6: 231.   [17] *MM*, 6: 219.

externally enforced law in the case of non-compliance with it. Those who reject such a prudential interpretation, on the other hand, can appeal to Kant's insistence that law and ethics are equally subject to the moral law, conformity with which cannot be based on prudential reasons:

> In contrast to the laws of nature, the laws of freedom are called moral laws. As directed merely to external actions in conformity to law, they are called juridical laws, but if they also require that the laws themselves be the determining grounds of action, they are ethical laws, and then one says that conformity with juridical laws is the legality of an action and conformity with ethical laws is its morality.[18]

Here Kant distinguishes between law and ethics in terms of their respective spheres of moral competence. Since *all* laws of freedom are laws of moral self-legislation, juridical laws *can* be self-legislated even though, in contrast to ethical laws, they are *also* externally enforceable. Hence the normative ground of juridical laws of freedom lies in subjects' capacity for self-legislation, not in an appeal to their prudential self-interest. It is, I think, fair to say that until recently the prudential interpretation of juridical legislation in the *Rechtslehre* has prevailed over non-prudential alternatives.[19] This is partly because of the general prevalence of prudentialist assumptions about agent motivation in the history of modern political thought, but also because of a genuine ambiguity in Kant's political writings, especially in some of his earlier, political essays.[20] None the less, there has recently been an upsurge in the non-prudential line of interpretation. In the following section I briefly contrast two representative positions from either camp, commenting on what I think wrong with both of them.

3 EXTERNAL FREEDOM: PRUDENCE OR VIRTUE?

Otfried Höffe has offered a sophisticated prudential reconstruction of the relation between external freedom and the categorical

---

[18] *MM*, 6: 214.

[19] For recent debate on this point see the exchange between Bernd Ludwig, 'Will die Natur unwiderstehlich die Republik?', and Reinhardt Brandt, 'Antwort auf Bernd Ludwig', *Kantstudien*, 88 (1997), 218–36. See also the exchange between Allen Wood, 'The Final Form of Kant's Practical Philosophy', and Paul Guyer, 'Justice and Morality', *The Southern Journal of Philosophy* (Supplement), 36 (1997), 1–28.

[20] Cf. Heinz-Gerd Schmitz, 'Moral oder Klugheit?', *Kantstudien*, 18 (1990), 413–34. See also Hella Mandt, 'Historisch–politische Traditionselemente in Kant'.

imperative.[21] Höffe recognises that any plausible interpretation must accommodate Kant's account of external freedom within the framework of the categorical imperative without in so doing reducing external freedom to internal freedom. Rejecting the subordination of politics to ethics, he advocates 'the juxtaposition of law [i.e. politics] and ethics, and their common subordination to the moral point of view, that is, the general categorical imperative'.[22] The suggested juxtaposition takes its cue from Kant's reference to different motivational incentives, on the basis of which Höffe distinguishes between two levels of the categorical imperative. At the first level we have the formulation of the categorical imperative as the supreme principle of morality in general, which makes no reference to motivational incentives at all: 'act only according to principles which can be conceived and willed as a universal law'.[23] At the second level, Höffe distinguishes between what he calls the 'categorical imperative of Virtue', and the 'categorical imperative of Law'. The former appeals to agents' good will as the requisite motivational incentive to 'act only according to maxims which can be conceived and willed as universal law'.[24] By contrast, the categorical imperative of Law merely enjoins agents to 'act externally only in agreement with principles that can be conceived and willed as universal law'.[25] Whereas the ethical imperative requires agents to make good willing their maxim of action, this is not necessary in the case of the juridical imperative: 'self-interest is sufficient for adherence to this principle'.[26]

Although Höffe's two-level distinction allows for the formal accommodation of external freedom within his revised structure of the categorical imperative, it is not clear that anything has been gained in substantive terms. Instead of showing that a conception of external freedom as autonomous willing and choosing is conceivable

---

[21] Otfried Höffe, 'Kant's Principle of Justice as Categorical Imperative of Law' in Y. Yovel, ed., *Kant's Practical Philosophy Reconsidered* (Amsterdam, Kluwer Academic Publishers, 1989), 149–67. For a more general statement of his Hobbesian reading of Kant, see also Höffe, ' "Even a Nation of Devils Needs the State": The Dilemma of Natural Justice' in H. Williams, ed., *Kant's Political Philosophy* (Cardiff, University of Wales Press, 1992), 120–42.

[22] Höffe, 'Kant's Principle of Justice', 153.

[23] Ibid., 156.   [24] Ibid.

[25] Ibid. By the 'categorical imperative of Law', Höffe means the universal principle of Right. Presumably, Höffe's somewhat idiosyncratic terminology is merely intended to emphasise the symmetry between his two second-level formulations of the categorical imperative.

[26] Ibid., 157.

within the constraints of the categorical imperative, Höffe has simply broadened the scope of the categorical imperative to include actions based on prudential motives. This is problematic, given Kant's insistence on the unconditional validity of the categorical imperative as a principle of pure practical reason that admits of no reference to sensible motives, including prudential motives.[27] Höffe's awareness of this difficulty is reflected in his tendency to equivocate between the sufficiency of self-interest as a motive for outward compliance with principles of justice, and the necessity of self-interest as the ground of those principles' normative justification. His initial claim that self-interest is sufficient for adherence to the categorical imperative of Law may amount to no more than a reminder of the external enforceability of principles of justice: if they are unwilling to act justly of their own accord, individuals can be compelled to act justly by means of the threat of sanctions. Here, the appeal to self-interest merely concerns the *enforcement* of principles of justice. This is consistent with an interpretation of the categorical imperative of Law as an unconditionally valid principle of pure practical reason: self-interest does not provide the normative ground of justice; appeal to it merely constitutes one possible means of ensuring compliance with the demands of justice. At other times, however, Höffe advances a much stronger claim, such as when he asserts that 'the enforcement of law, that is, what is morally right, or justice, *must coincide with* self-interest'.[28] Here, the equivocation between two possible readings is especially noticeable. Either Höffe is simply repeating the point that 'the enforcement of law' must coincide with self-interest in the form of sufficiently unattractive sanctions, or he is saying that the normative justification of the requirements of 'what is morally right, or justice' must coincide with self-interest. On the latter interpretation, the claim would be that, unless principles of justice do coincide with self-interest, no good reasons exist for adhering to

---

[27] Indeed, Höffe's two-level distinction raises questions as to the source of the so-called general formulation of the categorical imperative. On a plausible interpretation of the argument in the *Groundwork*, it is subjects' idea of duty, together with their capacity for autonomous willing, which accounts for the possibility of the categorical imperative. Since Höffe reserves these for the categorical imperative of Virtue, it is not clear what grounds the so-called general formula. This invites the view of the general formula as an externally stipulated principle of morality – hardly in keeping with Kant's principal claims regarding the source of morality and of moral agency.

[28] Höffe, 'Kant's Principle of Justice', 158.

them. In short, from self-interest at the level of law enforcement Höffe slides to self-interest at the level of normative justification.

Whichever interpretation Höffe intends, the structure of his systematic juxtaposition of law and ethics pushes him towards the stronger, normative interpretation. If what makes the categorical imperative of Virtue a principle of ethics is its appeal to the motivational incentive of ethical duty, then what makes the categorical imperative of Law a principle of justice must be its appeal to the motivational incentive of self-interest. Hence, when Kant claims that only that action is ethically worthy which is done from good will and from the maxim of duty,[29] Höffe should conclude, analogously, that only that action is just which is done from the motive of self-interest. But this conclusion is counter-intuitive – nor is it evident that support for it can be found in the text. Recall Kant's own remarks about different motivational incentives quoted in the section above. Kant does say that juridical lawgiving 'admits of an incentive other than the Idea of duty'. But this does not rule out the idea of duty as an equally possible incentive: in contrast to Höffe, Kant is not saying that the idea of duty pertains *only* to ethical lawgiving, and the incentive of self-interest *always* to juridical lawgiving. Kant's contention that juridical lawgiving *admits* of incentives other than duty indicates that his position is closer to Höffe's sufficiency argument than to the necessity argument. But the sufficiency argument is only concerned with sufficient means of law enforcement. Thus, when Kant says that these other incentives 'must be aversions, not allurements', the reference is to the threat of sanctions in the case of non-voluntary compliance with duties of justice. This negative reference to individuals' self-interest differs from some of Höffe's more positive references to self-interest as a motivational incentive whose demands principles of justice must acknowledge and satisfy. In short, Kant's references to different motivational incentives with respect to juridical lawgiving are restricted to the level of law enforcement and do not support claims about self-interest as the normative ground of justice.

Even if Höffe fails to provide a persuasive account of the distinctness between law and ethics as two separate spheres of morality, his resolve to resist the 'ethification'[30] of political agency is

---

[29] Cf. *Groundwork*, 4: 398.
[30] Höffe, 'Kant's Principle of Justice', 153.

extremely important. Höffe's resistance in this regard runs deep, and, although this sometimes takes an excessively Hobbesian expression, he rightly rejects the purchase of autonomy at the price of reducing external freedom to a version of internal freedom. The latter tendency is noticeable in Christine Korsgaard's recent piece on Kant and the ethics of political resistance.[31] Although Korsgaard does not address the motivational problem directly, she does reject readings of the *Rechtslehre* that make self-interest pivotal to the normative justification of the universal principle of Right. Korsgaard distinguishes between law enforcement and the normative justification of principles of justice in terms of what she calls 'procedural justice', on the one hand, and 'justice as a virtue', on the other. Procedural justice refers to the set of institutionalised procedures and principles of justice – the law of the land – whose coercive powers ensure general law-abidance. By contrast, justice as a virtue constitutes the normative basis for procedural justice: '[e]thics encompasses all of our duties. It is a duty of virtue to do the duties of justice from the motive of duty. In other words, justice itself is a virtue'.[32] Korsgaard concludes that, when they act prudentially, subjects act in mere conformity with procedural justice whose sanctions they are keen to avoid. But, when they act from the maxim of justice as a virtue, i.e. when they make it a duty of virtue to act justly, subjects are self-legislating agents of actions that are morally just instead of merely coinciding with justice. In this second case, subjects' just actions are autonomous.

Korsgaard's first claim is simply mistaken: morality, not ethics, encompasses all our duties according to Kant. The second claim sounds convoluted, at any rate it is misleading. Korsgaard implies that it is only when we make it our *ethical* duty to act justly that we are fulfilling our duties of justice from non-prudential motives. Now it is, of course, possible to make a virtue out of acting justly. In that sense it may even be possible to speak of ethics as encompassing all our duties. But, if someone makes a virtue out of acting justly, their actions are virtuous rather than (merely) just. The point is that, at least according to Kant, one can act justly without at the same time

[31] Christine Korsgaard, 'Taking the Law into Our Own Hands: Kant on the Right to Revolution' in Andrews Reath, Barbara Herman, and Christine Korsgaard, eds., *Reclaiming the History of Ethics. Essays for John Rawls* (Cambridge University Press, 1997), 297–328.
[32] Ibid., 317.

acting virtuously. This is precisely why the concept of Right abstracts from agents' maxims of action, focusing solely on *the form of external relations* between agents with respect to their choices. Hence, Korsgaard's conclusion does not follow that 'justice itself is a virtue', at least not if that is taken to mean that in the absence of virtue, there could be no justice. But the latter is what Korsgaard must mean when she identifies the 'virtue of justice' as the normative justification of the universal principle of Right. In so doing, Korsgaard effectively reduces law to ethics, and external freedom to internal freedom. If one can act justly only on condition that one is *ethically* minded to do so, the distinction between external freedom and internal freedom collapses.

One might think that something like Korsgaard's line of argument is the only way in which the autonomy of external freedom is to be had. At least Korsgaard does not reduce just action to prudential action. While she concedes that it is possible for agents to comply with the demands of justice from merely prudential motives, she also shows that it is possible to act justly from ethical grounds, and thus to act autonomously. None the less, like Höffe, so Korsgaard considers only two possible action incentives, viz. the ethical incentive and the prudential incentive. On both accounts, an action is either ethically motivated or done for prudential reasons. While Höffe's concern to uphold the distinction between law and ethics leads him to assign prudence to law and good will to ethics, Korsgaard's concern to preserve the morally binding character of justice leads her to conflate justice with virtue and law with ethics. But why should there not be further possible action incentives? Why should it not be possible for agents to honour their obligations of justice on the basis neither of prudential nor of ethical motives but merely in recognition and acknowledgement of the fact that they owe one another certain duties of justice? The problem is this: unless one can come up with an account of external freedom as autonomous willing and choosing, the prudential interpretation is difficult to avoid. But if one does not want to eliminate Kant's distinction between law and ethics, any conception of external freedom as autonomous willing and choosing must be distinct from internal freedom. What is required is a conception of autonomous willing and choosing that takes account of the specific requirements of political agency which distinguish external freedom from internal freedom.

4 EXTERNAL FREEDOM, DESIRES, AND NATURE

As I said, despite my disagreement with Höffe's prudential interpretation, he is right to insist on the distinction between ethics and law as two separate branches of morality. Höffe also recognises that upholding Kant's late distinction requires some adjustments regarding the account of freedom as autonomous willing initially developed in the *Groundwork*. But such adjustments should avoid making self-interest the distinguishing criterion of external freedom. Doing so merely adds fuel to the accusation that Kant entertains two conflicting conceptions of freedom, and invites the conclusion that Kant's endorsement of prudential motives in relation to external freedom amounts to a belated acknowledgement of the fact that political agency cannot be moral.

Likewise, if the conflation of law with ethics and of external freedom with internal freedom is to be avoided, this is because the requirements of political agency differ in important respects from those of ethical agency. The concept of desire provides an obvious starting-point for elucidating that difference. Kant's ethical writings are notorious for their seemingly dismissive attitude towards human desires and emotions. His relegation of the emotions to human beings' phenomenal nature, and his characterisation of them as obstacles to morality, have earned him much criticism. 'Kantian rationalism' is said to ignore the complexity and the subtlety of human emotions as an essential component of social interaction and moral conduct.[33] Such criticisms are not the exclusive preserve of those unsympathetic to Kant's moral philosophy in general. Kantians, too, often fault Kant for his crude 'psychological hedonism' in relation to individuals' desires and inclinations.[34] At the same time, this assessment of Kantian desires in his ethical writings is beginning to shift. In a recent paper, Andrews Reath has argued that Kant's account of happiness in relation to heteronomous willing bears little relation to the pleasure-seeking, hedonistic conception of desiring with which it is often associated.[35] Others, concerned to rebut

---

[33] See for example, Lawrence Blum, *Friendship, Altruism, and Morality* (London, Routledge & Kegan Paul, 1980); Victor Seidler, *Kant, Respect, and Injustice. The Limits of Liberal Moral Theory* (London, Routledge & Kegan Paul, 1986).

[34] Allen Wood, 'Kant's Compatibilism', 75.

[35] Andrews Reath, 'Hedonism, Heteronomy and Kant's Principle of Happiness', *Pacific Philosophical Quarterly*, 70 (1989), 42–72.

charges of Kant's 'formalism' and 'moral rigorism', point out that Kant's conception of the emotions and of their importance in human life is not as reductive as the standard picture assumes.[36] Moreover, and despite his formal derivation of the general principle of morality in the *Groundwork*, Kant's treatment of moral casuistry in the *Tugendlehre* demonstrates a sophisticated understanding of the positive contribution which individuals' emotions can make to moral judgements in particular circumstances.[37]

So far, these revised assessments of the emotions in Kant's ethics have not been matched by parallel revisions in the reception of desires in his political writings. If the motive of self-interest is generally considered more acceptable in the sphere of political agency, this is because desire-based action there tends to be associated with the quest for physical survival. The predominantly Humean psychology of the emotions in contemporary (Anglo-American) ethics tends to give way to the predominantly Hobbesian physiology of desires in politics. In practice, the psychological and physiological models complement one another; none the less the distinction indicates the different functions assigned to ethical and political desiring in principle. Thus, in ethics, subjects' desires refer primarily to their affective attitudes towards others: attitudes of sympathy and resentment, guilt, admiration, etc. These affective attitudes constitute agents' psychological responses to qualities, dispositions, and attitudes observed in others, which redound, in turn, on their own dispositions and attitudes towards them. In ethics, desires describe subject/subject relations. By contrast, desires in the context of political agency typically specify relations between subjects and objects, or, more properly, between subjects with regard to objects. Desires here have an economic function: they denote a relation of want between subjects and external objects, and a consequent relation of competition between subjects with regard to those objects. Since they are essentially object-oriented, desires in the political context often seem less intangible, more straightforward, than their psychologically complex counterparts in ethics. But the

[36] See, for example, Barbara Herman, 'Leaving Deontology Behind' in *The Practice of Moral Judgment*, 208–42; Susan Mendus, 'The Practical and the Pathological', *The Journal of Value Inquiry*, 19 (1985), 235–43; Onora O'Neill, 'Consistency in Action' in *Constructions of Reason*, chapter 5, 81–104.

[37] See, for example, Stephen Engstrom, 'Kant's Conception of Practical Wisdom', *Kantstudien*, 88 (1997), 16–43; and Roger Sullivan, 'The Influence of Kant's Anthropology on his Moral Theory', *Review of Metaphysics*, 49 (1995),77–94.

political conception possesses a complexity that arises from its own dynamic. Economic desiring is almost invariably conflictual, though it is so independently of the concept's affective functions: conflict stems from the relative scarcity of available objects of desire, and gives rise only derivatively to affective attitudes between subjects.

In what follows, I shall restrict my remarks to Kant's conception of desires and of desire-formation as they pertain to his account of external freedom; hence I shall be concerned only with the economic function of desiring and shall leave to one side their role in ethics. My principal concern is to argue that, at least in the *Rechtslehre*, Kant's remarks on subjects' capacity for desire point towards a conception of desire-based choice which is capable of meeting the requirements of autonomous willing and choosing. If such a conception of desire-based autonomous choosing is plausible, at least with respect to economic desiring, it should be possible to avoid the narrow dichotomy between prudential and ethical action incentives assumed by Höffe and Korsgaard. It should be possible to develop an account of external freedom which recognises the legitimate role of freely determined economic desiring as in accordance with the demands of morality, without in so doing collapsing law into ethics.[38]

Kant's most explicit remarks about desires occur in the general introduction to the *Metaphysics of Morals*, under the section entitled 'On the Relation of the Capacities of the Human Mind to Moral Laws'.[39] He there offers an arresting definition of the capacity for desire:

The *capacity for desire* is the capacity to be by means of one's representations the cause of the objects of these representations. The capacity of a being to act in accordance with its representations is called *life*.[40]

Two aspects about this definition stand out. The first is Kant's characterisation of the capacity for desire as *life*. The second is his

---

[38] To avoid confusion, I should emphasise that this is not to endorse Allison's advocacy of non-moral freedom. In contrast to Allison's account, the alternative conception here proposed views the limited spontaneity of agent deliberation as a necessary but not a sufficient condition for an act of choice to qualify as a freely determined choice. Only acts of choice which, in addition to deliberative spontaneity, reflect agents' acknowledgement of the constraints of pure practical reason, qualify as freely determined acts of choice.

[39] *MM*, 6: 211. The original German version refers to '*das menschliche Gemüt*'. *Gemüt* can be translated as referring to individuals' 'general temper', or 'temperament', or to their 'sensibilities' as well as to 'mind'. Gregor's translation of '*Gemüt*' as 'mind' emphasises its intellectual connotations, arguably at the cost of ignoring the term's sensible connotations.

[40] *MM*, 6: 211.

reference to a desiring being's capacity for *representation*. The equation of the capacity for desire with life is remarkable for its proximity to the Hobbesian conception of desiring as constituting part of a living being's 'vital motion'. For Hobbes, human beings are matter in motion – indeed, to be alive is to be in motion, such that a sure sign of death is the cessation of all bodily movement.[41] As a consequence, desiring, as that which keeps individuals in motion, is necessarily life-sustaining. A being that ceases to have desires is equivalent to a being that has ceased to be alive. At one level, Hobbes' physiological characterisation of desires as vital motion is extraordinarily crude, lacking the subtle psychology of desiring widely admired, for example, in Hume's account. At the same time, Hobbes' model is extremely sophisticated, not least because it takes him straight to his principal problem concerning the inevitably conflictual nature of economic (life-sustaining) desiring. As we shall see in the next chapter, Kant follows Hobbes in regarding individuals' desires for external objects as inevitably conflictual and as requiring a political solution. However, Kant's solution differs from Hobbes' proposed *Leviathan State*. Hobbes conceives his political solution in terms of an all-powerful sovereign who constrains individuals' pursuit of their desires by means of his irresistible force. By contrast, Kant's solution is premised on individuals' capacity to conceive and to acknowledge the authority of a general law of external freedom – the universal principle of Right – action in accordance with which makes possible the conflict-free coexistence of each with everyone else. One reason why Kant is able to replace Hobbes' principle of externally imposed legislation with a principle of external self-legislation is that his conception of individuals' capacity for desire is ultimately very different from that of Hobbes. A brief comparison between Kant's treatment of desires in the *Metaphysics of Morals* and in some of his earlier political and historical essays will help to locate the source of Kant's divergence from Hobbes.

It is in his earlier essays, and especially in some passages of the well-known *Perpetual Peace*, that Kant is at his most Hobbesian about individuals' desires and about human nature in general. Those who favour a Hobbesian interpretation of Kant's political philosophy like to draw attention to his remark in *Perpetual Peace* that 'the problem of

---

[41] Hobbes, *Leviathan* (Harmondsworth, the Penguin English Library, 1982), Part I, chapter 6.

setting up the state can be solved even by a nation of devils, so long as they are rational'.[42] Here we have an undisguised appeal to the rationality of prudential self-interest as the overriding motivational incentive to state foundation. But this should not detract from Kant's generally more ambivalent attitude towards individuals' desires and inclinations in the essays. As I said, in contrast to the traditionally unforgiving reception of Kant's ethics, recent reappraisals there attest him a more balanced view of the emotions. Even on the traditional reading, the picture is not altogether bleak. In Kant's ethics, the struggle between inclinations and reason is an agent-internal struggle with a high likelihood that the good willing agent will at least sometimes succeed in subordinating inclination to reason. By contrast, the terrain of *interindividual* strife and competitive desiring in the essays constitutes a much harsher environment. This is partly because, in contrast to the agent-centred perspective of his ethical writings, the essays adopt a historical perspective. Their principal concern is to assess the possibility of humanity's moral progress through gradual enlightenment by reason. While, in ethics, it should be of no concern to us how others act so long as we ourselves fulfil our moral duties, the adoption of such an inward-looking perspective is not possible with regard to historical and political agency. There the frustration, from indifference or from malevolence, by others of our well-intended attempts can be deeply demoralising. Viewed from a historical perspective, good willing agents are not merely struggling against their own desires and inclinations; they are also, and perhaps even more so, struggling against the ignorance and indifference of their fellow human beings upon whom the possibility of moral progress crucially depends. Thus, while the essays continue to conceive of individuals' desires and inclinations as belonging to their phenomenal nature, hence as subject to the causality of nature, the historical concerns of these writings add an interindividual dimension to the struggle between human nature and reason which is absent in his ethics.[43]

Embedded within this historical perspective is Kant's growing

---

[42] *Perpetual Peace*, 8: 366.
[43] Kant's awareness of the pitfalls of historical moral progress compared to individual good willing comes out most explicitly in his argument against Moses Mendelssohn in *Theory and Practice*, 8: 307–13. Although Kant argues against Mendelssohn that the hope for moral progress is not futile, he acknowledges the moral courage required of individuals when they act against the odds in the hope of historical progress.

awareness of the distinctly economic function of individuals' desires, which reveals itself in Kant's fascination with the growth of overseas commerce and trade. As is well known, in the phenomenon of trade Kant discerns, perhaps naively, the possibility of peaceful relations among nations. Even then, his views regarding the beneficial influence of economic interaction are ambivalent. Given its systemic character, the emergence of commerce cannot be traced back to the intentional actions of particular agents. Who then willed its emergence? Was it nature? Was it reason? Or was it the caprice and greed discernible in human nature? By the same token, it is not clear who or what wills the pacific ends Kant attributes to trade, or how these ends will be achieved. Will human agents achieve this end on the strength of their own good wills and sustained efforts to this effect, or will nature compel humanity to peace even against its own wishes? Is it a demand of reason, or a side-effect of nature that will ensure a peaceful outcome? *Perpetual Peace* fluctuates between different possible answers. At one point, Kant allies nature and reason against *human nature*, saying that nature 'will compel man to do that which he ought to do by the laws of freedom'.[44] Even then it remains obscure precisely how nature and/or reason will accomplish this feat. Sometimes Kant relies on systemic effects akin to Mandeville's famous 'private vices/public benefits' dictum, such as when he exclaims: 'thanks be to nature for fostering social incompatibility, enviously competitive vanity, and an insatiable desire for possession and even power'.[45] At other times he repudiates such prudential scheming, proclaiming that 'a true system of politics cannot take a single step without first paying tribute to morality'.[46]

I cannot here pursue Kant's fascinatingly ambiguous attitude towards individuals' (economic) desires in his political essays.[47] However, what is instructive about these ambiguities is the way in which they reveal the relative failure of Kant's ethics to accommodate the economic function of desiring. On the one hand, Kant holds on to his general conception of desires as part of human beings' phenomenal nature. On the other hand, given their life-sustaining function, economic desires cannot be overcome or

[44] *Perpetual Peace*, 8: 365.
[45] *Universal History*, 8: 2.   [46] *Perpetual Peace*, 8: 380.
[47] But see Flikschuh, 'Kantian Desires'. See also Martha Nussbaum, 'Kant and Cosmopolitanism' in James Bohman and Matthias Lutz-Bachmann, eds., *Perpetual Peace. Essays on Kant's Cosmopolitan Ideal* (Cambridge, MA, MIT Press, 1997), 25–58.

disciplined in precisely the same way in which it may be possible to discipline one's emotions in relation to one's ethical duties. As a result, the essays frequently indulge in descriptions of individuals' incorrigible greed and depravity, which give rise once to Mendelssohnian despair, at other times to Mandevillian cynicism about the general state of humanity. At the same time, it is clear that *whatever* individual agents' internal disposition towards each other – whether well-meaning or ill-intentioned – their economic desires are virtually bound to come into conflict with each other. In other words, despite his many expressions of moral disapproval, the essays reveal Kant's growing appreciation of Hobbes' insight into the *systemic* consequences of economic desiring, which may well be contrary to the agent's own intentions. The essays thus highlight the asymmetry between ethical and economic desires which arises from their different functions, and which means that the relation between economic desiring and practical reason in politics must be conceived differently from that between the emotions and practical reason in ethics.

If we conclude that Kant's ambivalent attitude towards economic desiring in the essays shows that he is hampered by his earlier assignment of desires to human beings' phenomenal nature, the specific requirements of economic desiring present a case for a partial rethinking of that initial ascription. In so far as economic desiring is acknowledged to be life-sustaining, it cannot be dismissed as morally illegitimate. But economic desiring sustains *human* life, and, in this respect, Hobbes' physiologically motivated tendency to equate human desires with animal drives might well be mistaken. Indeed, Kant's own sharp dichotomy between desires and reason in the *Groundwork* might be exaggerated. By this I do not mean to suggest that a naturally harmonious relationship obtains after all between the emotions, economic desiring and moral reasoning – a line of argument that is often pushed especially by communitarian criticisms of Kant. My claim is, rather, that Kant's growing recognition of the economic function of desiring pushes him towards the view of desire-formation as susceptible to reason. Far from being the human version of animal instincts, desiring is a distinctly rational capacity, i.e. one the capacity for which presupposes the capacity to reason. Indeed, this view of desiring as a product of reason does at times emerge in the essays themselves. In *Conjectural Beginnings*, Kant notes that, 'it is a peculiarity of reason that it is able, with the help of

the imagination, to invent desires which not only *lack* any corresponding natural impulse, but which are even *at variance* with the
latter'.[48] This is different not only from the Hobbesian notion of
desires as physiological drives stimulated by externally given 'trig-
gers' to action; the suggestion that reason creates desires also differs
from Kant's earlier attribution of desires to subjects' phenomenal
nature exclusively. In the *Rechtslehre*, this revised view of desiring as
requiring the capacity for cognition and judgement is even more
prominent.

5 EXTERNAL FREEDOM, DESIRES, AND REASON

One immediately striking difference between the essays and the
Rechtslehre is the omission in the later work of any reference to
sentiments such as individual greed, mutual hostility, and moral
depravity. In contrast to the colourful prose of the essays, the
approach to economic desiring in the *Rechtslehre* is dispassionate and
to the point. A second contrast is the return from the historical
perspective of the essays to the agent-centred perspective familiar
from Kant's ethics. The question of humanity's moral progress is not
raised; the *Rechtslehre* concerns itself solely with the obligations of
justice which individuals owe one another as a consequence of their
claims to external freedom. The requirement to enter with all others
into the civil condition follows from these agent-specific juridical
duties; the aim of the civil condition is to make possible conflict-free
coexistence, not to encourage the flourishing of ethics. In this
context, the *Rechtslehre* acknowledges the prima-facie legitimacy of
agents' economic desires. However, in so far as Kant does concede
their legitimacy, he also assumes their susceptibility to the demands
of reason. Economic desiring is susceptible to the demands of reason
because desiring itself is the product of a rational process, depending
on a desiring being's cognitive and evaluative capacities. Consider
once more Kant's definition of the capacity for desire:

> The *capacity for desire* is the capacity to be by means of one's representations
> the cause of the objects of these representations. The capacity of a being to
> act in accordance with its representations is called *life*.

Despite his similar equation of desiring with life, Kant does not

---

[48] *Conjectural Beginnings*, 8: 111.

entertain Hobbes' physiological conception of desiring as externally stimulated and internally transmitted vital motions which 'in pressing upon the brain and the heart', etc. eventually issue in outward bodily movement.[49] Kant does not think of agents as subject to the causality of their desires. Instead, he regards agents as the causes of their desires; at any rate, they have the capacity to be the causes of their desires. The reference to causality in the definition can be interpreted in two ways. In the first sense, being the cause of one's desires means no more than being causally efficacious in the attainment of the object of one's desire. One brings about the attainment of the object of one's desire by means of one's capacity for means–ends reasoning, combined with one's capacity for motor action. This meaning of 'being the cause of one's desires', which is roughly that at play in relation to heteronomous willing and instrumental reasoning, focuses on desire-attainment. However, Kant's definition is more concerned with desire-formation: at issue is not how we go about attaining desire-satisfaction, but what enables us to desire in the first place. Kant answers that it is *by means of one's representations* that one is the cause of one's desires, or, more specifically, that one is the cause of the *objects* of one's desires. Anyone familiar with the importance of the concept of representation in Kant's theory of knowledge will recognise the allusion to subjects' cognitive capacities in the present context. Subjects' capacity for desire presupposes, so the implication, their cognitive capacity to represent to themselves objects of their desires. Two points are thus worth bearing in mind when elaborating the status of subjects' representational capacities in relation to desire-formation. The first concerns the role of cognition in the representation of objects in general, including objects of desire. The second concerns the capacity for the imaginative representation of non-existent objects relative to desire-formation.

With respect to the first point, cognition of an object in its representation, we can refer once again to Stephan Körner's general characterisation of human beings as cognitively experiencing subjects. For Kant, from whom Körner borrows his description, human knowledge is representational in the sense that experience of sensibly intuited objects is conceptually mediated. Knowledge of objects does not result from the mere receptivity of the senses, but requires the activity of the understanding in the recognition of a sensible intuition

---

[49] Cf. *Leviathan*, Part I, chapters 1 and 6.

as an object of experience – what Körner refers to as the application of one's categorical framework to sensory perceptions. In more technical Kantian terminology, objective knowledge consists in the representation of a sensible intuition under the concept of an object. What is important in the present context is the emphasis on human understanding as an *active* power or capacity. It is only in virtue of their capacity to bring a sensible intuition under the rules of the concept of an object, that subjects can cognise an external object as such. This general view of the cognitive structure of experience must extend to objects of desire as well: the recognition of a sensibly given intuition as an object of desire requires subjects' application of the rules of the understanding (i.e. concepts) to that intuition. However, Kant does not think of these cognitive operations as more or less automatic processes. As we saw in chapter 1, not only are human beings cognitively experiencing subjects; they are also aware of themselves as such. Hence, experience of empirical reality is conscious such experience: 'It must be possible for the "I think" to accompany all my representations'.[50] But, if this applies to the cognition of empirically objects in general, it must apply to subjects' cognition of the objects of their desire. Subjects not only form and have desires, they are also aware of themselves *as* forming and *as* having desires. In short, given his general theory of knowledge of objects, Kant must think of object-oriented desiring as requiring complex cognitive and evaluative capacities both in subjects' recognition of an object of their desire, and in their awareness of themselves as desiring subjects. The importance to Kant of the cognitive component of desire-formation is emphasised in his distinction in the *Metaphysics of Morals* between 'concupiscence' and 'desire'. While concupiscence, as akin to animal instinct, 'is always a sensible modification of the mind' which can stimulate to action, 'it has not yet become an act of the capacity for desire'. Only 'the capacity for desiring in accordance with concepts is called the capacity for doing or refraining from doing what one pleases'.[51] This suggests that someone who cannot form and act in accordance with a conception of the object of their desire, does not choose and act on the basis of a capacity for desire.

The second point I want to touch on concerns the relation between desires and the productive imagination. Kant's definition

[50] *CPR*, B131.   [51] *MM*, 6: 213.

makes no direct reference to sensibly given intuitions of objects. The capacity to represent to oneself possible objects of desire does not appear to require the actual presence of a corresponding desire-stimulating sensible intuition. Presumably this does not mean that subjects do not also form representations of objects of desire on the basis of sensible intuitions along the lines just suggested. None the less, the capacity for desire in general depends primarily on subjects' cognitive and imaginative capacities, rather than on sensible stimulation. We can form a conception of a possible object of desire even in the absence of sensible stimuli. This creative aspect of desire-formation is often neglected in physiological and even in psychological accounts of desire-formation. At the same time, a large number of our desires are ones we end up not acting upon: we can imagine desirable objects or states of affairs which we desire to obtain but the obtaining of which we judge to be impossible. Likewise, we are able to entertain desires 'in the imagination' without desiring their realisation. Finally, many of the desires we do act on relate to not as yet existent objects of desire. Our ability to form a conception of their desirability by means of the imagination guides our attempt to bring about their actual realisation. In sum, although in one sense we are the causes of the objects of our desires merely by being causally efficacious in bringing about the attainment of the objects of our desires, this sense is secondary to Kant's meaning of 'being the cause of'. In its principal meaning, rational beings' cognitive and imaginative capacities enable them to form a conception of (not as yet existent) objects of desire, making them the causes of the desires they come to have.

These remarks are not meant to deny that desiring requires more than the cognitive capacities for objective representation and for productive imagination. Obviously, there must be something that distinguishes the conception of an object of desire from the conception of objects in general. Nor do all of our imaginations hinge on things or states of affairs which we desire. In addition to cognitive capacities, conative (psychological and physiological) criteria must be included in a comprehensive account of desire-formation. I do not deny this, but here focus on what Kant's reference to representations implies about desire-formation that physiological and psychological accounts tend to deny or ignore. Of course, even then Kant's remarks on the cognitive dimension of desire-formation are suggestive rather than exhaustive; his observations are sparse and obscure, requiring much interpretation. Even so, Kant's remarks in the introduction to the *Metaphysics of Morals* show that the attribution to him of a cognitive conception of desire-formation is not without textual support. Recall the original question: how is it possible for desire-based choice and action to count as free in the sense of being autonomously determined, i.e. determined in accordance with the laws of freedom? So far, I have argued that it is a necessary condition of desire-based but freely determined choice that the process of desire-formation depend, at least to some extent, on subjects' cognitive capacities. I mean this not just in the sense that it may be rational for one to have a particular desire, i.e. that some rationally valued end justifies one having the relevant desire as a means to that end. Not just *having* a desire, but even *forming* a desire must reflect cognitive processes at work, of which the agent is aware and over which they possess at least a degree of reflective control.[52] None the less, even if desiring does presuppose cognitive and imaginative capacities on the part of the desiring agent, this is evidently not sufficient for non-prudential desiring. Rational desiring is not morally constrained desiring merely in virtue of being rational. One can be a rationally desiring agent in the meaning of the term here suggested without being someone who desires in accordance with the requirements of pure practical reason. Still, in so far as rational desiring presupposes the agent's awareness of themselves as a rationally desiring subject, such awareness implies an ability to reflect on and to evaluate one's desires, including the way in which one came to have them. Rational desiring implies evaluative desiring. This requirement for evaluative desiring is implicit in Kant's somewhat obscure distinction between 'interests of inclination' and 'interests of reason'.

Both interests of inclination and interests of reason belong to the category of practical pleasure. In the *Metaphysics of Morals*, Kant distinguishes in passing between practical pleasure and aesthetic pleasure. The imaginative aspects of desire-formation are most apparent in relation to aesthetic pleasure. Aesthetic pleasure 'is not connected with any desire for an object, but is already connected with a mere representation that one forms of an object (regardless of whether the object of representation exists or not)'.[53] Aesthetic pleasure thus constitutes a more abstract, contemplative kind of

---

[52] See footnote 8, above.   [53] *MM*, 6: 212.

pleasure than that which accompanies our practically efficacious capacity for desire. The latter is practical pleasure, i.e. pleasure in relation to action. In the case of practical pleasure, the desire which accompanies the feeling of pleasure can either 'precede the determination of the will', or it can 'follow upon the determination of the will'. Where the desire precedes will determination, Kant speaks of an 'interest of inclination'; where the desire follows upon the determination of the will, we have an 'interest of reason'. The distinction between interests of inclination and interests of reason invokes that between heteronomous willing and autonomous willing in the *Groundwork*. In the case of an 'interest of inclination', desire-formation is pathologically affected. Experienced as a 'sensible modification of the mind',[54] an antecedent feeling of pleasure stimulates desire-formation. This does not mean that pleasurable sensation and desire-formation are *identical*. The representation of a pleasurable sensation as a possible object of desire requires the application of the rules of the understanding in the cognition of the object. Even where practical desiring is pathologically affected in the sense of being stimulated by the senses, the transformation of a pleasurable sensation into the judgement of an object of desire requires cognitive capacities on the part of the agent.

In addition to cognitive capacities, practical desiring also requires evaluative capacities: the subject must judge whether and if so how the desired object is practically attainable. With regard to interests of inclination, the relevant rules of judgement are those associated with heteronomous willing and with the hypothetical imperative. The subject evaluates the possible realisation of the conceived object of desire in terms of the means necessary to its attainment. Crucially, this form of desire-evaluation makes no reference to the effects on others of one's pursuit and attainment of the object of one's desire. Desire-evaluation in accordance with the hypothetical imperative is rational but means–ends oriented: in that sense the will is determined by material practical principles, i.e. by practical principles which are responsive to the subject's sensibly stimulated representation of the object of their desire.

Where the feeling of pleasure 'follows upon an antecedent determination of the capacity for desire', Kant speaks of an 'interest of reason'. Here the feeling of pleasure does not consist of a sensible

---

[54] *MM*, 6: 212.

modification of the mind. It is 'sense-free inclination' based on 'intellectual pleasure'.[55] Sense-free pleasure arises from the acknow-ledgement of one's moral duties and from acting on them without resentment. In the case of 'interests of reason', desire-formation is restrained by something which gives rise to a feeling of intellectual pleasure in virtue of its influence on desire-formation: desire-formation is restrained by principles of pure practical reason. Kant's allusions to the categorical imperative at this stage indicate that this second mode of desire evaluation includes a moral dimension. In contrast to merely instrumental desire-evaluation, this second mode implies agents' willingness to form and pursue their desires in a manner which is cognisant of the possible effects on others of one's desire-based actions. While this does not mean that subjects cease to pursue the objects of their desires, desire-pursuit is constrained by moral considerations. Of course, agents are capable only of con-straining their desires in the appropriate manner if desire-formation is susceptible to reason in the manner sketched above. If desire-formation were purely pathological, i.e. if desires were not suscep-tible to reasoned constraint, agents would either have to abstract from their desires completely when acting in accordance with the demands of pure practical reason, or the constraint would have to be externally imposed. The first alternative leads to Kant's conception of ethically good action; the second alternative amounts to a conception of external legislation. Only the third possibility here suggested provides the resources for a conception of external freedom as desire-based but autonomous choice and action which reduces neither to internal freedom nor to 'alien' legislation and enforcement of the requirements of morality.

6 CONCLUSION

The aim of this chapter has been to sketch a possible interpretation of external freedom as based on autonomous choice and action without reducing it to Kant's conception of internal freedom. This aim was motivated by the need to acknowledge the distinctive and legitimate role of economic desires in relation to political agency whilst resisting the conclusion that political agency must therefore be based on prudential self-interest. The latter is a conclusion that is

---

[55] *MM*, 6: 212/213.

frequently drawn, though not always wisely so. Indeed, even Hobbes, to whom the inference from self-interest to external legisla-tion is usually attributed, is far more difficult to pin down on this point than is often assumed. If Hobbesian agents are so constituted that they can act only from self-interest, it is notoriously difficult to understand how Hobbes' precepts of right reasoning could ever get them out of the state of nature. Similar difficulties confront those who attribute prudential incentives to Kant's political agents: if the universal principle of Right is an externally given principle of juridical legislation, rather than one which is grounded in agents' capacity for autonomy, who then is the legislator? Given Kant's general conception of freedom as a shared idea of pure practical reason, we must assume that it is finite rational beings themselves who conceive of and act on the universal principle of Right in virtue of their capacity to constrain their actions in accordance with reason's 'order of ideas'.

Of course, much of what I have said about desire-formation in relation to external freedom remains sketchy and provisional. More-over, even if one concedes that there is some basis – or even only some need – for attribution to Kant of a conception of autonomous economic choice and action, it is clear that economic desiring can never be 'sense-free' to the extent required for an interest of reason in the strict sense. Since economic desiring is inevitably object-oriented, it is impossible for agents to abstract from material considerations in their economic choices and actions. This is why Höffe is right to resist the 'ethification' of external freedom, and to argue instead for a partial revision of Kant's initial formulation of the categorical imperative as the supreme principle of morality. If the sphere of law or politics does form a distinct branch of morality, such that it must be possible for agents to legislate principles of external freedom for themselves, then the supreme principle of morality, from which such external legislation must be derived, must acknowledge the legitimacy of economic desiring in relation to external freedom. Indeed, when he considers the universal principle of Right as the external version of the categorical imperative in Part I of the *Rechtslehre*, Kant does acknowledge the complications introduced to his initial framework by agents' legitimate claims for external objects of their choice. In attempting to deal with these difficulties, Kant appeals to the famously obscure 'postulate of practical reason with regard to Right', which he characterises as an 'a priori extension of pure practical reason'.[56] It is the task of the next chapter to interpret the meaning of this extension of the categorical imperative in relation to external freedom, and to explicate what it means for economically desiring agents to be cognisant of the effects of their choices on the conditions for choice of others. This takes us to the heart of the *Rechtslehre*, namely to Kant's justification of individual property rights and of their resulting obligations of justice to one another.

[56] *RL*, 6: 247.

The 'Lex Permissiva': property rights and political obligation in the 'Rechtslehre'

Postulate of Practical Reason with Regard to Right: It is possible for me to have any external object of my choice as mine, that is, a maxim by which, if it were to become a law, an object of choice would *in itself* (objectively) have to belong to no one (*res nullius*) is contrary to Right . . . Reason wills that this hold as a principle, and it does this as *practical* reason, which extends itself a priori by this postulate of reason.   (*RL*, 246, 247)

I INTRODUCTION

Chapter 2 offered an account of Kant's metaphysics of freedom as an idea of reason; chapter 3 focused on the concept of external freedom in relation to the categorical imperative and autonomous willing.[1] I pointed to a difficulty that arose for Kant's initial exposition of positive freedom in connection with his subsequent distinction between internal and external freedom, namely the latter's apparent endorsement of desire-based choices as free choices. This endorsement conflicts with the distinction in the *Groundwork* between heteronomous willing and autonomous willing. In order to resolve this difficulty, I suggested that in the *Metaphysics of Morals* Kant entertains, or at least gestures towards, a conception of desiring and desire-based choices which aligns the capacity for desire closer than previously with subjects' cognitive and evaluative capacities. While this does not mean that all desire-based actions are autonomous – interests of inclination are determined heteronomously – the revised account allows for the possibility of autonomously determined, desire-based choices. I suggested that this

---

[1] This chapter is partly based on my earlier paper on 'Freedom and Constraint in Kant's Metaphysical Elements of Justice', *History of Political Thought*, 20 (1999), 250–71.

creates conceptual space for an account of political obligation that relies neither on prudential nor on ethical incentives, but that appeals to agents' reflective acknowledgement of their obligations of justice towards one another. The aim of the present chapter is to develop a more detailed analysis and defence of this alternative account of the grounds of political obligation in the *Rechtslehre*.

The argument in chapter 3 was confined to Kant's conception of economic desiring in relation to external freedom; I said nothing about the function of desiring in Kant's ethics. Even with regard to economic desiring in the *Rechtslehre*, my claim is not to have given an accurate reconstruction so much as a possible interpretation of Kant's definition of the capacity for desire. My contention is that, if we take seriously Kant's characterisation of law and ethics as two equal if distinct branches of morality, it must be possible to accommodate external freedom under the categorical imperative without in so doing reducing law to ethics. In other words, Kant must possess something like the conception of economic desiring proposed in chapter 3 if his account of external freedom is to be consistent with the general requirements of moral self-legislation.

When turning to the heart of the *Rechtslehre*, namely Kant's deduction of individuals' property rights and their resulting obligations of justice, interpretation rather than reconstruction is virtually unavoidable. As I said in the introductory chapter, the main reason behind the almost complete neglect, until recently, of the *Rechtslehre* is the distorted state of the argument in the published text itself. A lot of dedicated work by individual Kant scholars has gone into the effort of sifting the argument proper from illicitly included preliminary notes and provisional drafts in the published text. Many have puzzled over the correct (as against the published) sequence of individual paragraphs in their efforts to reconstruct a clear line of argument. Such efforts have, in turn, generated debates as to what would count as the ultimately correct sequence.[2] These are highly specific scholarly and philological issues, which I shall not engage with in this book. Even so, they should warn anyone who is

---

[2] See especially Gerd Buchda, 'Das Privatrecht Immanuel Kants'; also Friedrich Tenbruck, 'Über eine notwendige Textkorrektur in Kants "Metaphysik der Sitten"', *Archiv für Philosophie*, 3 (1949), 216–20. Buchda and Tenbruck established independently of each other the illicit inclusion of some of Kant's preliminary notes in sections 4–8 of §6, Section I in the *Rechtslehre*. Their findings are discussed in Gerd-Walter Küsters, *Kants Rechtsphilosophie. Erträge der Forschung* (Darmstadt, Wissenschaftliche Buchgesellschaft, 1988). See also Thomas Mautner, 'Kant's Metaphysics of Morals: A Note on the Text', *Kantstudien*,73 (1981), 356–9.

interested in the political thought contained in the *Rechtslehre* against too confident a conclusion that they have succeeded in offering the definitive analysis of what Kant said or meant to say, where, how, and why. This is so especially in view of the fact that the revival of interest currently enjoyed by the *Rechtslehre* is not unrelated to Rawls' and Habermas' respective Kantian credentials in relation to the problem of political justification. Whether one thinks of Kant as the 'most adequate of all social contract theorists',[3] or takes his conception of the *Rechtstaat* to be the 'most democratic of all such conceptions',[4] it is as well to be aware of the fact that one is reading the *Rechtslehre* through the lenses of one's own political outlook and substantive concerns.[5] This is not to say that one interpretation is as good as any other – indeed, the next chapter will argue that there is less support for contractarian interpretations of the *Rechtslehre* than is often assumed by current interpretations of the text. Still, a political interpretation is not the same as either historical reconstruction or scholarly exegesis, and the present book belongs to the first category of possible approaches to Kant's work. It will not, therefore, escape readers that the following interpretation of Kant's account of political obligation is shaped by a focus on his cosmopolitanism. In fact, the resonance of Kant's cosmopolitanism with current problems of international or global justice constitutes a second reason for renewed interest in the text.[6] I shall argue, however, that Kant does not so much provide support for as produce an alternative to current liberal approaches to global justice. In contrast to the latter's tendency to treat global justice as an extension of domestic justice, Kant argues that domestic justice is not possible in the absence of global justice. The primacy of the cosmopolitan perspective shapes even Kant's justification of individual property rights, which is one reason why there is little support for a contractarian interpretation of Kant's account of political obligation. Accordingly, this chapter will focus on what Bernd Ludwig has identified as 'the theoretical

---

[3] See, for example, Patrick Riley, 'On Kant as the Most Adequate of the Social Contract Theorists', *Political Theory*, 1 (1973), 450–71.

[4] This is the conclusion reached by Ingeborg Mauss, 'Zur Theorie der Institutionalisierung bei Kant' in Gerhard Köhler, ed., *Politische Institutionen im Gesellschaftlichem Umbruch* (Opladen, Westdeutscher Verlag, 1990), 358–85.

[5] Reinhardt Brandt cautions against commentators' tendency to conflate their own political concerns with those of Kant in 'Die Politische Institution bei Kant'.

[6] See, for example, the collection of essays in Otfried Höffe, ed., *Zum Ewigen Frieden* (Berlin, Akademie Verlag, 1995); also James Bohman and Matthias Lutz-Bachmann, eds., *Perpetual Peace. Essays on Kant's Cosmopolitan Ideal* (Cambridge, MA, MIT Press, 1997).

novum of the *Rechtslehre*',[7] namely the 'postulate of practical reason with regard to Right'. It is by means of this postulate that Kant succeeds in deriving individuals' (global) obligations of justice towards one another directly from their claims to external objects of their choice, rendering redundant any contractual political agreement to that effect.

However, philosophically potent though the postulate may be, it is also extremely obscure. Much of the reason for this is that its proper place in the argument is a matter of considerable debate. Having distinguished between political interpretation and scholarly reconstruction, it is therefore equally important to point out that the two approaches influence one another. Even if the following argument offers a political interpretation, the sequence of relevant sections in the text obviously impacts on the plausibility of the interpretation offered. If the postulate is central to the argument, its disputed position in the text is not irrelevant. Still, since the concern here is not to settle that dispute, it suffices to point out that my interpretation of Kant's property argument is based on Ludwig's revised edition of the *Rechtslehre*.[8] Ludwig's revisions are the result of what he refers to as his philological reconstruction of the text,[9] which he proffers in support of his rearrangement of a relatively small though not negligible number of paragraphs. This is obviously not uncontentious. None the less, the most important of the proposed changes in the present context, i.e. the relocation of the postulate from §2 of Section I, chapter 1, to §6 does enhance the overall coherence of Kant's property argument. In the rest of the chapter I shall assume §6 to be the correct place in the text for the postulate.

Apart from Ludwig, the second Kant scholar whose work has influenced my reading of the postulate is Reinhard Brandt. In an important paper on the postulate, Brandt draws attention to Kant's characterisation of it as a *lex permissiva* or permissive law. Brandt

[7] Bernd Ludwig, 'Der Platz des rechtlichen Postulats der praktischen Vernunft innerhalb der Paragraphen 1–6 der Kantischen Rechtslehre' in Reinhard Brandt, ed., *Rechtsphilosophie der Aufklärung* (Berlin, de Gruyter, 1982), 218–32.

[8] Ludwig, ed., *Metaphysische Anfangsgründe der Rechtslehre*, by Immanuel Kant. As noted in the Introduction (footnote 9), Ludwig's amended edition is now available in English translation by Mary Gregor. Building on the findings of Buchda and Tenbruck (see footnote 2, this chapter), Ludwig recommends the relocation of §2 of Section I (which contains the 'Postulate of Practical Reason with regard to Right') into §6. The incorporation of §2 into §6 thus replaces the paragraphs 4–8 of §6. For discussion and defence of these changes see Ludwig, *Kants Rechtslehre*, 60–5 and 102–15.

[9] Ibid., 4–6.

interprets permissive laws as laws that provisionally authorise actions the commission of which are, strictly speaking, prohibited.[10] This is an acute reading of the postulate, which puts Brandt in a position to offer a plausible explanation of Kant's obscure references to the postulate as an 'a priori extension of pure practical reason'.[11] My interpretation of the postulate as a preliminary reflective judgement concerning the grounds of political obligation is indebted to Brandt's analysis of the postulate as a *lex permissiva*.

Despite these debts, my interpretation of the postulate differs from those of Ludwig and Brandt in so far as I place particular emphasis on the relation between freedom and nature in the *Rechtslehre*. In this connection, I want to make good the promise of chapter 2, where I said that acquaintance with the third antinomy in *CPR* will assist one's appreciation of the structurally similar antinomy of Right which Kant introduces in the course of his property argument. Put in a nutshell, the principal argument in this chapter is that the postulate, as *lex permissiva*, offers a provisional solution to the antinomy of Right. In so doing, the postulate makes possible a determinate solution to the problem of Right. This determinate solution is grounded in subjects' reflective recognition of their obligations of justice towards one another. Hence, the general sequence of the argument below is from conflict of Right to provisional Right, and from provisional Right to determinate, or peremptory Right. The corresponding technical terms are, 'the antinomy of Right'; the distinction between 'empirical possession' and 'intelligible possession'; the postulate as *lex permissiva*; and the universal principle of Right understood as a reflective judgement of practical reason. Before turning to the, at times, unavoidably technical debate, I begin with some general remarks on the distinctiveness of Kant's approach to the problem of property rights when compared to more conventional liberal accounts. These remarks will elucidate Kant's crucial distinction between inner mine and outer mine.

2 INNATE RIGHT AND ACQUIRED RIGHTS

The most familiar aspect of Kant's justification of property rights is probably his rejection of the labour theory of property, which is

---

[10] Reinhard Brandt, 'Das Erlaubnisgesetz, oder: Vernunft und Geschichte in Kants Rechtslehre' in Brandt, ed., *Rechtsphilosophie der Aufklärung*, 233–75.
[11] *RL*, 6: 247.

usually associated with John Locke. In the *Rechtslehre*, Kant dismisses that view, 'which is so old and still so widespread, [according to which] a right to things is a right directly against them, as if someone could, by the work he expends on them, put things under an obligation to serve him and no one else'.[12] Kant's dismissal of 'the old view' has to do with his definition of the concept of Right as a concept of pure practical reason. I have already mentioned the concept of Right in chapter 3, where I drew attention to Kant's specification of it as concerned solely with the external form of relations between the choice (*Willkür*) of one to that of another.[13] It follows from this definition that the concept of Right, as a concept of pure practical reason, can hold only between beings whose capacity for choice makes them susceptible to reason. Since inanimate objects are not susceptible to reason, it is a mistake to define relations of Right as holding between subjects and objects. Property rights specify a three-way relation between subjects with regard to objects rather than a two-way relation between subject and object.

In fact, Kant faults the Lockean view on two counts: first, in thinking that property rights denote a direct relation between subject and object; and, second, in assuming that a unilateral act of empirical acquisition (such as the act of investing one's labour in the object) can establish a rightful claim against all others to that object. Property rights are neither empirically grounded, nor can they be established unilaterally. The 'old view' makes these mistakes because it fails to distinguish between 'innate rights' and 'acquired rights'.

---

[12] *RL*, 6: 269. It may be misleading to attribute this view of property rights to Locke himself. According to Locke, it is ultimately God who grants his industrious subjects property rights over the land which they labour in obeyance of His command to multiply the fruits of the earth. On Locke's theological justification, property rights specify a relation between subject, God, and object. Locke's more secular successors may be the more appropriate reference points for the view rejected by Kant. For contemporary exponents of the secularised 'Lockean view', see, for example, Robert Nozick, *Anarchy, State and Utopia* (Oxford, Basil Blackwell, 1974), chapter 7, 149–231, 171–93; Hillel Steiner, *An Essay on Rights* (Oxford, Basil Blackwell, 1994), chapters 6 and 7, 188–265; Samuel Wheeler, 'Natural Body Rights as Property Rights', *Noûs* 14 (1980). Indeed, in some of his earlier writings (especially in his 'Reflections on the Beautiful and the Sublime'), Kant himself advocated a version of the labour theory of property rights – his rejection of the 'old view' is therefore an exercise in self-criticism as much as anything else. For comment and evaluation of this shift in Kant's thinking, see Reinhard Brandt, *Eigentumstheorien von Grotius bis Kant* (Stuttgart: Frommann-Holzboog, 1974), 167–79; Kenneth Baynes, 'Kant on Property Rights and the Social Contract', *The Monist*, 72 (1989), 433–53; Mary Gregor, 'Kant's Theory of Property', *The Review of Metaphysics*, 41 (1988), 757–87.
[13] See chapter 3, section 2.

Again, we have already encountered the innate right to freedom when examining Kant's conception of external freedom:

Freedom (independence from being constrained by another's choice), in so far as it can coexist with the freedom of every other in accordance with a universal law, is the only original right belonging to every man by virtue of his humanity. This principle of innate freedom already involves the following authorisations, which are not really distinct from it: innate equality . . .; hence, a man's quality of being his own master (*sui iuris*), as well as being a man beyond reproach (*iusti*), since before he performs any act affecting rights he has done no wrong to anyone; and finally, his being authorised to do to others anything that does not in itself diminish what is theirs so long as they do not want to accept it.[14]

Innate equality; the quality of being beyond reproach (*Unbeschol-tenheit*); and independence from the arbitrary will of another thus define a person's inner mine, or their internal *suum*, which is theirs merely in virtue of their humanity. I said in chapter 3 that the concept of external freedom is *derived from* the innate right to freedom, and I shall come back to this in a moment. For now the important point is this: although the innate right implies subjects' right to freedom of choice and action, including property rights, the latter are not contained in the innate right to freedom. In contrast to Locke's specification of a person's internal *suum* as comprising their right to life, liberty, and property, Kant does not include a right to external possessions in a person's *suum*. The right to external mine is not contained in what is internally mine, but falls under the category of acquired rights.[15] Since the *Rechtslehre* is concerned solely with acquired rights, a person's internal *suum* strictly falls outside the scope of its discussion.[16] None the less, the universal principle of Right clearly is derived from the innate right to freedom. Recall that, according to this principle:

Any action is right, if it can coexist with everyone's freedom in accordance with a universal law, or if on its maxim the freedom of choice of each can coexist with everyone's freedom in accordance with a universal law.[17]

In so far as a person's independence from another's arbitrary will affirms their capacity for freedom of choice and action, the universal principle of Right regulates relations between subjects with respect to their external actions. The question is whether lawful external

---

[14] *RL*, 6: 237/238.   [15] *RL*, 6: 258.
[16] *RL*, 6: 238.   [17] *RL*, 6: 230.

freedom implies more than just freedom of movement in general, i.e. whether it includes a right to particular external objects of one's choice. This is where Kant's departure from the old view becomes interesting. On the one hand, he denies that the right to external possessions is contained in a person's innate right or internal *suum*. On the other hand, both the universal principle of Right and the innate right to freedom from which that principle is derived, imply the acknowledgement of individuals' freedom of action and choice. But the acknowledgement of subjects' capacity for choice in relation to external action invites the further claim to possible *objects* of one's choice. Thus, although Kant denies that the *right* to external possessions is contained in a person's internal *suum*, he must acknowledge that individuals' *claims* to such a right indirectly arise from what *is* contained in their innate right to freedom. This leaves him with two problems. Since he denies that a right to external objects is contained in individuals' internal *suum*, he needs to show, first, that a different kind of connection is conceivable between a person's innate right and their claim to external objects of their choice which, though not an innate right, possesses prima facie validity. This leads him to distinguish between the conception of empirical possession and that of intelligible possession. But, even if a conception of intelligible possession is conceivable, and even if a person's claim to external objects of their choice possesses prima facie validity, this does not suffice to demonstrate such a claim's compatibility with the requirements of the universal principle of Right. Thus, Kant's second task is to show how individuals' potentially conflicting claims to external objects *can* coexist with one another in accordance with the universal principle of Right. Kant does not clearly distinguish between these two related but distinct aspects of justification.[18] He says that:

> The question, How is it possible for something external to be mine or yours? resolves itself into the question, How is merely rightful (intelligible) possession possible?, and this in turn, into the third question, How is a synthetic a priori proposition of Right possible?[19]

I shall interpret this obscure passage as calling for a two-step argument, where the answer to the first question depends on

---

[18] For an illuminating discussion, see Peter Baumgarten, 'Zwei Seiten der Kantschen Begründung von Eigentum und Staat', *Kantstudien*, 85 (1994), 147–59.
[19] *RL*, 6: 249.

answering questions two and three. In order to show how external mine or yours is possible (question 1), we must first establish the prima facie validity of individuals' rights claims (question 2). Secondly, we must demonstrate the actual legitimacy of these claims by showing their compatibility with the universal principle of Right (question 3). The first task begins with Kant's distinction between empirical possession and intelligible possession, issuing in the formulation of the antinomy of Right. I turn to this in the next two sections. The solution to the antinomy, and the vindication of the legitimacy of individuals' rights claims, depends on the postulate of practical reason with regard to Right, or the *lex permissiva*. This will be dealt with in sections 5 and 6.

3 THE ANTINOMY OF RIGHT: THE FORMAL ARGUMENT

Kant introduces the distinction between empirical possession and intelligible possession in §1 of Section I, following a preliminary definition of rightful external possession:

That is rightfully mine (*meum iuris*) with which I am so connected that another's use of it without my consent would wrong me. The subjective condition of any possible use is possession.[20]

We have seen that the universal principle of Right defines another's action as wrong only in so far as that action constitutes a violation of my right to freedom. This means that another's use of an external object of my choice is unlawful only if their use of it without my consent constitutes a violation of my freedom. Given Kant's denial that the right to external possessions of my choice is *contained in* the innate right to freedom, the claim to lawful external possessions depends on a possible *connection between* my innate right and external objects: 'Something external would be mine only if I may assume that I could be wronged by another's use of a thing *even though I am not in [physical] possession of it*'.[21] Thus, while Locke argues that something external becomes mine because it becomes part of myself as a result of my mixing my labour with it, for Kant the object cannot be thus incorporated into my internal *suum*, but remains physically distinct from me. None the less, if rightful possession is to be possible, a special kind of connection must obtain between subject and object, which would entitle the subject to prevent others from

---

[20] *RL*, 6: 245.   [21] *RL*, 6: 245.

using the object without the subject's consent. The question is what sort of connection this would have to be.

The conception of empirical possession falls short of the required connection. Empirical possession only establishes a contingent connection between subject and object. It puts me in possession of an object only so long as I have immediate physical control over it. I might be in empirical possession of an apple, for example, where my holding it in my hand establishes a physical connection between myself and the apple. If someone comes along and 'wrests the apple from my hand', they are indeed doing me wrong 'with regard to what is internally mine'.[22] Their wresting amounts to a transgression against the physical inviolability of my person. However, once the apple is out of my hand the connection between myself and the object is severed, and I have no basis for claiming it back as rightfully mine. The apple has passed from my empirical possession of it to the empirical possession of the other, with whom the object is now physically connected.

Matters would be different on a conception of intelligible possession. Here, my claim to ownership would not depend on my physical detention of the object: '*intelligible possession* (if this is possible) is possession of an object *without holding it* (*detentio*)'.[23] On this conception I could claim the apple as mine 'only if I [could] say that I possess it even though I have put it down, no matter where'.[24] My taking someone else's apple into my physical possession would not entitle me to claim rightful ownership over it. Conversely, I could put my apple on the table, leave the room, return after an hour, and all the while claim it as rightfully mine. The conception of non-empirical possession denotes a non-physical connection between my innate right to freedom and external objects of my choice. Here, someone's taking an object, which I intelligibly possess, into their empirical possession would constitute a violation of my freedom even in the absence of a simultaneous transgression against my physical inviolability as a person.

Kant's distinction between the two conceptions of possession is intuitively plausible.[25] At a pre-reflective level we tend to think of

---

[22] *RL*, 6: 248.   [23] *RL*, 6: 245.   [24] *RL*, 6: 247.

[25] None the less, secularised versions of the Lockean justification of property rights continue to prevail in contemporary liberal theory, especially among libertarians, who usually start from the dual premise of individuals' natural right to freedom and self-ownership rights. For references, see note 12 above. Those opposed to the libertarian perspective usually

ownership in terms of someone's physical possession of this or that object. On reflection, we also recognise that more than physical detention is involved: I can park my car, leave my house, loan out my tool kit, and still claim rightful ownership over all of these things even when I am not in immediate physical possession of them. But, even if it is intuitively plausible, this does not suffice to show that intelligible possession is indeed justifiable. This takes us to the antinomy of Right in §7:

The *thesis* says: It *is possible* to have something external as mine even though I am not in possession of it.

The *antithesis* says: It *is not possible* to have something external as mine unless I am in possession of it.

Solution: Both propositions are true, the first if I understand, by the word possession, empirical possession (*possessio phaenomenon*), the second if I understand by it purely intelligible possession (*possessio noumenon*).[26]

The thesis defends a conception of intelligible possession; the antithesis advocates a conception of empirical possession. The solution's ruling, that both propositions are true, inverts the positions' respective conceptions of possession, implying some form of reconciliation between them. This unexpected and unexplained inversion has given rise to considerable debate and confusion. Indeed, the entire formulation of the antinomy is deeply obscure and is not helped by the fact that, having stated it, Kant passes over it without further comment. In order to gain some insight into the structure of the dispute, we must look back to the discussion of the third antinomy in *CPR*.[27] Recall that an antinomy is a conflict of reason in which two opposed philosophical positions derive conflict-

repudiate both libertarian premises, arguing for property rights on the basis of need, or efficiency, or sometimes as a means to individual autonomy. See, for example, Jeremy Waldron, *The Right to Private Property* (Oxford: Clarendon Press, 1988); Stephen Münzer, *A Theory of Property* (Cambridge University Press, 1990); John Christman, *The Myth of Property. Towards an Egalitarian Theory of Ownership* (Oxford University Press, 1994). The libertarian tendency to appeal to both Locke and Kant in support of their arguments betrays a tendency to conflate Locke's natural right to freedom with Kant's innate right to freedom. It is important to distinguish between them. While libertarians are often criticised for departing from question-begging premises, Kant's conception of innate right to freedom as a right which individuals possess 'merely in virtue of their humanity' is grounded in his metaphysics of freedom as a (shared) idea of reason. Whether or not one finds Kant's account defensible is a separate question – the point is that, given his metaphysical presuppositions, Kant is an unlikely proponent of a libertarian conception of individual freedom as a natural right.

[26] *RL*, 6: 255.   [27] See chapter 2, section 2.

ing conclusions from mutually accepted premises. We can provisionally assume that, as in *CPR*, so in the *Rechtslehre* the antinomy pitches
the broadly rationalist position of the thesis against the broadly
empiricist position of the antithesis. I shall further assume that the
universal principle of Right forms the shared premise from which
the two positions derive their conflicting conclusions concerning the
legitimacy or otherwise of external possessions. Finally, since Kant's
contention that thesis and antithesis are both true resembles his
solution to the third antinomy in *CPR*, we can expect the antinomy
of Right to be resolved through the formulation of a third perspective, which takes on board aspects of thesis and antithesis without
fully endorsing either position.[28]

Even with these hints regarding the structure of the antinomy, its
subject-matter remains obscure. This may be why the antinomy of
Right has not received much attention in the literature. A noticeable
exception is Wolfgang Kersting's searching paper, 'Freiheit und
Intelligibler Besitz'.[29] Kersting's reading of the antinomy relies
heavily on Kant's innumerable preliminary notes to the *Rechtslehre*
which contain several different sketches of the dispute and which
shed some light on its possible function in the published text. None
the less, Kersting is insufficiently mindful of the fact that the sketches
in the preliminary notes do not overlap with the argument in the
Rechtslehre. More specifically, Kersting privileges the position of the
thesis, dismissing the antithesis as erroneous – a conclusion that
conflicts with Kant's contention that both propositions are true.
Before assessing Kersting's proposed solution, I shall summarise his
exposition of the conflict itself.

In the preliminary notes, thesis and antithesis both accept the
innate right to freedom of each and the universal principle of Right
derived from it. Both accept the Kantian view that the right to
external possession is not contained in a person's internal *suum*. They
differ over the possibility of a non-analytic but necessary connection
between the innate right to freedom and the right to external
possessions. The antithesis claims that no such necessary connection

---

[28] For the sake of completeness, note also a discrepancy between the third antinomy and the
antinomy of Right, namely that the latter does not explicitly employ the strategy of indirect
proof.

[29] Wolfgang Kersting, 'Freiheit und Intelligibler Besitz: Kants Lehre vom Synthetischen
Rechtssatz a priori', *Zeitschrift für Philosophie*, 6 (1981), 31–51. An amended version of the
same discussion can also be found in Kersting, *Wohlgeordnete Freiheit*, 233–41.

obtains, and that possession of external objects of one's choice cannot be in accordance with the universal principle of Right. By contrast, the thesis insists that a necessary connection between innate right and external possessions does obtain, and that possession of external objects of one's choice must be in accordance with the universal principle of Right.

According to the antithesis, 'it appears to be contained in the expressions themselves that it is impossible for an external object of my choice to be mine, i.e. that others could, through their use of objects outside of me, violate my freedom' (*AK* 23: 231).[30] The crucial point here is that the impossibility of property rights is said to be 'contained in the expressions themselves'. The antithesis' negative conclusion regarding a right to external possessions rests on its denial of an analytically necessary relation between freedom and external possessions, where this is construed in Kant's standard meaning of 'analytic containment'. On this understanding of analyticity the principal difficulty consists in the fact that 'internal' and 'external' are mutually exclusive predicates. Something is either internal or external: it cannot be both at the same time. More specifically, an internal right cannot contain an external right. Since the innate right to freedom refers to a person's internal *suum*, and since the universal principle of Right rules out as unlawful only those actions by others which transgress against my freedom, it is impossible that someone's use of external objects could constitute a violation of my freedom. For such a violation of my freedom to be possible, 'I would have to be able to think of myself as subject as simultaneously invested in an object outside of me'; I would have to 'think of myself as in two places at the same time'.[31] But this is impossible. Since 'internal' and 'external' are mutually exclusive predicates, the universal principle of Right cannot without contradiction affirm that someone's use of an external object of my choice without my consent constitutes a violation of my innate right to freedom. This does not mean that the antithesis cannot countenance any form of external possession at all. It can accept the conception of empirical possession which supposes no more than a *contingent* connection between subject and object. Thus the antithesis can allow for 'possession in use' which grants

---

[30] Kant quoted in Kersting, 'Intelligibler Besitz', 33. The numbers in brackets refer to the relevant volume and pages of the Prussian Academy edition containing Kant's preliminary notes on the *Rechtslehre*.

[31] Kant quoted in Kersting, 'Intelligibler Besitz', 34.

subjects' temporary possession of particular external objects for the satisfaction of their basic needs – what Brandt refers to as a form of 'communal possession' or 'primitive communism' (*Besitzkommunismus*).[32] However, the antithesis cannot allow individuals' *exclusive* right to external objects of their choice.

In contrast to the antithesis, the thesis does make a case for exclusive possession as in accordance with the universal principle of Right. It does so by challenging the antithesis' conception of freedom: 'the [antithesis] is to be rejected because it is contrary to the idea of freedom itself'. Indeed, the antithesis 'destroys freedom as a positive capacity'.[33] This complaint evokes Kant's contention that we can have insight into the grounds of freedom only from a practical perspective. In a convoluted passage, the thesis contends that a denial of the practically necessary presuppositions of freedom amounts to a denial of the right to freedom itself:

[According to the antithesis] the subject would be entitled only to the use of its inner determinations. But since the relation in which the subject stands to external objects means that the use of these inner determinations depends on the availability to the subject of external objects [of its choice], it would, according to the antithesis, be lawful to hinder someone from having those inner determinations without which it would be impossible for them to avail themselves of their freedom. (*AK* 23: 309/10)[34]

The claim is that the antithesis both acknowledges and denies subjects' use of their 'inner determinations' in relation to their right to freedom. But what are these inner determinations? In so far as the thesis emphasises a conception of freedom as a positive capacity, it is reasonable to conjecture that the determinations in question refer to freedom as a practical capacity of the will – more specifically to the will's capacity to exercise its power of choice in relation to external objects. The antithesis destroys freedom as a positive capacity by failing to acknowledge the will's capacity for choice in relation to external objects as a necessary presupposition of subjects' exercise of their freedom. With its reference to the necessary presuppositions of freedom, the thesis makes a pitch for a non-analytic necessary

---

[32] Cf. Brandt, *Eigentumstheorien*, 187–8. 'Possession in use' is also what Kenneth Westphal seems to have in mind when he argues that Kant's justification of property rights in the *Rechtslehre* does not go beyond the justification of usufruct rights – what Westphal refers to somewhat obscurely as 'choses in possession'. See Westphal, 'Do Kant's Principles Justify Property or Usufruct?', *Jahrbuch für Recht und Ethik*, 5 (1997), 142–94.

[33] Kant quoted in Kersting, 'Intelligibler Besitz', 35.

[34] Ibid.

connection between freedom and external possessions. On this view, the issue is not whether or not the right to external possessions is *contained* in the innate right to freedom, but whether the latter *presupposes* the former. The thesis answers in the affirmative: unless acknowledging subjects' right to freedom includes an acknowledgement of the necessary presuppositions of freedom as a practical capacity of the will, one effectively denies subjects their right to freedom. Finally, the thesis' affirmation of freedom as a practical capacity of the will in relation to external objects holds out the prospect of a non-empirical connection between subject and object. The legitimate possession of an external object does not depend on physical detention, but is grounded in a particular relation of the will to the object. If such a non-empirical connection between will and object is conceivable, an intelligible conception of possession may be possible.

In summarising the dispute sketched in the preliminary notes, it is tempting to side with the thesis and against the antithesis. The thesis invokes Kant's conception of freedom as a positive capacity and as a practical capacity of the will. Moreover, its rejection of mere analytic necessity in favour of a non-analytic but necessary connection between freedom and external objects appears to align the thesis with central tenets of Kant's critical philosophy. Indeed, this is just the conclusion drawn by Kersting when he asserts that the thesis 'disposes of the antithesis'[35] by exposing as inadequate the latter's conception of freedom, and by demonstrating the possibility of a conception of intelligible possession. Kersting believes his conclusion to be supported by the postulate of practical reason as formulated in the *Rechtslehre*:

Postulate of practical reason with regard to Right: It is possible for me to have any external object of my choice as mine, that is, a maxim by which, if it were to become a law, an object of choice would *in itself* (objectively) have to belong to no one (*res nullius*) is contrary to Right.[36]

I shall consider the postulate in detail in sections 5 and 6 below; here I simply want to comment on Kersting's interpretation of it in relation to the antinomical dispute as expounded in the preliminary notes. At first sight, Kersting does have a point: in denying that a general prohibition of exclusive possession could be rightful the postulate does appear to reject the conclusion of the antithesis.

---

[35] Ibid., 37.   [36] *RL*, 6: 246.

Indeed, in the comments immediately following the postulate, Kant reiterates the considerations advanced by the thesis in the preliminary notes. If it were not rightful to claim external objects of my choice as mine, 'freedom would be depriving itself of the use of its choice with regard to an object of choice'. Since we can have knowledge of our freedom only as a practical capacity, 'it is an *a priori* presupposition of practical reason to regard and treat any object of my choice as something that could objectively be mine or yours'.[37] These remarks lend support to Kersting's conclusion in favour of the thesis. But Kersting goes much further when he claims that:

[The postulate affirms] the right to dominion [*Herrschaftsgewalt*] over external objects [as] a natural entitlement of freedom of choice [which] cannot be lawfully restricted. Any legal regulation must be rejected, whose norms restrict or even deny freedom's right of dominion over the realm of objects. The postulate constitutes a transcendental relation of Right [*tranzendentales Rechtsverhältnis*] between freedom of choice as such and external objects; it confers upon freedom of choice an absolute legal power [*Rechtsmacht*] over external objects.[38]

This conclusion is too strong for two reasons. First, the postulate mentions neither a 'transcendental relation of Right', nor subjects' 'absolute legal power' over objects. It only asserts that subjects' claims to external objects of their choice cannot be contrary to Right. Kersting's contention that the postulate establishes a legal relation is premature and goes beyond what is explicitly stated by the postulate. Second, Kersting conflates the position of the thesis in the preliminary notes with that of the postulate in the *Rechtslehre*. Yet, while the thesis of the preliminary notes may plead subjects' 'absolute legal power over external objects', this is not a claim which the postulate of the *Rechtslehre* could vindicate. The reason for this is obvious: on Kersting's account, the thesis defines intelligible possession in terms of the will's relation to external objects. His subsequent conclusion, that the postulate confers on subjects 'the right of dominion' over objects, comes close to depicting property rights as a relation according to which subjects obligate objects.[39] But this is

---

[37] *RL*, 6: 246.

[38] Kersting, 'Intelligibler Besitz', 38. See also, *Wohlgeordnete Freiheit*, 243.

[39] This tendency to construe relations of Right in terms of subject/object relations is especially marked in the earlier paper, 'Intelligibler Besitz', where Kersting suggests that the denial of subjects' power of dominion over objects would amount to attributing freedom to objects by rendering them '*herrenlos*', i.e. 'without master', or 'masterless' (37, 38). This

just the old view of property rights explicitly rejected by Kant. Since what is at issue is the possibility of rightful external possession in accordance with the universal principle of Right, and since the concept of Right specifies a relation between subjects who are susceptible to reason, the disagreement cannot be about whether or not subjects have dominion over objects. The crucial question must be whether individuals' claims to external possessions can be legitimate in the sense of being compatible with the equally valid claims of everyone else.

Kersting is overly hasty in his dismissal of the antithesis and unqualified support for the thesis. He overlooks the fact that the position of the thesis in the preliminary notes falls short of Kant's requirements for rightful external possession in the *Rechtslehre*. The next section offers an alternative interpretation of the antinomical dispute in relation to the postulate. I shall suggest that the postulate does take into account the antithesis' reservations against exclusive external possessions. While these reservations do not suffice for a denial of the right to possession, they correct the thesis' oversight concerning the intersubjective dimension of lawful external possession. Far from dismissing the antithesis and endorsing the thesis, the postulate acknowledges that 'both propositions are true'.

4 THE ANTINOMY OF RIGHT: THE SUBSTANTIVE ARGUMENT

My disagreement with Kersting concerns not his formal analysis of the antinomy so much as the substantive conclusion he draws from it. I agree with him that the dispute in the preliminary notes focuses on the possibility or otherwise of a non-analytic but necessary connection between subjects' innate right to freedom and external objects of their choice. Since, in contrast to the thesis, the antithesis fails even to consider the possibility of such a connection, it is not unreasonable to conclude in favour of the thesis. Indeed, it may be Kersting's eagerness to establish the critical credentials of Kant's philosophy of Right which encourages him in this conclusion. I have argued that this is mistaken. The thesis does gesture towards an intelligible relation between the subject's will and external objects of its choice. However, this cannot as yet constitute a rightful relation

particular claim is withdrawn in *Wohlgeordnete Freiheit*, where Kersting emphasises that the postulate 'is not intended to defeat a purported rights claim on the part of objects' (248).

for the simple reason that Kant defines the concept of Right in terms of a subject/subject relation. Similarly, even if the antithesis' conclusions are unacceptable as they stand, this need not mean that this position advances no valid reasons in cautioning against the right to exclusive external possessions. These remarks suggest that neither thesis nor antithesis are either completely mistaken or wholly correct. Both raise valid points, but neither amounts to a 'critical solution' in the Kantian sense of the term.

This situation is analogous to that of the third antinomy, where thesis and antithesis represent two pre-critical philosophical positions – rationalist and empiricist – whose reconciliation is effected through the introduction of a third alternative. In fact, the analogy between the third antinomy and the antinomy of Right does not just concern their formal structure, but extends to their respective substantive content as well. Recall that chapter 2 characterised the debate between thesis and antithesis in *CPR* as a conflict between freedom and nature. While the thesis insisted that freedom must be possible, the antithesis objected that entertaining such an idea threatens the unity of experience. In the antinomy of Right, we confront a similar conflict between the claims of freedom and the constraints of nature, though this time from a political (rather than a cosmological) perspective. It is worth emphasising that, like the thesis, so the antithesis claims that its negative conclusion about possible external possession follows from the universal principle of Right. The universal principle of Right does not just affirm the innate right to freedom of each; it also stipulates that the exercise of the freedom of each must be compatible with the equal right to freedom of everyone else. Since the thesis' advocacy of exclusive possession focuses on the right to freedom *of each*, it is not implausible to assume that the antithesis' opposition to individual property rights hinges on their implications for the equal right to freedom *of others*. While the thesis contends that, given the conception of freedom as a practical capacity of the will, a right to external possessions must be possible, the antithesis objects that, given the unavoidable constraints of nature, no such right is possible.

In pursuing this line of argument, I shall emphasise the position of the antithesis. This is partly in order to correct for an imbalance in Kersting's account, which privileges the thesis. More generally, however, Kant has a reputation among critics and supporters alike for favouring abstract argument over contextual considerations with clear practical implications.[40] Often an interest in philosophical abstraction is equated with disinterest in practical concerns. Throughout the preceding chapters I have tried to show that this equation cannot be applied to Kant's philosophy. Both his epistemological conception of cognitively experiencing subjects who must presuppose a mind-independent world of sensible experience, and his moral conception of finite rational beings who are subject to certain limitations, are abstract conceptions. But neither reflect a philosophical position that is removed from practical concerns. The same holds for the *Rechtslehre*. Kant's troubled concern with the unavoidable constraints of nature and their implications for relations of Right between subjects is expressed at a very high level of abstraction, rendering his argument demanding but also extremely powerful. Consider his remark that:

> The concept of merely rightful possession is not an empirical concept (dependent upon conditions of space and time) and yet it has practical reality, that is, it must be applicable to objects of experience, knowledge of which is dependent upon those conditions.[41]

This remark, which occurs in the same paragraph as the antinomy, highlights the tension between the concept of Right as a concept of pure practical reason, and the empirical conditions of its application. Although the concept itself can be analysed independently of empirical conditions, its practical application is subject to these conditions. Note that the reference here is to the *unavoidable* conditions of empirical reality – space and time – rather than to the merely empirical, or empirically contingent conditions referred to in the *Groundwork* in connection with agents' subjective desires and inclinations. The empirical constraints at issue in the *Rechtslehre* are not subjective, motivational constraints whose influence upon the

---

[40] Kant's reputation here is based on his rhetorical question in *Groundwork* whether we 'do not think it a matter of the utmost necessity to work out for once a pure moral philosophy completely cleansed of everything that can only be empirical and appropriate to anthropology?'(4: 389). However, the passage is usually quoted out of context. Kant's claim is not that empirical conditions 'don't matter', or that the end of philosophical inquiry into the grounds of morality should not be practical. Instead he complains of those 'self-styled creative thinkers', who substitute for the discipline of reasoned argument 'a mixture of the empirical and the rational in unknown proportions, even to themselves' (4: 388). Such approaches do morality a disservice by offering quick fixes in place of thoroughgoing inquiry. For a defence of abstraction in Kant's ethics, see Onora O'Neill, 'Constructivism in Ethics' in *Constructions of Reason*, 206–18. See also O'Neill, 'Abstraction, Idealization, and Ideology' in J. D. G. Evans, ed., *Moral Philosophy and Contemporary Problems* (Cambridge University Press, 1988), 55–69.

[41] *RL*, 6: 253.

will it is possible for agents to control or overcome. Instead, the
constraints refer to the external conditions of agency in general: they
determine the conditions of human agency which, as such, are not
subject to modification through agents' wills. In this context, Kant's
analogy in the introduction to the *Rechtslehre* is intriguing, between a
'mathematical construction' and the 'construction of the concept of
Right'. In 'pure mathematics', he claims, 'we cannot derive the
properties of its objects immediately from concepts but can discover
them only by constructing concepts'.[42] Our conceptual grasp of
mathematical constructions depends on their intuitive representation
in space and time. The figurative representation we draw of a
triangle enables us to abstract from the particular representation to
the general mathematical laws which it instantiates. Similarly, 'it is
not the concept of Right but the *construction* of that concept, that is,
the presentation of it in pure intuition a priori',[43] which enables us
to determine its defining features and necessary presuppositions.
Like the concept of a triangle, so the concept of Right consists of all
its constitutive features and presuppositions considered together. But
the precise constellation of these features and presuppositions, and
their relations to each other, is not immediately obvious to us. The
concept of Right is not a given, but is a construct of practical reason:
its possible construction depends on our ability to render a representation of its necessary presuppositions and conditions. On the one
hand, our capacity for abstraction depends on our capacity for
intuitive representation in space and time: our capacity to acknowledge the concept of Right as an (abstract) concept of pure practical
reason depends on our capacity to represent this concept to ourselves under the conditions of its application. On the other hand, the
fact that we are able to come up with intuitive representations of
theoretical and of practical concepts depends on given background
conditions that make such representation possible in the first place.
Our representations of mathematical concepts depend upon and are
constrained (according to Kant) by time and space as necessary
forms of intuition for us: without time and space, no mathematical
construction would be possible for us at all. By the same token, time
and space constrain our mathematical possibilities by imposing
limits on the representations we can construct.

But what are the relevant background conditions and constraints

---

[42] *RL*, 6: 233.   [43] *RL*, 6: 233.

with regard to the practical construction of the concept of Right? Kant's analogy draws attention to the spatio-temporal constraints of theoretical and practical constructions alike. Just as our representation of the figure of a triangle is subject to the constraints of three-dimensional space, so the practical construction of the concept of Right is subject to spatial and temporal constraints, albeit considered in terms of their significance for practical reason. In the passage in question, acknowledgement of spatio-temporal constraints in relation to the concept of Right is expressed in terms of the notion of 'thoroughgoing reciprocal coercion':[44] the right of each is delimited by the equal right of everyone else. In the given context, thorough-going reciprocal coercion invokes a spatial image according to which the free action space of each is delimited and constrained by the equal action space of everyone else. A much more explicit reference to the relevant spatio-temporal constraints can be found in a passage which occurs much later on and which pertains to the cosmopolitan dimension of Kant's property argument mentioned at the beginning of this chapter. Kant there asserts that:

The spherical surface of the earth unites all the places on its surface; for if its surface were an unbounded plane, men could be so dispersed on it that they would not come into any community with one another, and community would not then be a necessary result of their existence on the earth.[45]

Here we have an image of *unavoidable* empirical constraints, abstractly conceived, attention to which is essential to the practical construction of the concept of Right. The earth's spherical surface is that empirically given space for possible agency within which human beings are constrained to articulate their claims to freedom of choice and action. It is not a subjectively given, *merely* empirical condition, which is in principle open to modification by human willing and agency. To the contrary, the global boundary constitutes an objectively given, unavoidable condition of empirical reality within the limits of which human agents are constrained to establish possible relations of Right. If this is a plausible line of thought, we can interpret the antinomical conflict as a potentially fruitful dispute in which the two positions attempt to offer exhaustive representations of the concept of Right by considering, from their respectively limited perspectives, its necessary presuppositions and conditions of realisation.

[44] *RL*, 6: 233.   [45] *RL*, 6: 263.

Recall that the universal principle of Right forms the shared premise of thesis and antithesis alike. We know that, according to the thesis, external possession must be consistent with this principle, since freedom as a practical capacity of the will presupposes subjects' power of choice in relation to external objects. But what are the considerations that move the antithesis to *deny* a possible connection between innate freedom and external objects? In contrast to the thesis' emphasis on the claims to freedom of each, the antithesis emphasises the implications of such unilateral claims for the freedom of everyone else. Under conditions of unavoidable empirical constraint (i.e. the earth's spherical surface) any exercise of choice by one compromises the freedom of everyone else by removing from availability to them external objects of their possible choice. From the perspective of the antithesis, exclusive possession of external objects of one's choice is incompatible with the freedom of everyone else and cannot, therefore, be in accordance with Right.

The advantage of reformulating the antinomy of Right in these terms is that we end up with a real conflict of practical reason. Thesis and antithesis both make valid points concerning property rights in relation to the universal principle of Right. In emphasising a non-empirical but necessary relation between external objects and subjects' power of choice, the thesis defends a broadly rationalist position which treats the will's capacity for choice as a sufficient condition for a legitimate claim to exclusive possession. By contrast, the antithesis adopts a broadly empiricist outlook when it rejects as illegitimate anything but a contingent and hence temporary connection between innate right and external objects, arguing that under conditions of unavoidable empirical constraints, the exclusive possession of external objects of their choice by some inevitably compromises the equal right to freedom of everyone else. Given the valid objections which either position advances against its opponent, neither can offer a feasible solution to the problem of external freedom. The search for a third alternative becomes compelling.

5   THE 'LEX PERMISSIVA' AS A 'DARK PRELIMINARY
JUDGEMENT'

On the interpretation developed above, the antinomical dispute leaves us with two equally unpalatable alternatives. Either we exercise our freedom of choice and accept our actions' unavoidable effects on the possible choices of others, or we respect others' equally valid claims to freedom and desist from exercising our freedom of choice and action. In the first case, we violate the compatibility requirement of the universal principle of Right; in the second case, we effectively deny any right to freedom of choice and action at all. At this stage, we must return to the 'postulate of practical reason with regard to Right':

It is possible for me to have any external object of my choice as mine, that is, a maxim by which, if it were to become a law, an object of choice would *in itself* (objectively) have to *belong to no one* (*res nullius*), is contrary to Right.

As Kersting says, the postulate appears to affirm the position of the thesis. Indeed, apart from the familiar remarks about freedom as a positive capacity, Kant goes on to make a more explicit point against the antithesis when he adds that a general prohibition against external possession cannot qualify as a principle of practical reason. Since principles of practical reason are action guiding, the antithesis' prohibition of individuals' freedom of choice and action in relation to external objects cannot qualify as such a principle.[46] So the thesis wins by default: If the general prohibition against external possession of the antithesis cannot qualify as a law of practical reason, the general permission of external possession must be rightful.[47]

But on the present interpretation of the antinomy the postulate's apparent affirmation of the thesis remains worrying. After all, the thesis' position also entails a violation of the universal principle of Right by compromising the equal right to freedom of everyone else. Strictly speaking, however, the postulate does not endorse the *rightfulness* of the thesis. The postulate only says that in so far as its general prohibition would be contrary to Right, external possession *must be possible*. This still falls short of saying that the position of the thesis is rightful. Consider Kant's characterisation of the postulate as a *lex permissiva*:

This postulate can be called a permissive principle [*lex permissiva*] of practical reason, which gives us an authorisation that could not be got from mere concepts of Right as such, namely to put all others under an

---

[46] *RL*, 6: 246.

[47] According to Ludwig, Kant's remark that pure practical reason can issue only 'formal laws', i.e. either a general permission or a general prohibition, and that the position of the antithesis cannot qualify as a law of external freedom, constitutes a *decisive* reason in favour of the thesis. See Ludwig, *Kant's Rechtslehre*, 112–13.

obligation, which they would not otherwise have, to refrain from using certain objects of our choice because we have been the first to take them into our possession. Reason wills that this hold as a principle, and it does this as practical reason, which extends itself a priori by this postulate of reason.[48]

This is an odd solution to the conflict. The postulate as *lex permissiva* authorises us to put others under an obligation to refrain from using external objects of our choice *simply because we have been the first to take them into our possession*. But to cite an act of unilateral, empirical acquisition as the ground of legitimate external possession violates thesis and antithesis alike. Neither thesis nor antithesis regards empirical acquisition as sufficient for a legitimate claim to exclusive possession. By permitting unilateral acts of empirical acquisition *and* by counting them as legitimate, the postulate's special authorisation amounts to a violation of the universal principle of Right on both counts! In drawing attention to this provocative result, Reinhard Brandt has argued that the function of the *lex permissiva* is precisely to permit a provisional violation of the universal principle of Right. According to Brandt, Kant regards the commission of an act of injustice as a necessary condition of the possible establishment of relations of justice between persons.[49] Brandt advances this interpretation of the *lex permissiva* in the context of a more general discussion of state formation, where he claims that Kant shares Hobbes' view that state foundation is necessarily based on the use of force: in the absence of a Romulus who is prepared to use violent means, state formation would not, and perhaps could not, occur.[50] Kant parts company with Hobbes in regarding the use of force as insufficient for political *legitimation*. None the less, on this view, state foundation *precedes* political justification. However, this is not to advocate *ad hoc* legitimation: Brandt's analysis of the *lex permissiva* hinges on his reading of the postulate as a type of practical judgement peculiar to the context of political agency.

Especially insightful in this context is Brandt's finding that, according to Kant, permissive laws 'obtain in natural law [*im Naturrecht*], not in ethics'.[51] With this suggestion, we have a first indication of the *lex permissiva* as an extension of the categorical

---

[48] *RL*, 6: 247.   [49] Brandt, 'Das Erlaubnisgesetz', 245–7.
[50] Ibid., 267. It is not clear whether Brandt regards the use of violence as logically necessary to state-foundation, or merely as inevitable in practice.
[51] Ibid., 244.

imperative's initial formulation in the *Groundwork*. Brandt's point of departure is Kant's distinction between prescriptive laws and prohibitive laws in relation to the categorical imperative. In ethics, the categorical imperative prescribes some types of action while prohibiting others. Yet between prescription and prohibition a wide range of possible actions remain, which are morally indifferent. Should the moral law legislate with respect to the latter by instituting so-called 'permissive laws' that specify all those actions whose commission is neither prescribed nor prohibited but left to the discretion of the agent? In the *Tugendlehre*, Kant emphatically rejects this idea. The demand for ethical legislation with regard to morally indifferent actions is 'concern with petty details which, were it admitted into the doctrine of virtue would turn the government of virtue into tyranny'.[52] Apart from substantive considerations about undermining the purpose of moral principles in the *Tugendlehre*, Kant offers some systematic considerations against permissive laws in a long footnote in *Perpetual Peace*. He notes that:

All laws embody an element of objective practical necessity as a reason for certain actions, whereas a permission depends only upon practical contingencies. Thus, a permissive law would be a compulsion to do something which one cannot be compelled to do, and if the object of the law were the same as that of a permission, a contradiction would result.[53]

Kant evidently believes that the concept of law in relation to actions which are merely permissible (i.e. neither prescribed not prohibited) verges on incoherence: such laws would contain no grounds for their necessitation. Surprisingly, the same footnote goes on to consider the possibility of permissive laws in relation to 'practical necessity'. By this time, the discussion has shifted from practical laws in general to 'natural right' (*Naturrecht*). Kant intimates that the commission of certain political actions, though strictly speaking unlawful, 'are nevertheless honest'.[54] Such an action's 'honesty' in the face of its unlawfulness is a reference not to ignorance of the law but to the unavoidability of the action *despite* knowledge of the law. In the sphere of law, or politics, there are unlawful actions which are none the less honestly committed because committing them is unavoidable under the circumstances. A few footnotes further on Kant is more explicit. He raises the possibility of permissive laws in relation to political judgement,

---

[52] *TL*, 6: 409.   [53] *Perpetual Peace*, 8: 348.   [54] *Perpetual Peace*, 8: 348.

asking whether it may not sometimes be permissible for a sovereign to delay the reform of an existing system of positive law even when the latter is known to conflict with the requirements of pure practical reason. After considering the issue, Kant concludes that such delays may indeed be permissible under certain circumstances, i.e. when political conditions are such as to make it either impossible or imprudent to institute changes whose effects, though well intended, would be politically disruptive. This does not justify the sovereign in postponing reforms indefinitely; the special permission to rule contrary to natural law holds only as long as circumstances make it impossible to rule otherwise:

> Permissive laws of reason allow a state of public right to continue, even if it is affected by injustice, until all is ripe for a revolution or has been prepared for it by peaceful means. For any legal constitution, even if it is only in small measure lawful, is better than none at all, and the fate for a premature reform would be anarchy. Thus political wisdom, with things as they are at present, will make it a duty to carry out reforms appropriate to the ideal of public Right.[55]

What is interesting about these passages is Kant's shift from the rejection of permissive laws in ethics on the grounds of 'practical contingencies', to their endorsement in the sphere of law on grounds of 'practical necessity'. Permissive laws in ethics refer to morally indifferent actions and should not, for that reason, be subject to moral legislation. But permissive laws in politics refer to actions which, though not morally indifferent, cannot be classed either under prescriptive laws or under prohibitive laws. Instead, they apply to actions which, though they are strictly speaking unlawful, must be regarded as provisionally lawful on the grounds that political circumstances leave open no other option. Permissive laws count as provisionally just; they are valid in anticipation of and in preparation for the institutionalisation of laws that do accord with the requirements of pure practical reason.

Despite its suggestiveness, the discussion of permissive laws in *Perpetual Peace* is tangential to the text's principal concerns and remains confined to footnotes. As Brandt points out, Kant characterises permissive laws as a type of *empirical* political judgement and as indicative of particular sovereigns' political wisdom and foresight. While he does hint that permissive laws, as a third possible class of

---

[55] *Perpetual Peace*, 8: 374, footnote.

law, 'automatically present themselves within the systematic division of reason', he fails to expand on these remarks in the context of the discussion in *Perpetual Peace*.[56]

Nor is Kant very explicit about the systematic status of the *lex permissiva* in the *Rechtslehre*. However, he there refers to the postulate as an 'a priori extension of principles of practical reason'.[57] Here the principle in question can only be the universal principle of Right. Hence the postulate, as a permissive law of practical reason within the sphere of law, can be taken to extend the systematic divisions of (practical) reason' initially developed in the *Groundwork*. In the sphere of law, permissive laws mediate between the prescriptive laws and the prohibitive laws of pure practical reason. Permissive laws apply to actions which, though not morally indifferent, cannot be classed either under obligatory actions or under the prohibited actions. They serve as provisionally valid principles of action with respect to political problems that stand in need of a solution but for which no solution readily presents itself. As such, they count as provisionally just, i.e. as just in anticipation of a more permanent solution in which the constraints of empirical reality are reconciled with the demands of pure practical reason. In borrowing from Kant's preliminary notes, Brandt evocatively characterises permissive laws as 'dark preliminary judgements', whose role it is to identify the path to a determinate or conclusive practical judgement:

Preliminary judgements form part of our most obscure representations. Every determinate judgement of ours is based on a dark, preliminary judgement which we reach beforehand. The latter guides us in our search of something determinate. Someone in search of undiscovered shores, for example, will not simply sail into the seas. Before embarking, he will already have formed a preliminary judgement about his likely destination. Preliminary judgements precede determinate judgements.[58]

Permissive laws are tentative attempts at practical political judgement, the urgency and necessity of which subjects recognise and acknowledge, but the determinate form of which they are not as yet able to discern. The question is why such preliminary judgements are required in connection with the justification of property rights. A possible answer to this question lies in the relation between the antinomy of Right and the postulate as *lex permissiva*.

---

[56] Brandt, 'Das Erlaubnisgesetz', 243.   [57] *RL*, 6: 247.
[58] Kant quoted in Brandt, 'Das Erlaubnisgesetz', 247.

6 REFLECTIVE JUDGEMENT AND POLITICAL OBLIGATION

Brandt's characterisation of the *lex permissiva* as a dark preliminary judgement allows us to make some sense of Kant's claim that the postulate constitutes an a priori extension of the categorical imperatives as it applies to political judgement and agency. On this reading, the postulate mediates between prescriptive and prohibitive laws of practical reason: the *lex permissiva* provisionally counts as permissible an action that is strictly speaking prohibited. I now want to connect Brandt's interpretation of the postulate with my analysis of the antinomical property dispute. This will show how agents' reflective recognition of their obligations of justice results from the peculiar solution to the antinomy proposed by Kant through the *lex permissiva*.

Of particular importance to this final step in the argument is the practical nature of Kant's solution. As with his conception of freedom as an idea of pure practical reason, of which we can have no theoretical knowledge, but whose reality we must assume for practical purposes, so Kant enigmatically asserts of the concept of Right that 'theoretical principles about external objects that are mine or yours get lost in the intelligible and represent no extension of knowledge'.[59] Given our limited knowledge, we are capable only of constructing a *practical* solution to the problem of Right: but this much we are constrained to do. Even so, the situation does not look promising. We have seen that, although neither of the two proffered solutions to the dispute satisfies both requirements of the universal principle of Right, the formal constraints on principles of practical reason compel us to make a choice between them. Since the solution advocated by the antithesis cannot serve as a principle of practical reason, the postulate provisionally embraces the thesis. It does so despite the fact that this position, too, entails a violation of the universal principle of Right. The question is why this solution should none the less be deemed legitimate. Following Brandt, we can interpret the *lex permissiva* as a preliminary judgement that tentatively authorises what is strictly speaking a violation of the universal principle of Right. The special authorisation to take into empirical possession external objects of one's choice counts as provisionally legitimate in so far as such acts might point towards a possible solution to this otherwise impossible situation. But what induces us

[59] *RL*, 6: 252.

to entertain this hope? In order to see the reasoning behind this provisional authorisation, we must construct the postulate's authorisation as a practical solution to the problem of Right under conditions of unavoidable empirical constraints.

Consider again the thesis' omission of any reference to affected others. Although the thesis insists that its conception of intelligible possession constitutes a necessary presupposition of freedom as a practical capacity of the will, it construes the conception of intelligible possession as a subject/object relation. It thus fails to acknowledge that rightful possession is subject to the possible acknowledgement of its rightfulness by all affected others with whose freedom it must be compatible. I now want to suggest that, rather than merely endorsing the thesis, the postulate as *lex permissiva* corrects it with regard to its crucial oversight. While the *lex permissiva* does authorise individuals' acts of unilateral empirical acquisition, it does not in so doing concede authority to individuals' unilateral wills. Individual wills' 'power of dominion' does not rest on a 'natural entitlement of freedom', as Kersting suggests. Instead, the authority behind the postulate's special authorisation is grounded in reason itself: *reason* wills that the postulate hold as a principle of pure practical reason. But if it is *reason* which authorises this special permission, then those whom the *lex permissiva* authorises to take into possession external objects of their choice must be acting within the constraints of reason. This means that their actions are subject to the demands of their possible justification to others.

Consider, then, a situation in which I acquire an external object of my choice, and appeal to my authority, under the *lex permissiva*, to oblige you to refrain from using that object without my consent. Since in appealing to the postulate I base my demand on the authority of reason, you can inquire into the grounds of my demand's justification. I refer you to the argument of the thesis, which affirms my right to external possession as a necessary presupposition of my innate right to freedom. But you appeal to the argument of the antithesis by reminding me of your equally valid right, which I have *already* compromised through my initial act. What is crucial here is my recognition of my prior violation of your freedom as an unavoidable consequence of the exercise of my freedom. My attempt to demonstrate to you that you are now (subsequent to my acquisition) under an obligation of justice towards me leads me to recognise that I am already (as a result of my acquisition) under an obligation of justice towards you. The reflective judgement made possible by the *lex permissiva* is not that it confirms me in my claim of your obligation towards me, but that it alerts me to the fact of my prior obligation towards you. In this way, my obligations of justice towards you follow as a direct corollary of my exercise of my freedom of choice and action.

It is important to emphasise that this account of freedom as directly obligation-entailing differs from contractarian arguments about the agreed reciprocal recognition of each other's rights to freedom. On the contractarian argument, my recognition of your right to freedom is conditional upon your recognition of my equal right. Where such reciprocal recognition is not forthcoming, no obligation obtains. On the present interpretation, my obligations of justice towards you result from the consequences for you of my acting under conditions of unavoidable empirical constraint. Since I cannot choose not to act (remember that the prohibition of action under the antithesis cannot qualify as a principle of practical reason), and since my actions inevitably affect your possible agency, I do not need to obligate myself: I am obliged:

> The universal law of Right (*Rechtsgesetz*), so act externally that the free use of your choice can coexist with the freedom of everyone else in accordance with a universal law, is indeed a law (*Gesetz*), which lays an obligation on me, but it does not at all expect, far less demand, that *I myself* should limit my freedom to those conditions just for the sake of this obligation; instead, reason says only that freedom *is* limited to those conditions . . . and it says this as a postulate which is incapable of further proof.[60]

Admittedly, Kant's tendency to personify reason by way of referring to reason 'saying this' or 'willing that' is somewhat peculiar. He evidently regards not only all our thinking, but also all our actions as subject to the authority of reason. However, there is no need to interpret the authority of reason in terms of an externally imposed rationality demand, which emanates from a transcendently given authoritative source. Kant's view of the authority of reason, which we have the capacity to recognise and to acknowledge (but whose demands we are equally at liberty to ignore), relates to his conception of humans as finite rational agents. I shall come back to the latter in chapter 6. For now, it suffices to point out that what makes Brandt's characterisation of the *lex permissiva* as a dark

---

[60] *RL*, 6: 252.

preliminary judgement so powerful an articulation of Kantian practical reasoning is its sensitivity towards agents' capacity to mobilise the resources of their own reasoning. In construing the *lex permissiva* as a solution to the antinomical conflict of Right, this chapter has tried to show how it is possible for finite rational agents to come to a reflective understanding of the constraints of their situation without rendering them helpless and inactive in the face of these constraints. The *lex permissiva* makes possible what one might call a recognitional shift in agents' perception of their situation, leading them from their unilateral claims to freedom to an acknowledgement of their duties of justice towards one another. This acknowledgement by agents that the duties of justice impose constraints on their claims to freedom makes possible the practical construction of the concept of Right in the form of civil society. Pure practical reason forms an order of ideas of its own:

Possession in anticipation of and preparation for the civil condition . . . is provisionally rightful possession, whereas possession found in an actual civil condition would be conclusive possession. . . . The way to have something external as one's own in a state of nature is physical possession that has in its favour the rightful presumption that it will be made into rightful possession through being united with the will of all in a public lawgiving, and in anticipation of this holds comparatively as rightful possession.[61]

There are echoes here of the claim attributed by Brandt to Kant, according to which state foundation is necessarily based on force, or injustice. However, the initial violation of others' freedom of choice and action provisionally authorised by the postulate as *lex permissiva* does not endorse 'the right of the strongest'. Its provisional status indicates that the postulate serves as a principle of transition from a condition of lawlessness to one of lawful freedom. The completion of that transition from provisional Right to peremptory Right, and the cosmopolitan form which this takes, are the subject-matter of the next chapter.

---

[61] *RL*, 6: 257.

CHAPTER 5

The general united will and cosmopolitan Right

All men are originally (i.e., prior to any choice that establishes a right) in a possession of land that is in conformity with Right, that is, they have a right to be wherever nature or chance (apart from their will) has placed them . . . The possession by all men on the earth that precedes any acts of theirs which would establish rights is an *original possession in common*, the concept of which is not empirical and dependent on temporal conditions.

(*RL*, 6:262)

I INTRODUCTION

The previous chapter interpreted the *lex permissiva* as a 'dark preliminary judgement' of pure practical reason. The postulate's provisional authorisation of unilateral acquisition leads to agents' reflective acknowledgement of the fact that any exercise of their freedom of choice and action entails obligations of justice towards others. On the one hand, given my innate right to freedom as a positive capacity, it must be possible for me to claim external objects of my choice as mine. On the other hand, given the constraints of nature, any such act of choice compromises the equally valid claims to freedom of everyone else. Subjects' obligations of justice towards one another are a direct corollary of their exercise of freedom of choice and action. One might characterise this judgement as requiring a recognitional shift from a conception of intelligible possession as a subject/object relation, to one which acknowledges that rightful possession defines a relation between subjects with regard to external objects of their choice. But although the postulate shows that agents' exercise of their external freedom is obligation entailing, it says nothing about how this obligation is to be discharged. It thus falls short of a conclusive solution to the problem of Right. One clue is, however, given in Kant's remark that:

A unilateral will cannot serve as a coercive law for everyone with regard to possession that is external. Only a collective general (common) and powerful will can provide everyone this assurance.[1]

Even though unilateral acquisition is unavoidable, a unilateral will cannot establish a claim of Right. Since the provisional authorisation of unilateral acquisition under the *lex permissiva* presupposes the possibility of intelligible possession understood as a subject/subject relation, the postulate implies the idea of an omnilateral will. This is a will capable of representing the intersubjective character of intelligible possession as a concept of pure practical reason. The validity of the postulate's special authorisation thus depends on a possible omnilateral will as that which grounds the conception of intelligible possession. A less formal way of putting it is to say that, while the *lex permissiva* shows *that* a conception of intelligible posses-sion must be possible, the idea of the general united will shows *how* it is possible. Kant sums up the relation between postulate and general will in terms of the distinction between provisional Right and peremptory Right: unilateral acquisition under the postulate is provisionally rightful in so far as it 'has in its favour the rightful presumption'[2] that it will become peremptory Right. Peremptory Right is the civil condition.

There is widespread agreement within the literature that the idea of the general united will is pivotal to the transition from provisional Right to peremptory Right. The question is how the legislative authority of this general will is to be conceived. Two possible but divergent interpretations have been canvassed. Each draws on either of two supplementary ideas introduced by Kant in connection with the general united will. The first of these interpretations effectively equates the idea of the general will with the idea of a social contract – I shall refer to this as the contractarian interpretation. The second strategy links the idea of the general will with the idea of original possession in common – I shall call this the natural law reading. On the first interpretation, the general will is the product of a contractual agreement between subjects to reciprocal recognition of the equal right of each to external objects of their choice. Legislative authority is *conferred on* the general will by unilateral wills through an act of establishment: the contractual union of unilateral wills creates the legislative authority of the general will. It is an

---

[1] *RL,* 6: 256.   [2] *RL,* 6: 257.

implication of this interpretation that obligations of justice are assumed voluntarily, and that the legitimacy of these obligations depends on their having been so assumed. By contrast, the natural law reading construes the general will as an antecedently given legislative authority which is grounded in the idea of original possession in common, and which assigns to each individual their rightful portion of external possessions from the common stock. Natural law arguments typically derive political obligations from purportedly universal features of human nature or from the structure of human needs as discerned by reason. But, although discernible *by* human reason, the grounds of obligation are not the product *of* human reasoning. In non-secular natural law theory, they ultimately originate in the will of God, which reveals itself to human reason in the laws of nature. The metaphysical basis of *secular* natural law theory is rather more elusive: it is often not clear what exactly replaces God's will as the antecedently given source of authority.[3] Secular natural law theory might be classed as a kind of moral realism, whose specific political obligations supervene on the determinate facts of human nature. In any case, as an *antecedently given* legislative authority, however conceived, the general united will of the natural law interpretation *confers legitimacy upon* subjects' unilateral choices and actions.

Textual evidence is available for both strands of interpretation, thus making plausible two conflicting accounts of the grounds of political obligation. Kant's evasiveness concerning the precise status of the general united will is particularly unhelpful here, as is his unexplained resort to the two mentioned supplementary ideas at different points in the text. The almost casual characterisation of the general united will as an a priori idea of pure practical reason means that it does not fit neatly into the framework of either tradition of political thought. On the one hand, the apriority of the will signals its status as an unconditionally valid principle of legitimation. This exceeds the conditional validity of contractually incurred obligations. Yet the view of the general will as an *idea of reason* is equally in tension with natural law assumptions about the antecedently given

---

[3] For an insightful analysis of Kant's break with natural law thinking, see Mary Gregor, 'Kant on "Natural Rights"' in Ronald Beiner and William James Booth, eds., *Kant and Political Philosophy: The Contemporary Legacy* (New Haven, Yale University Press, 1993), 50–75. Charles Covell reaches similar conclusions in his comparative analysis of Kant and the natural law tradition of international law in *Kant and the Law of Peace* (London, Macmillan, 1998).

grounds of obligation which are discovered by, though not 'produced by' human reason. Given these difficulties, a more promising approach may be to derive the idea of the general united will from the structure of Kant's property argument. In adopting this approach this chapter pursues two parallel aims. One is to show that the idea of the general will constitutes the justificatory ground of the conception of intelligible possession upon which the *lex permissiva* depends. Elucidating the relation between postulate and general will is therefore the principal interpretative concern of this chapter. The second, more substantive aim hinges on the connection between the general will and the cosmopolitan scope of obligations of justice. Here it is worth noting that Kant sinks the idea of the general united will in the idea of original possession in common. While the references to original possession in common do not make Kant a natural law thinker, the fact that common possession refers to the earth's spherical surface betrays his cosmopolitan orientation. In this latter respect, an affinity clearly does exist between Kant and the natural law tradition. However, neither the idea of original possession in common nor that of the general united will are antecedently given. Instead, both are to be located in subjects' capacity for reflective practical deliberation and judgement.

The next section begins with an overview of contractarian and natural law interpretations of the Kantian idea of the general will. Section 3 analyses the concept of 'original acquisition' and its implications for the idea of original possession in common. In that context, I consider and reject Leslie Mulholland's natural law interpretation of the *Rechtslehre*.[4] Section 4 offers an interpretation of the cosmopolitan scope of the general united will in relation to the idea of original possession in common. Section 5 argues that Kant's cosmopolitanism sets his approach to justice apart from the contractarian tradition. In short, the *Rechtslehre* cannot be assimilated either under the natural law tradition or under social contract theory.

2 GENERAL WILL, CONTRACT, AND NATURAL LAW

As I said, much of the current literature on the *Rechtslehre* favours a contractarian framework of justification according to which the move from provisional Right to peremptory Right is the product of

[4] Leslie Mulholland, *Kant's System of Rights* (New York, Columbia University Press, 1990).

an explicit agreement to that effect among affected subjects.[5] The assumed motivations for entering into such contractual agreement differ, depending on how the relevant textual passages are interpreted. The sections most frequently alluded to are the 'Hobbesian paragraphs' 41–2, in which Kant speaks darkly of the threat which each poses to the other by their very nature. Hence 'no one need wait until they become prudent through bitter experience'[6] of a course of events (i.e. the war of all against all) whose inevitability anyone can foresee who but reflects on the proclivities of human nature. Since these paragraphs form the transition from *Private Right* to *Public Right*, they are obvious candidates for a contractarian interpretation of the exit from the natural condition into civil society. Individuals' entrance into public, coercible relations of Right with one another is a matter of prudential foresight even where the war of all against all is not (yet) an actual condition. One problem with this interpretation concerns the complete absence of rights in the typical Hobbesian state of nature.[7] This makes it difficult to account for Kant's distinction between provisional Right in the pre-civil condition and peremptory Right in civil society within a Hobbesian contractual framework.

A less pessimistic, though still contractarian diagnosis of the desirability of moving from one condition to the other can be gleaned from Kant's more Lockean remarks about the need for a common judge with powers to adjudicate between parties' conflicting rights claims. On this view, the principal reason for moving from the natural to the civil condition is not wolf-like human nature, but the inconveniences which result from the absence of common standards of judgement.[8] Relations of publicly agreed peremptory Right secure the enjoyment of the provisional rights which each already possesses in the natural condition. In contrast to the Hobbesian reading, the Lockean interpretation tends to give *too much*

---

[5] Recent contractarian interpretations include: Otfried Höffe, 'The Dilemma of Natural Justice'; Wolfgang Kersting, *Wohlgeordnete Freiheit*; Jeffrie Murphy, *Kant: The Philosophy of Right* (London, Macmillan, 1970); Allen Rosen, *Kant's Theory of Justice* (Ithaca, Cornell University Press, 1993).

[6] *RL*, 6: 307.

[7] Cf. Hobbes, *Leviathan*, Part I, chapters 13 and 14.

[8] *RL*, 6: 312: 'Unless one wants to renounce any concepts of Right, the first thing one has to resolve upon is the principle that one must leave the state of nature, in which each follows his own judgement, unite oneself with all others . . . subject oneself to a public lawful external coercion, and so enter into a condition in which what is to be recognised as belonging to one is determined *by law* and is allotted to one by an adequate *power*.'

weight to provisional rights in the pre-civil condition. Kant's view that provisional rights count as rightful *in anticipation of* relations of peremptory Right differs from the Lockian affirmation of *natural* rights to property in the state of nature. Since unilateral acquisition in the natural condition is only conditionally rightful, entrance into the civil condition amounts to more than the institutional secure-ment of what Locke, but not Kant, regards as individuals' natural rights.

However, the principal difficulty with contractarian interpreta-tions concerns the tension between the unconditional validity of Kant's a priori *idea* of a contract in contrast to the conditional validity of a contractual agreement, and the contractarian focus on domestic justice to the exclusion of cosmopolitan Right. The latter conflicts with Kant's insistence on the systematic connection between domestic Right, international Right and cosmopolitan Right. I shall return to these contrasts between Kant and social contract theory towards the end of the chapter. Here I simply want to draw out some of the general differences between contractarian and natural law approaches to the Kantian idea of the general will. Admittedly, Kant's allusions to the idea of the social contract *as well as* to the idea of the general united will invite confusion, not least because both ideas pertain to the discussion of political obligation and state legitimation. Treating them as interchangeable may seem like the most natural reading. None the less, they should not be conflated with one another. Kant introduces these ideas at different points in the argument. While the social contract is mentioned at the transition from *Private Right* to *Public Right*, the general will figures more prominently – and arguably more systematically – in the property argument of *Private Right*.

Its occurrence in the property context has been emphasised by Leslie Mulholland, who makes a case for a natural law interpretation of Kant's account of political obligation. The natural law influence is especially evident in Kant's conjunction of the idea of the general will with the idea of original possession in common. The assumption of initial common ownership figures prominently in natural law deriva-tions of individual property rights. The most pertinent natural law representative in this respect is Hugo Grotius (1583–1645), who introduces the notion of common ownership in the context of a property argument that begins from a global perspective. *The Rights of War and Peace* begins with the supposition that 'God originally gave the earth to all in common',[9] so that all might derive their sustenance from it. Although there is no explicit right to exclusive possession, common ownership implies exclusive property rights in so far as sustenance requires the individuation of resources. Grotius' account focuses on explaining as in accordance with natural justice the individual distribution of what God originally gave to all in common. He combines natural necessity with social advantageousness. On the one hand, the individuation of the common stock is unavoidable: each mouthful of food taken from the common stock constitutes an act of unilateral acquisition whose legitimacy God must be presumed to have intended. On the other hand, individual distribution of the common stock also turns out to be mutually advantageous, since it 'satisfies the desire for commodious living'. Men 'departed from the primaeval state of holding all things in common' because 'it was found inconvenient' to abide by the initial arrangement. In light of the manifest advantages of individual possession, 'men agreed that whatever anyone had occupied should be accounted his own'.[10]

Grotian agreements are not of the hypothetical kind which characterise social contract theory. They constitute a series of actual, more or less *ad hoc* agreements between consenting parties, and they are restricted to the division of the common stock. They are not explicitly concerned with state foundation or with the legitimation of political authority. The individuation of common property develops from 'first occupation'. Grotius recounts what he takes to be a historically actual progression from primitive common ownership to individual property rights, with correspondingly increasing levels of civilisation. Moveable objects (e.g. animals) are divided up first, the division of immovable property (i.e. land) comes last. Human history develops from the hunter stage to nomadic life and only then into settled communities, leading finally to the formation of states. The acquisition of property through occupation is justified partly on grounds of necessity and partly by agreement. Occupation precedes agreement, so that agreement ratifies a process that is already more or less complete.[11]

---

[9] Grotius, *The Rights of War and Peace*, Book.II, chapter 2.   [10] Ibid.
[11] Interpretations of the status of contracts in Grotius differ. Compare Reinhard Brandt, *Eigentumstheorien*, chapter 1, 31–40; Richard Tuck, *Natural Rights Theories* (Cambridge University Press, 1979), chapter 3, 58–82; Steven Buckle, *Natural Law and the Theory of Property: Grotius to Hume* (Oxford, Clarendon Press, 1991), chapter 1, 1–52.

A notable natural law influence on Kant is a shared preoccupation with acquisition through occupation, though, as we shall see, Kant finds occupation considerably more problematic than Grotius. There is also a superficial similarity between Grotius' move from *de facto* unilateral occupation to the general endorsement of its legitimacy, and Kant's view of the relation between provisional Right and peremptory Right. However, Grotian agreements are conventional and based on 'commodious living'. As a consequence, individuals' titles to exclusive possession are not irrevocable. Under conditions of extreme hardship, 'rights of necessity' permit a (temporary and limited) return to common possession. This is so largely because, for Grotius, rights in external possessions retain their strong connection with basic human needs. Since, for Kant, the concept of Right pertains to the *form* of relations of choice between subjects, he cannot accommodate substantive 'rights of necessity' within his theory of justice.[12]

More interesting than the similarities are the discrepancies, especially those that indicate Kant's *conscientious* departure from natural law assumptions. For Grotius, the division of land comes last and indicates the process of state formation. By contrast, Kant argues that original acquisition of land necessarily *precedes* the acquisition of anything else. For related reasons, Kant's highest level of public Right consists in global relations of justice between *individuals*, whereas Grotius restricts his account to relations of justice between *states*. But one difference in particular is of systematic importance. Its significance is best explained with reference to Grotius' ambiguity concerning the metaphysical grounds of natural law obligations. Grotius is notorious for his contention that the laws of nature would be valid even if one were to concede the inconceivable, i.e. the non-existence of God. This ambiguity is reflected in Grotius' mixed methodology, which combines what he calls the 'a priori method' with the 'a posteriori method'. While the former 'refers the proof of things touching the laws of nature to certain fundamental conceptions which are beyond question', the latter method appeals to 'the testimony of philosophers, poets, historians'.[13] In his subsequent account, Grotius frequently supports his a priori claims with appeals to a posteriori evidence drawn primarily

---

[12] Cf. Kant's remarks on 'equivocal Rights' at *RL*, 6: 234.
[13] Grotius, *Prolegomena to the Three Books on the Law of War and Peace*, sections 39–40.

from scripture, thus treating the Old Testament as though it were humankind's history book.

I mention Grotius' mixed methodology because it exemplifies some of the metaphysical ambiguities which are also discernible in contemporary natural law theory. As we shall see, Mulholland's interpretation of Kant is a case in point. More generally, however, the strategy of verifying a priori principles by appeal to supposed historical facts has earned natural law theory a reputation for political conservatism, whereby what *happens to be* the case as a matter of fact is vindicated as what *ought to be* the case as a matter of natural law. This tendency towards political conservatism is noticeable in Grotius' explanation of the move from primitive common possession to individual division: individual division is an a priori requirement of (God's) laws of nature because, if it were not, it would not have occurred as a matter of historical fact. In this regard, the point of contrast with Kant is arresting. Kant argues the other way around, moving from *the fact* of individual acquisition to *the idea* of original possession in common. This deliberate inversion of the natural law sequence from common possession to individual acquisition is of considerable political consequence. It suggests that the idea of original possession in common and that of the general united will should not be interpreted along the lines of natural law metaphysics: their respective functions are radically different. More significantly, the inversion draws attention to the contrast between Kant's forward-looking political perspective and Grotius' conservative outlook. While, for Grotius, common possession gradually gives way to human beings' separation into individual households and distinct nations, Kant argues that unilateral acquisition obligates individuals and nations towards each other, entailing his conception of the *Weltbürger* and of cosmopolitan Right. This systematic difference between Kant and natural law theory will be of importance in the discussion of original possession in common below.

3 ORIGINAL ACQUISITION AND ORIGINAL POSSESSION IN COMMON

Despite the influence on him of natural law theory, Kant's reversal of the conventional sequence from common ownership to individual possession marks the distinctness of his approach to the general united will as an idea of practical reason. Indeed, Kant emphatically

distances himself from the view of common ownership as a historically actual state of affairs. The idea of original possession in
common 'is not an empirical concept, dependent upon temporal
conditions, like that of a supposed primitive possession in common
(*communia primaeva*)'; it is 'a practical rational concept' which 'contains a priori the distributive principle'[14] of the general united will.
The principal difficulty lies in establishing exactly how the latter
idea is to be thought of as contained in the former. I begin with an
analysis of Kant's concept of original acquisition, focusing on
subjects' original acquisition of a place on the earth. I then examine
Mulholland's natural law interpretation of the relation between
original possession in common and general will. This will set the
scene for an alternative account of the relation between original
possession in common and general will in the next section.

3(a) Original acquisition

Kant's claim in §12 of chapter 2, Section I, that 'first acquisition of a
thing can only be acquisition of land'[15] is best examined in light of
the problem of original acquisition discussed in §10. The focus of §10
is on 'the general principle of external acquisition'. As noted in
chapter 4, a person's innate right and their acquired rights are
conceptually distinct. While each person possesses the innate right to
freedom in virtue of their humanity, rights to external possessions
are acquired rights. Although the postulate affirmed that taking into
possession external objects of one's choice must be possible, nothing
specific was said about the process of acquisition itself. The discussion of acquired rights in §10 offers what may be called a regressive
analysis of this process, beginning with a statement of the general
principle of acquisition, and issuing in the concept of original
acquisition. It is the latter concept that concerns us here. The
passage starts with a preliminary delimitation of what is meant by
something's being externally mine:

I acquire something when I bring it about (*efficio*) that it becomes *mine*.
Something external is originally mine which is mine without any act that
establishes a right to it. But that *acquisition* is original which is not derived
from what is another's.[16]

---

[14] *RL*, 6: 262.   [15] *RL*, 6: 261.   [16] *RL*, 6: 258.

Acquired rights are those which I acquire as a result of some action whereby I bring it about that something becomes mine. Acquisition in the civil condition would be by means of a contract through which the right to a thing is transferred from the current owner to the new owner. Here, an acquired right to an external object is derived from what is another's by means of an act that establishes a right to it. However, the present focus is on *original* acquisition, which is prior to the civil condition. Immediately following the above remark, Kant continues that, 'nothing external is originally mine, but it can indeed be acquired originally, that is without being derived from what is another's'. That nothing external *is* originally mine follows from the distinction between innate right and acquired rights. If it *were* originally mine, it would not be acquired, but would be part of my innate right. But if it were part of my innate right it could not be external to me, since nothing external can be part of my innate right. Hence, anything which is external to me, and which I claim as mine, must fall under the category of acquired rights.

Where what is acquired is not derived from what is another's, it is acquired originally. But how can something be originally acquired in the sense of not being derived from what is another's? Such a claim makes sense only on the assumption of a historically primeval state of affairs in which nothing belongs to anyone (*res nullius*). On this assumption, one could posit a generation of first acquirers who acquire external possessions through the occupation of unoccupied land and movable possessions. This process would eventually result in a situation where occupation is complete, such that nothing can any longer be non-derivatively acquired. But Kant not only insists that his argument is not to be understood historically, he also appears to reject the notion of *res nullius*. In §10 we hear that 'a condition of community (*communio mei et tui*) of what is mine and yours [i.e. a condition of *rightful* possession] can never be thought to be original but must be acquired (by an act that establishes an external right), although *possession of an external object can originally be in common*'.[17] Where original possession in common can or must be thought, one cannot also think an original condition in which

---

[17] *RL*, 6: 258, emphasis added. Gregor translates the relevant section as 'possession of an external object can originally be *only* possession in common'. Although it would support the present interpretation, the original text only says that external possession *can be* original and common: '*obwohl der Besitz eines äußeren Gegenstandes ursprünglich und gemeinsam sein kann*'.

nothing belongs to anyone (*res nullius*). But, where original possession in common *is* thought, acquisition of things by anyone has to be thought of as derived from what is held in common. It is not obvious why such acquisition should be referred to as original acquisition rather than as being derived from what is everyone's.

In sum, the situation is puzzling. On the one hand, Kant denies that anything external can *be* mine originally. Possession of external objects falls under the category of acquired rights. On the other hand, he claims that something external can be originally *acquired*, i.e. acquired without being derived from what is another's. Yet, in so far as Kant also says that possession of external objects can or must originally be held in common, it is difficult to see how anyone can acquire anything originally in the sense of not acquiring it from what is either someone's or everyone's.

Perhaps we should ignore for the moment the issue of original possession *in common*. Recall that only those things are originally acquired which are acquired through no act that establishes a right to them. Since the concept of Right specifies relations between subjects with regard to objects, nothing that belongs to someone can be rightfully acquired by another without an act that establishes a right to it. This suggests that something which is acquired originally cannot be acquired from what belongs to any *particular* other. In so far as original acquisition is acquisition without an act that establishes a right to it, it is non-rightful acquisition. However, since original acquisition is not derived from what belongs to any particular other, it is not acquisition in violation of (established) relations of mine and yours. Perhaps then, original acquisition is non-derivative and without an act that establishes a right to it because it precedes mine/thine relations. One way of putting it is to say that original acquisition, as acquisition without any act that establishes a right to it, is *unbescholten* or blameless: one acquires the object in question through no fault (or act) of one's own. This interpretation of original acquisition as 'blameless acquisition' (*unbescholtene Erwerbung*) becomes more plausible when considered with reference to the acquisition of land.

3(b) Original acquisition of land

The condensed remarks on acquisition of land in §12 are no less puzzling than those on original acquisition discussed above. Land, which refers to 'all inhabitable ground', is the 'substance' upon which all movable external objects depend as its 'inherences'. The contention is that possession of movable objects presupposes possession of land:

> For suppose that the land belonged to no one: I could then remove every movable thing from its place and take [that place] for myself until the thing has disappeared completely, without thereby infringing upon the freedom of anyone else who is not now holding [the thing].[18]

The reference to the 'complete disappearance' of the thing is especially cryptic. But, suppose my car is parked on the pavement in front of my house. Although I own the car, I do not own the bit of pavement upon which it is parked. However, presumably the pavement is owned by *someone*, maybe the city council. I might have a contractual arrangement with the council that entitles me to use part of the pavement for parking my car. Given such rights of occupancy, I can prevent others from coming along and removing my car from that place so that they may park their car on it. Now, suppose that I have parked my car along a bit of the road where parking is prohibited. The city council can remove my car without asking my permission and without infringing my rights in my car. None the less, their right to tow away my car without my permission compromises my powers of control over it. The general thought behind §12 is that lack of control over the land on which my possessions are placed compromises my rights in those possessions.[19]

Now consider the situation of squatters. Since squatters neither own nor rent the land they occupy, they can be moved off it at any time and without prior notice. Their movable possessions need not be infringed to render possession and use of them insecure. The mere fact that squatters have nowhere to put their belongings makes them vulnerable to the arbitrary choices of others. But squatters are not merely insecure with regard to their movable possessions. After all, it is not just their possessions, but they themselves who can be arbitrarily moved from place to place. What squatters lack, or are denied a right to, is a place on the earth. While it is important that one have a piece of land on which to place one's possessions, it is imperative that one have a place on the earth upon which to place

---

[18] *RL*, 6: 262. Gregor translation slightly amended.

[19] Cf. Ludwig, *Kants Rechtslehre*: 'The acquisition of any external object – including that of movable objects – presupposes possession of a piece of land' (127).

oneself. Without a right to a place on the earth one will find oneself in the situation of a squatter who gets pushed from place to place. Even though one will not literally 'disappear completely' from the face of the earth, in the absence of others' acknowledgement of one's right to be there, one might as well not be there. It is this – having an acknowledged right to a place on the earth – which is affirmed as original acquisition in §13:

All men are originally (i.e. prior to any act that establishes a right) in a possession of land that is in conformity with right, that is, they have a right to be wherever nature or chance (apart from their will) has placed them.[20]

In contrast to Grotian first occupation for the purpose of settlement and cultivation, original acquisition in the *Rechtslehre* refers to persons' entrance into the world as physically embodied beings.[21] A place on the earth is distinct from and therefore external to the person who occupies it. It is something which one acquires. But this acquisition is not the result of an act of choice. No one chooses to be born, and no one can be held responsible for their physical entrance into the world. Each has entered the world, and occupied a place in it 'apart from their will'. In so doing, no one has *derived* their place on the earth from what was someone else's: each person's acquisition of a place on the earth is original in virtue of the fact that it is *they* who occupy it. Hence, what is unjust about the situation of squatters is not that they have not acquired a place on the earth, but that they are denied rightful possession of what is theirs by virtue of their entrance into the world. Original acquisition of a place on the earth is blameless acquisition, i.e. acquired through no act of choice. As we shall see, however, the fact that original acquisition is acquired blamelessly does not render it devoid of obligations.

3(c) Original possession in common

Subjects' acquisition of a place on the earth is *unbescholten*, i.e. acquired apart from their will, and merely in virtue of their physical entrance into the world. Physically embodied beings are constrained to occupy a portion of space on the earth, and that portion cannot simultaneously be occupied by anyone else. Still, it is not evident

---

[20] *RL*, 6: 262.
[21] This point is also emphasised by Hans-Georg Deggau, *Die Aporien der Rechtslehre Kants* (Stuttgart, Frommann-Holzboog, 1983), 135.

why the *right* to a place should immediately follow from such unavoidable physical occupation. After all, Grotius, too, regards occupation and consumption as unavoidable in the face of individuals' natural needs for sustenance. None the less, the division of common property depends on general consent: 'men *agreed* that whatever anyone had occupied should be accounted his own'. For Kant, by contrast, original acquisition, though a consequence of unavoidable physical occupation, is at the same time 'taking into possession'.[22] While occupation results from physical necessity, taking into possession is a unilateral declaration of Right: I proclaim this place as *mine*. The point is well expressed by Mulholland when he says that, although subjects enter the world *apart* from their will, they also enter it *with* a will.[23] Subjects not only occupy land, but they also claim entitlement to the land they occupy.

This reference to subjects' capacity for choice and to their consequent unilateral declaration of Right complicates matters immensely. If it were simply the case that subjects' entrance into the world unavoidably included their blameless occupation of a place on the earth, the principle of equal need could be introduced as that consensual principle of distribution in accordance with which each is assigned a determinate place on the earth, thus ensuring the sustenance of each. The unilateral declaration by each of such a title to their place has more far-reaching implications than those of a needs claim – it is a declaration of Right based on an act of choice (i.e. I *will* this place to be mine). The evident difficulty here is that such a unilateral declaration of Right conflicts with the simultaneous characterisation of original acquisition as acquisition *apart* from one's will. If one has acquired one's place apart from one's will and without an act that establishes a right to it, how can one none the less claim rightful possession of it? At this point, Kant's repeated reiterations, that unilateral acquisition is necessary and unavoidable, but that a unilateral will cannot serve as a coercive law for everyone, suggest that the argument has run aground. On the one hand, 'original acquisition of an external object of choice is taking control of it (*occupatio*) and as original, is the result of a unilateral choice'.[24] On the other hand, 'by my unilateral choice I cannot bind another

[22] *RL*, 6: 258.
[23] Mulholland, *Kant's System of Rights*, 279–80.
[24] *RL*, 6: 258. Note that the reference to 'choice' here is inconsistent with the earlier characterisation of original acquisition as acquisition 'apart from one's will'.

to refrain from using a thing'.[25] A little later the same point is repeated: 'original acquisition of an external object, and hence too of a specific and separate piece of land, can take place only through taking control of it (*occupatio*)'. But 'the [unilateral] will can justify external acquisition only in so far as it is included in a will that is united a priori and that commands absolutely'.[26]

It is this apparent deadlock between the fact of unilateral declaration and the requirements of omnilateral legislation which has led Mulholland to detect a dramatic reversal in Kant's final position from contractarian premises to a natural law conclusion:

Kant attempts to maintain the prime insight of the social contract tradition, that of the validity of the deed principle, and yet tries to preserve the idea of natural law theory: that laws are not mere conventions, but are reasonable principles which depend in part on human nature. However, Kant cannot have it both ways. Strictly, it is the natural law doctrine, which depends on rational consistency, and not the deed principle, that forms the basis of Kant's account of acquired rights and political obligation.[27]

What Mulholland refers to as the 'deed principle' derives from his own view that their capacity for deliberate agency distinguishes persons from mere things by making them capable of incurring obligations. On this basis, Mulholland attributes to Kant the further view that persons incur obligations *only* as a result of their voluntary actions: 'The deed principle asserts that one person may not obligate another to do some action unless the other does something voluntarily which, because of a rule, allows the other [*sic*] to obligate him.'[28] Mulholland's formulation of the deed principle, as well as his textual evidence for it are obscure.[29] Presumably, the rule alluded to is the

---

[25] *RL*, 6: 261.   [26] *RL*, 6: 263.
[27] Mulholland, *Kant's System of Rights*, 267.   [28] Ibid., 136.
[29] To avoid confusion, I should emphasise that Kant nowhere formulates anything like the deed principle; the formulation is Muholland's own. In the general introduction to the *Metaphysics of Morals*, Kant defines 'deed' as follows: 'An action is called a *deed* in so far as it comes under obligatory laws and hence in so far as the subject, in doing it, is considered in terms of his freedom of choice. By such an action the author is regarded as the author of its effect, and this, together with the action itself, can be *imputed* to him, if one is previously acquainted with the law by virtue of which an obligation rests on these' (*MM*, 6: 223). Mulholland may have had this passage in mind when formulating his own deed principle. The problem is that the passage states virtually the opposite of what Mulholland intends with his deed principle. For Kant, deeds are actions which fall under obligatory laws, whereas Mulholland's account construes obligatory laws as resulting from voluntary deeds of individuals. In fact, Mulholland derives his principal support for the 'deed principle' from what he detects as a tension between two of Kant's formulae of the categorical imperative in the *Groundwork*: 'The problem in Kant's treatment stems from the two criteria of rightness of actions which he develops in the *Foundations of the Metaphysics of Morals*: the

universal principle of Right in accordance with which individuals reciprocally restrict their freedom of choice and action. None the less, the wording remains ambiguous. The actual formulation suggests a non-contractarian view whereby agents *incur* obligations as a result of some other voluntary actions of theirs. This would not be incompatible with the interpretation advanced in the previous chapter, according to which individuals' choices and actions are obligation *entailing*: X is in a position to obligate Y as a consequence of an antecedent, voluntary act committed by Y. However, Mulholland explicitly characterises the deed principle as a contractarian principle of voluntarily *assumed* obligation. On this view, subjects assume obligations in virtue of a voluntary act to that effect, and the obligations are valid for that reason. Since Mulholland links the deed principle to Kant's reference to subjects' capacity for choice, since he associates the concept of freedom of choice and action with social contract theory, and since he explicitly characterises the deed principle as a contractarian principle, it is reasonable to conclude that he intends the second interpretation of the deed principle.

One purpose of Mulholland's construction of the deed principle is to show that, from a contractarian perspective, the problem of unilateral original acquisition remains irresolvable: 'any [original] acquisition must involve the imposition of an obligation on all others to refrain from the object in question. However, if others have performed no deed through which they acquire this obligation, they are immune from being obligated.'[30] Again, this way of putting it is confusing.[31] On the face of it, my deed of original acquisition would seem to constitute sufficient grounds for my incurring obligations

law of nature principle and the principle of humanity as an end in itself. The latter requires that a person not obligate another without the other performing a voluntary action, usually consent. The former bases obligations on the idea of what maxims can be willed to be universal laws in conformity with the restrictions imposed by nature' (*Kant's System of Rights*, 14). This is an idiosyncratic interpretation of the relation between the formulas of the categorical imperative. Mulholland's equation of the formula of universal law with a natural law principle conflicts with Kant's principal contention, that the principles of morality are principles of reason, not prescriptions of nature. Similar reservations against Mulholland's interpretation are voiced by Daniel Weinstock, 'Natural Law and Public Reason in Kant's Political Philosophy', *Canadian Journal of Philosophy*, 26 (1996), 389–411.

[30] Mulholland, *Kant's System of Rights*, 253.
[31] Thus, it is plausible to hold that someone can freely *assume* an obligation which they did not have before; it is equally plausible to hold that someone can *incur* an obligation as a result of some action of theirs. But it is difficult to see how an action committed by X entails that X wants to impose an obligation on Y, which X cannot impose on Y because Y has not performed an action which would make it possible for X to impose an obligation on Y as a result of X's action. Yet this is what Mulholland's formulation suggests.

towards others. But Mulholland thinks that original acquisition leads me to claim that *others* are obligated towards me. Yet, since others have committed no deed in virtue of which I could obligate them, my claim to my place as mine obligates no one, but remains utterly futile. In the face of the evident failure of this peculiar argument, Kant is said to 'abandon' the deed principle in favour of 'the natural law principle of rational consistency'. According to the revised view, obligations of justice are not incurred voluntarily, i.e. as a result of a deliberate deed to that effect. Instead, 'the basis of morality lies in an already determined structure which rational beings have by nature'.[32] By now Mulholland has replaced individuals' capacity for choice with the principle of need: 'Since each person *needs* to use land, each as a rational being must will the law that land be usable.'[33] The result is a modified natural law position, whereby my realisation that I need to use land must, as a matter of consistent reasoning, bring me to realise others' equal needs. In so far as each realises that everyone needs land, the general united will constitutes that 'natural law principle of rational consistency' in accordance with which the common stock is distributed equally among all. Each is assigned an equal portion of land based on the mutually recognised principle of need.

There is considerable insight in Mulholland's focus on the ambiguous status of original acquisition. As already mentioned, the principal difficulty lies in accepting 'blameless occupation' and 'unilateral declaration' as belonging to the same concept. While occupation happens apart from one's will, declaration is an expression of one's will: it is not obvious how both can be features of original acquisition simultaneously. None the less, the attribution of a deed principle to Kant is contrived, depending on an equivocation between two quite different conceptions of the relation between freedom and obligation. According to the first possible conception, subjects incur obligations towards others in virtue of their capacity for choice and action. According to the second, subjects are free agents who are bound only by freely assumed obligations. Though both positions are implicit in Mulholland's formulation of the deed principle, the proposition that the capacity for freedom entails obligations differs from the claim that obligations are freely assumed. The latter conception captures an essential aspect of

---

[32] Mulholland, *Kant's System of Rights*, 111.   [33] Ibid., 280.

contractarianism; yet Kant adopts the former conception of the relation between freedom and obligation. The attribution to Kant of a contractarian deed principle is thus spurious.

Mulholland's tendency to conflate the two views probably has to do with his independent complaint that Kant's *formal* definition of the concept of Right contains no reference to need as a *substantive* principle of justice. Hence, the oscillation which he detects in the text, between a contractarian emphasis on freedom of choice and a natural law appreciation of human needs, reflects his own preference for the natural law position. But there are considerable costs to equating Kant's final position with a natural law argument. For one thing, it commits Mulholland to the textually implausible substitution of the idea of freedom with the principle of need. This move, which Mulholland is compelled to make in consequence of his assumption that commitment to freedom of choice signals commitment to contractarianism, is contrary to Kant's definition of the concept of Right as specifying the form of relations of choice between subjects. But it also remains unclear how exactly Mulholland conceives the status of the general united will as an idea of reason. The noted natural law ambiguity concerning the relation between nature and reason is exemplified in Mulholland's claim that the grounds of political obligation lie in an *already determined structure* which rational beings have by nature. It is ambiguous whether the 'already determined structure' refers to human reason, or whether it refers to the structure of their physical needs, or both. Given his natural law commitments, Mulholland presumably intends the already determined structure to be the discernment by human reason of human needs. The general united will then constitutes a principle of reason whose necessity derives from subjects' reasoned insight into the structure of human needs: the structure of needs determines the requisite distributive principle. The general united will thus results from human reflection on the conditions of human existence rather than being antecedently given by the will of God, for example. This coheres with Mulholland's characterisation of the general united will as a principle of rational consistency which distributes land in accordance with the equal needs of each. But, even if this interpretation avoids the problematic notion of a general will as antecedently given, there remains something uncannily Grotian about Mulholland's account. On the suggested interpretation, the general will does not merely take the structure of human needs into account: to the contrary, the general will is *determined* by that structure. Mulholland's conception of the general united will might thus be described as a form of moral realism, where political obligations supervene as rational requirements on the determinate facts of human nature. What lends this interpretation of Mulholland's position plausibility is the fact that he conceives the function of the general united will in typical natural law terms: it is that distributive principle which divides the common stock in accordance with the principle of equal need. We start with original common possession and end up with individual property in accordance with a distributive principle whose validity derives from the already determined structure of human nature. This entirely ignores the fact that the argument in the *Rechtslehre* proceeds *from* unilateral original acquisition *to* the idea of original possession in common, not vice versa.

4 THE GENERAL UNITED WILL AS AN A PRIORI IDEA OF REASON

Mulholland is right to reject a contractarian solution to the problem of original acquisition, but he is right for the wrong reasons. His natural law substitution of the principle of need for the idea of freedom rests on a misunderstanding of the Kantian conception of freedom of choice and action. None the less, Kant's approach to the idea of the general united will under cover of the *further* idea of original possession in common is deeply obscure. The proliferation of ideas of reason is especially unhelpful in view of the fact that Kant nowhere bothers to specify their exact status. Although he alludes to their apriority as ideas of pure practical reason, nothing is said about how these ideas arise, or what justifies our entertaining them. Are the ideas of the general united will and of original possession in common (and, for that matter, the idea of the social contract) *necessary* ideas of pure practical reason? Are they of the same order of apriority as the idea of freedom itself? Or are they more like heuristic devices – action-guiding constructions of reason which assist practical deliberation, but which are not necessary ideas of reason in the strong sense of possessing unconditional validity for all finite rational beings?[34]

---

[34] Mary Gregor tries to grapple with some of these obscurities in *The Laws of Freedom* (Oxford, Basil Blackwell, 1963), chapters 1 and 2, 1–33.

There is no space here to consider in detail the ambiguous status of the three supplementary ideas of reason and the supposed relation between them. However, one plausible – if provisional – strategy suggests itself in Körner's notion of a categorial framework as consisting in a person's organisation *and stratification* of their theoretically and practically supreme principles. 'Stratification' here indicates the hierarchical ordering of a person's lower-order practical principles in relation to their practically supreme principle. In Körner's own terminology, lower-order practical principles are said to be dominated by practically supreme principles in the sense that commitment to the former implies commitment to the latter, but not vice versa.[35] When adapting Körner's general model to Kant's metaphysics of freedom in chapter 2, I designated freedom as an idea of pure practical reason as Kant's practically supreme principle. If we apply Körner's further distinction between practically supreme principles and lower-order practical principles to the present context, Kant's three supplementary ideas of reason (the idea of a general united will, of the social contract, and of original possession in common) might be thought of as lower-order or derivative practical principles that are dominated by the practically supreme principle of freedom. On this account, the metaphysically supreme idea of freedom, which is valid for all finite rational beings as such, dominates derivative ideas of practical reflection whose claim to validity is restricted to a subset of finite rational beings, i.e. finite rational *human* beings. This is, admittedly, a somewhat rough-and-ready adaptation of Körner's stratification model to Kantian ideas of reason. It remains to be explored quite how the supplementary ideas are 'dominated' by the idea of freedom. Moreover, the present sketch tells us nothing about the relation between the three supplementary ideas. None the less, the general outline of the suggested strategy does have its merits. First, the stratification model prevents a proliferation of metaphysically supreme ideas without denying the connection between supreme idea and dependent ideas. It preserves the systematic relation between Kant's otherwise seemingly *ad hoc* proliferation of 'ideas of reason'. Second, the suggestion that, in contrast to metaphysically supreme practical ideas, lower-order ideas are restricted in scope to a subset of finite rational beings fits well with the oft-noted sensitivity of the *Rechtslehre* towards

---

[35] Cf. Körner, *Metaphysics. Its Structure and Function*, 11–14, and 22–4.

specifically *anthropological* conditions and circumstances. None the less, to say that ideas of practical reflection are *sensitive* to specifically human conditions and constraints is not to say that they are *determined* by these constraints. The thought is rather that ideas of practical reflection mediate between metaphysically supreme ideas and the specific conditions of their practical application. Recall here Kant's remark in the third antinomy, that the idea of freedom represents the capacity of reason to 'frame an order of ideas of its own'.[36] Although practical reason must be cognisant of the constraints of nature, its principles and ideas are not determined by those constraints. Instead, principles and ideas of practical reason offer a practically deliberative response to the constraints of nature as they pertain to the realm of human agency.

The characterisation of the general united will as an idea of practical reflection is in keeping with the relation between postulate and general will sketched earlier on. If the postulate stands to the general will as a preliminary judgement does to a determinate judgement, both form aspects of a single reflective judgement that frames the laws of external freedom under conditions of human agency. But how does the *further* idea of original possession in common fit into the suggested relation? As I said, Kant sinks the idea of the general united will into the idea of original possession in common: the former is contained in the latter as 'the principle in accordance with which alone men can use a place on the earth in accordance with principles of Right'.[37] In what follows, I shall suggest that the idea of original possession in common forms a bridge between postulate and general united will. If the postulate shows *that* a conception of intelligible possession must be possible, the general united will shows *how* such a conception is possible by drawing on the idea of original possession in common.

My starting-point is the regressive analysis in section 3 above, from acquisition of objects in general to original acquisition of a place on the earth. Recall that, according to the postulate, every unilateral act of external acquisition is obligation entailing. But one's acquisition of external objects presupposes one's original acquisition of a place on the earth. In contrast to acquisition in general, which is an act of choice, original acquisition takes place apart from one's will. The crucial question is whether original acquisition, like

---

[36] *CPR*, A548/B576. [37] *RL*, 6: 262.

acquisition in general, is obligation entailing. I think, for Kant, the answer has to be 'yes'. In so far as one's place on the earth is something which, though occupied by one's physical self, is external to one, it cannot be part of one's innate right. If it is not part of one's innate right, it is an acquired right. If it is an acquired right, it stands in need of justification to others.

This contention, that entrance into the world is obligation entailing sounds excessive. After all, original acquisition is *blameless* not least because it is entirely unavoidable: one can hardly be held responsible for it. But, if one is not responsible for one's original acquisition, how can one be required to take responsibility for having acquired it? The answer is put crisply by Karlfriedrich Herb and Bernd Ludwig when they say that human beings enter the world as 'subjects of Right', that is, as 'beings who are subject to obligations which are neither innate nor freely assumed through an act that establishes an obligation'.[38] Our obligations of justice are not innate because they are acquired, i.e. they arise as a result of our physical occupation of a place on the earth. They are not freely assumed because the acquisition is original, i.e. happens apart from our will. But the reason why being under such originally acquired obligations of justice is not itself an injustice is that we are capable of acknowledging and of discharging these obligations. To put it more pointedly, we are under obligations of justice in virtue of our capacity to frame an idea of an order of just relations between subjects. Consider in this context the full passage in §13, partially quoted above, concerning original possession in common:

All men are originally (i.e., prior to any choice that establishes a right) in possession of land that is in conformity with right, that is, they have a right to be wherever nature or chance (apart from their will) has placed them. This kind of possession (*possessio*) – which is to be distinguished from residence (*sedes*), a chosen and therefore an acquired lasting possession – is possession in common because the spherical surface of the earth unites all the places on its surface; for if its surface were an unbounded plane, men could be so dispersed on it that they would not come into any community with one another, and community would not then be a necessary result of their existence on the earth. The possession by all men on the earth that precedes any acts of theirs which would establish rights (that is constituted by nature itself) is an original possession in common (*communio possessionis originaria*), the concept of which is not empirical and dependent upon

---

[38] Karlfriedrich Herb and Bernd Ludwig, 'Naturzustand, Eigentum und Staat', *Kantstudien*, 83 (1994), 283–316, 294.

temporal conditions, like that of a supposed primitive possession in common (*communio primaeva*), which can never be proved. Original possession in common is, rather, a practical rational concept which contains *a priori* the principle in accordance with which alone men can use a place on the earth in accordance with principles of Right.[39]

Kant's treatment of original possession in common in this passage brings out two points of contrast with the natural law tradition. The first, more obvious point refers to Kant explicitly distancing himself from an historical interpretation of common possession as a form of primitive communism. The idea of original possession in common describes a form of 'disjunctive possession in common' (*disjunktiver Allgemeinbesitz*). The *fact* of unilateral original acquisition precedes the *idea* of original possession in common. As a practical rational concept, the latter constitutes a mental representation of the unavoidable if problematic acquisition by each of a place on the earth: given the earth's spherical surface, subjects cannot avoid coming into contact with one another as a result of their respective occupations. It is the *disjunctive* unity of all the places on the earth that gives rise to the idea of original possession in common. The second and related point of contrast refers to the difference between a material principle of distribution, such as Mulholland's principle of equal need, and a formal principle of distribution, such as Kant's principle of Right in terms of the equal claim to external freedom of each. What is at stake in the above passage is evidently *not* the division of the common stock. Instead, the idea of original possession in common depicts the relations of systematic interdependence that obtain between individuals in virtue of the unavoidable unity of places on the earth.

In sum, the idea of original possession in common comprises two elements. The disjunctive element constitutes the formal representation of the unavoidable physical occupation by each of a place on the earth – the earth's spherical surface is depicted as made up of individual spaces each of which represents the equally valid claims to external freedom. The uniting element represents a reflective acknowledgement by agents of the relations of interdependence obtaining among them in consequence of unavoidable individual occupancy. In showing that the disjunctive unity of all the places on the earth entails relations of systematic interdependence, the idea of

[39] *RL*, 6: 262.

original possession in common offers a *generalised* version of the conception of intelligible possession. Where the postulate tended to portray obligations of justice as a bilateral relation between unilateral acquirers and those whose freedom is compromised as a result, the idea of original possession in common shows these relations to be omnilateral (*allseitig*): given the unity of all the places on the earth any act of injustice committed by one 'is felt even in the remotest corner of the earth'. Secondly, where the postulate assumed that obligations of justice result from particular acts of choice and acquisition, the idea of original possession in common shows that obligations are originally acquired: we are under obligations of justice towards one another merely in virtue of our entrance into the world and in virtue of our capacity to acknowledge and to act on these obligations. The idea of the general united will thus emerges from the regressive analysis of acquisition in general under the postulate to original acquisition of a place on the earth as its necessary presupposition. The bridging function of the idea of original possession in common demonstrates the conditions of systematic interdependence among individuals as original acquirers and hence as subjects of Right. As such, the idea of the general will constitutes an acknowledgement both of the necessity of a system of public lawgiving in accordance with which the legitimate claims of each to a place on the earth can be recognised, and of the possibility of its realisation through entrance into the civil condition. The idea of original possession in common is not a depiction of how things initially were (prior to distribution and individuation), but of how they ought to become: disjunctive possession in common does not represent the gradual division of an original common stock. To the contrary, it is a coming together of unilateral wills under the legislative authority of an omnilateral will in consequence of the acknowledgement of the necessity of a system of public lawgiving that can do justice to the claims of Right of each.

5 CONTRACTUALISM OR COSMOPOLITANISM?

So far I have argued against a natural law interpretation of the idea of the general united will. The general united will should not be interpreted as an antecedently given source of legislative authority, discovered by, but not resulting from, human reason. Nor should it be construed as a moral fact which supervenes on human nature. As an idea of practical reflection, the general united will results from subjects' acknowledgement of the necessity of a system of public lawgiving under conditions of human coexistence as they are represented in the idea of original possession in common. It is important to emphasise the implicit reference to the idea of freedom, i.e. to reason's capacity to frame an order of ideas of its own. In principle, the idea of the general united will could fail to emerge – subjects could fail to reflect on the necessary conditions of peaceful coexistence. Alternatively, even if the idea of the general united will did arise, subjects could still fail to act on it. Whether or not subjects acknowledge the necessity of instituting relations of Right among themselves is fundamentally up to them. As Kant puts it, 'given the intention to be and to remain in a state of externally lawless freedom, men do *one another* no wrong at all when they feud among themselves; for what holds for one also holds in turn for the other, as if by mutual consent'.[40]

But if entrance into the civil condition is a matter of free volition, why not construe it in contractual terms? Why not say that subjects agree among themselves to set up a system of law which ensures that the rights claims of each are respected and secured? Why must they acknowledge the necessity of Right rather than merely agree on its desirability? That it is necessity, not desirability, which is at stake is indicated in Kant's use of italics: though men may do '*one another*' no wrong if they act unjustly as if by mutual consent, 'in general they do wrong in the highest degree by wanting to be and to remain in a condition that is not rightful'. Yet what does it mean to say they do wrong 'in the highest degree'? Is this not to invoke a transcendent source of lawgiving after all, from the perspective of which the rights and wrongs of human actions are judged?

Mulholland is not alone in finding Kant confused between the two major traditions of political thought. The view that Kant champions free choice only to clamp down on it with claims about uncondi-tional obligation is widespread. Commentators often think them-selves constrained to choose between social contract theory and natural law theory, or between a more liberal and a more conserva-tive reading of the *Rechtslehre*. From the perspective of Kant's property argument, the reasons for the attested confusion are not difficult to identify. They concern the noted obscurity of the concept

---

[40] *RL*, 6: 308.

of original acquisition with its simultaneous references to acquisition apart from one's will and acquisition as an expression of one's will. If natural law thinkers emphasise the first aspect of original acquisition, contractarian interpretations focus on the second aspect, where the requirement for mutual agreement follows from respect for individuals' capacity for choice. In this final section, I shall argue that, just as one should resist a natural law interpretation of the grounds of political legitimation, so one should resist reducing Kant's argument to a contractarian strategy of justification. My reasons for rejecting a contractarian reading relate to Kant's cosmopolitan perspective: contractarian interpretations undermine Kant's cosmopolitanism. As a matter of casual observation, one may note that those who adopt a contractarian framework of interpretation often pay little attention to Kant's cosmopolitanism. This is despite the fact that Kant himself clearly thinks the latter indispensable to any adequate system of Right:

> Since the earth's surface is not unlimited but closed, the concepts of the Right of a state and of a Right of nations lead inevitably to the Idea of a Right of all nations (*ius gentium*) or cosmopolitan Right (*ius cosmopoliticum*). So if the principle of outer freedom limited by law is lacking in any of these three possible forms of rightful condition, the framework of all the others is unavoidably undermined and must finally collapse.[41]

Kant does not share the widespread view that we can turn our attention to the issue of cosmopolitan Right only *after* we have settled the matter of domestic justice. The grounds of cosmopolitan justice are identical with those of domestic justice: both follow from the claim to external freedom of each under conditions of unavoidable empirical constraints. Instead of distinguishing between different theories of justice for the domestic and the international contexts, Kant refers to different *levels* of institutionalising his cosmopolitan conception of Right. The question is whether the neglect of the cosmopolitan perspective by contractarian interpreters is accidental, or whether it is a consequence of the contractarian perspective itself. While it is reasonably uncontentious to say that a strong historical connection obtains between the rise of social contract theory and the consolidation of distinct nation states, this need not mean that contractarianism forecloses the cosmopolitan perspective at the conceptual level. At the same time, it is difficult to avoid the

---

[41] *RL*, 6: 311.

suspicion that the contractarian perspective encourages such conceptual closure.

One indication of such closure is the element of exclusivity which attaches to ordinary contractual agreements as exchange relations. The terms of a contractual agreement are usually thought to apply only to those party to it. Being party to a contract depends not only on one's own willingness to exchange, but equally so on others' willingness to exchange with one. Hence, membership is not unconditional: one has to be able to offer something others might want. Some of the anti-cosmopolitan implications of this classic form of the social contract as an exchange relation are indicated in Hobbes' suggestion that, if nothing else, subjects of a single commonwealth will be united in the thought of a common enemy whose exclusion from the social compact constitutes sufficient incentive for those included in it to exchange mutual assurances with one another. Contemporary Hobbesians usually appeal to more general considerations of mutual advantage. It would not be prudent, but foolish to enter into binding obligations with those who pose no threat to one's interests, or whose co-operation cannot benefit one in any tangible ways: one would be giving up something in return for nothing.[42]

However, even this more general form of prudential reasoning is rejected by many contemporary contractarians as a misconstrual of what is essential about the social contract as a *special kind of contract*. This is not the promise of mutual advantage, but the requirements of political consensus as a condition of political legitimation. The idea of contractual agreement expresses the moral conviction that no one ought to be subject to laws which they would not or could not have consented to themselves.[43] This interpretation of the social contract as expressing the requirement of political consensus may be less vulnerable to the charge of exclusivity. The view of the contract as an exchange relation is replaced by the view of it as a forum for reasonable agreement: a sufficient condition of membership is willingness to reach agreement on reasonable terms. But, if reasonable

---

[42] See, for example, David Gauthier, *Morals by Agreement* (Oxford, Clarendon Press, 1986). For a critique of the 'mutual advantage' approach see Brian Barry, *Theories of Justice*, 66–76.

[43] The most sophisticated defence of this form of consensual contractarianism is Thomas Scanlon's *What We Owe to Each Other* (Cambridge, MA, Belknap Press of Harvard University Press, 1998), especially chapter 5, 189–247.

agreement is the aim, why must it take the form of a contract of mutual assurance?[44]

There is an ambiguity surrounding the consensual interpretation of the social contract, which the exchange model does not suffer from. The latter specifies the grounds of political obligations as the product of contractees' reciprocal exchange of obligations. The social contract establishes political obligations that did not obtain prior to the contract. In the case of the consensus model, it is less clear in how far the contract establishes political obligations, and in how far it merely establishes consensus regarding the system of public lawgiving to be adopted in honouring obligations which are valid irrespective of any contractual agreement. Most contemporary consensus contractarians tend towards the former view, where consensus grounds obligations of justice. The exchange model's assumption of prudential self-interest is replaced with a moral desire for reasonable agreement. Consensus theorists often advocate the supposed desire for reasonable agreement as a specifically Kantian motive for agreement. Arguably, however, the idea of the social contract as employed in the *Rechtslehre* is more properly interpreted as an idea of reason which guides the process of public lawmaking *within* civil society, rather than as a device which grounds the obligation to *enter* civil society.[45]

The case against the stronger interpretation of the social contract as the source of political obligations is usually made on the basis of its incompatibility with Kant's property argument. Some of the difficulties of contractarian interpretations in relation to the property argument can be illustrated with reference to two recent contributions on the subject, one by Kenneth Baynes[46] and the other by Kevin Dodson.[47] Both Baynes and Dodson perceive an intrinsic connection between Kant's property argument and his supposedly contractarian account of political obligations. Both think Kant confused between natural law theory and contractarianism, and

---

[44] This question is raised by Thomas Nagel, 'Rawls on Justice'; also by Ronald Dworkin, 'The Original Position', both in Norman Daniels, ed., *Reading Rawls* (Oxford, Basil Blackwell, 1975), 1–15 and 16–52.

[45] Cf. Herb and Ludwig, 'Naturzustand und Staat'; Daniel Weinstock, 'Natural Law and Public Reason'. See also, more generally, Ernest Weinrib, 'Law as Idea of Reason' in Howard Williams, ed., *Kant's Political Philosophy*, 15–49.

[46] Kenneth Baynes, 'Kant on Property Rights and the Social Contract'.

[47] Kevin Dodson, 'Autonomy and Authority in Kant's *Rechtslehre*', *Political Theory*, 25 (1997), 93–111.

both resolve the attested confusion in favour of contractarianism. Both advocate versions of the consensual, obligation-grounding interpretation of the contract. However, it is worth recalling that the idea of the social contract does not figure in the relevant property passages, but makes its appearance only in the much later transition from *Private Right* to *Public Right*.[48] Baynes and Dodson thus rely on a questionable equation of the idea of the general united will with the idea of a social contract. Given the general will's relation to the idea of original possession in common, the success of the equation depends on offering a plausible contractarian interpretation of original possession in common. Yet neither author seems to me to succeed in this task.

Dodson's principal contention is that Kant's conception of intelligible possession as denoting a subject/subject relation commits him to a consensual and *therefore* to a contractarian account of property legitimation: 'property is possible *only* in civil society'.[49] By this Dodson means to claim more than that publicly acknowledged and coercively enforceable property rights require a system of public lawgiving. In his view, the consensual basis of property right reveals as unintelligible Kant's distinction between provisional Right in the natural condition and peremptory Right in the civil condition. For Dodson, property rights are *either* innate and naturally given *or* consensual and socially established. In so far as they depend on a conception of intelligible possession, they must be consensual. If they are consensual, they presuppose civil society. If they presuppose civil society, there can be no provisional property rights in the pre-civil condition. Hence, the provisional/peremptory distinction canvasses two mutually exclusive alternatives of property legitimation, indicating confusion on Kant's part.[50] Suitably corrected, Dodson reconstructs Kant's argument as follows: intelligible possession is based on consensus; consensus requires a united general will; a united general will results from the voluntary contractual union of

---

[48] This is not entirely accurate: Kant does mention the idea of a contract in section 19 of *Private Right* (*RL*, 6:272–3). However, the contract under discussion is not the social contract, but a commercial transaction between two parties. The discussion concerns possible forms of rightful exchanges of their acquired rights between rights holders – it does not relate to the problem of original acquisition or to the grounds of political obligation more generally. Contractual relations of exchange of the kind discussed thus presuppose civil society.

[49] Dodson, 'Autonomy and Authority', 102.

[50] Ibid., 105.

unilateral wills: hence property rights are legitimated contractually. However, Dodson's conclusion is premised on what arguably amounts to a self-contradictory interpretation of original possession in common. This is what he says:

Our right to property is based on our innate common possession of land and the corresponding general will permitting private possession. We have only one innate right, and any right to an external object is an acquired right based on positive law. . . Any acquisition of property outside the legal framework of civil society is nothing but an arbitrary usurpation.[51]

To begin with, Dodson's characterisation of original possession in common as *innate* conflicts with Kant's explicit reminder that this is *not* how the idea is to be interpreted. More importantly, Dodson accepts Kant's claim that we have only one innate right – i.e. the innate right to freedom – and that all rights to external objects are acquired rights. But it is then inconsistent of him to speak of *innate* common possession of land. Since the latter falls under the category of acquired rights, the possession of land, common or otherwise, cannot be innate. On the one hand, Dodson is compelled to assume innate common possession, since he rejects the possibility of provisionally rightful unilateral possession. On the other hand, the innatist interpretation undermines rather than supports his contention that individual property rights are based *solely* on contractual consensus. If land is co-owned *innately*, some form of property rights clearly must precede their consensual and contractual individuation under positive law. If Dodson wants to insist that property rights derive solely from positive law, he should have denied that anyone owns anything at all in the pre-civil society. But the latter is evidently not Kant's position, for whom original acquisition, hence provisional Right, is unavoidable in the pre-civil condition.

Like Dodson, Kenneth Baynes, too, believes that 'property rights require the united agreement of all as this is represented in the idea of the social contract'.[52] Property rights are based on agreement rather than on an acknowledgement of their necessity. But Baynes is more sensitive to the status of the social contract as an idea of reason. While Dodson regards property rights as based exclusively on positive contractual law, Baynes acknowledges that 'the original contract is qualitatively different from all other agreements'. Far

<hr />

[51] Ibid., 104.
[52] Baynes, 'Property Rights and Social Contract', 444.

from being voluntary, it is, as Kant says, an end 'which all *ought* to share'.[53] But Baynes transposes the Kantian quote from its original place in the text to the property argument. As a result, he, too, equates the general will with the social contract. He must then account for the role of original possession in common:

The notion of common ownership serves as a presupposition or condition of the social contract and must itself be viewed as part of the original or innate right which all have simply in virtue of being born on the earth.[54]

Again, there is the slide from external objects as an acquired right to common possession of land as an innate right, though, in contrast to Dodson, Baynes remains closer to Kant in interpreting the presupposition of common possession as resulting from individuals' entrance into the world. But, if original common ownership is a necessary presupposition for the possibility of individual property rights, it is not the contract but common possession which serves as the ultimate ground of such rights. If the contract is an end which all *ought* to share, it is not clear whether this means that the agreement of all is required for the recognition of individual property rights, or whether all are required to agree to such recognition. In the latter case, it may be less misleading not to speak of a contract at all.

In contrast to Dodson, Baynes is aware of the ambiguities that surround the idea of a social contract as an end which all ought to share. The suggestion that the idea of the contract is a moral requirement which is binding *prior to* any actual contractual agreement puts paid to the notion of a contractually incurred obligation. This ambiguity of the idea of the contract as an unconditional moral requirement persists even where its function is construed as applying to public lawmaking *within* civil society rather than as the ground of the political obligation to *enter* civil society. There is no space here to consider the idea of the social contract as a relation between legislator and subjects; interested readers may consult Daniel Weinstock's insightful discussion of the issue. What I want to consider here is why, despite Kant's own omission of the social contract in the context of the property argument, so many interpreters feel compelled to slip it in. The contractual move at this juncture adversely affects Kant's distinctive idea of disjunctive possession in common.

[53] Ibid. (See also *RL*, 6: 315.)
[54] Baynes, 'Property Rights and Social Contract', 441.

While none of the above shows that a contractarian interpretation necessarily rules out the cosmopolitan perspective contained in the idea of original possession in common, it does prevent that perspective from coming into focus. As far as I can see, the neglect of the cosmopolitan perspective is a consequence of two related features about consensual contractarianism. The first of these concerns the general tendency to think of the social contract as a single act of establishment, which is based on voluntary agreement, and whose purpose it is to signal a definitive transition from one condition to the next. The social contract demarcates the boundary between a lawless condition and a lawful condition. This view of civil society as resulting from a single act of establishment persists even when the social contract is thought of as a hypothetical thought experiment rather than as an actual historical event. My reservations here do not concern the abstract quality of the idea of the contract, and its supposedly corrosive effects on organic conceptions of society. My objection is more in line with that raised by Herb and Ludwig. According to them, an exact point of transition from the natural condition to the civil condition is absent in the *Rechtslehre* precisely because of the cosmopolitan perspective contained in the idea of disjunctive original possession in common. It is because original acquisition is unavoidable that a provisional right to such possession does exist in the natural condition, and it is because such a right is only provisional that entrance into the civil condition is obligatory. But such entrance into (cosmopolitan) society cannot happen through a single act of establishment. In so far as subjects' unilateral acts of acquisition in the natural condition *anticipate* the civil condition, the strict dichotomy between 'natural condition' and 'civil condition' disappears and is replaced by the distinction between provisional Right and peremptory Right. Instead of a strict demarcation between provisional Right and peremptory Right, Kant envisages the gradual but steady transformation of provisional into peremptory Right as a process of reform which will eventually encompass the spherical surface of the earth as a whole. The coming together of peoples in the idea of disjunctive possession in common envisages a gradual dismantling of boundaries that hinder the development of relations of Right between subjects:

With Kant's account, the conception of the individual state as the paradigm of civil society and of peremptory mine–thine relations begins to lose its importance. For Kant the individual state constitutes a transitional phase in the development towards global relations of Right. While the individual state appears like a *status civilis* from the confined local perspective, it remains a condition of merely provisional mine and thine from the enlarged global perspective.[55]

The conception of relations of Right as a process of development and reform rather than as a single act of establishment tends to be lost sight of in contractarian interpretations. The second feature of contractarianism as potentially detracting from the global perspective relates to its overwhelming focus on intersubjective consensus as the only important condition for political agreement. At least where it is based on the conviction that no one should be subjected to laws to which they *would not* have consented, the focus on consensus tends to encourage the view that any political arrangement is in principle realisable so long as subjects agree to its desirability. From a global standpoint, such neglect of unavoidable empirical constraints is a luxury which few can afford. That individuals should not be subjected to laws which they would not have consented to is a legitimate political concern, but that there are constraints which no physically embodied finite rational being can avoid (unless this be at the expense of others), and that such constraints impose limits on what can reasonably be demanded or consented to is no less important a fact of political life. Yet the search for consensus often eclipses attention to unavoidable constraints. This privileging of consensus to the neglect of other, equally important considerations may be one reason for the relative failure of contemporary distributive theories when extended to the global context. With regard to the *Rechtslehre*, the contractarian neglect of conditions of unavoidable constraint is indicated in a noticeable failure to thematise Kant's powerful and recurring image of the earth's spherical surface as a limiting condition of consensus.

6 CONCLUSION

Though more could be said about natural law and contractarian interpretations of the general united will, it is time to bring this long chapter to a close. My own reservations against contractarian readings of the *Rechtslehre* focus on their neglect of Kant's cosmopolitan perspective. None the less, none of the considerations advanced in

[55] Herb and Ludwig, 'Naturzustand und Staat', 313–14.

the previous section show that contractarian readings of Kant are impossible in principle, or that the idea of the social contract plays no role at all in the text. What I do hope to have shown is the relative failure of contractarian attempts to replace the idea of the general united will with that of the social contract in the context of Kant's property argument. The fact that contractarians find themselves constrained to attempt this move in the first place attests to the importance, in terms of grounding political obligation, of the property argument. The fact that such moves do not on the whole succeed gives credence to those interpreters who perceive the role of the social contract in the *Rechtslehre* to lie, not in founding political society, but in regulating the process of lawmaking within it. More generally, this chapter has tried to account for the relation between the postulate and the idea of the general united will by focusing on the bridging idea of original possession in common. I have argued that the obscure but distinctive concept of original acquisition as comprising both occupation (apart from one's will) and declaration (of one's will) leads to a reversal of traditional natural law accounts from innate possession in common to property individuation. As an idea of reflective practical reason, disjunctive possession in common represents a coming together of subjects in the recognition of the necessity of working towards the realisation of cosmopolitan Right. The essential claim is that subjects are under obligations of Right in virtue of their capacity to acknowledge and discharge these obligations within the unavoidable constraints of the earth's spherical surface.

CHAPTER 6

The metaphysics of Kant's cosmopolitanism

Since the earth's surface is not unlimited but closed, the concepts of the Right of a state and of a Right of nations lead inevitably to the Idea of a *Right for all nations* (*ius gentium*) or *cosmopolitan Right* (*ius cosmopoliticum*). So if the principle of outer freedom limited by law is lacking in any of these three possible forms of rightful condition, the framework of all others is unavoidably undermined and must finally collapse. (*RL*, 6: 311)

But the rule for this [cosmopolitan] constitution, as a norm for others, cannot be derived from the experience of those who have hitherto found it most to their advantage . . . it certainly requires a metaphysics. Even those who ridicule metaphysics admit its necessity, though carelessly, when they say, for example, as they often do: 'the best constitution is that in which power belongs not to men but to law'. For what can be more metaphysically sublimated than this very Idea?' (*RL*, 6: 355)

I INTRODUCTION

Over the course of the last two chapters I have argued that both the justification of individual property rights and the account of individuals' ensuing obligations of justice are broached by Kant from a cosmopolitan perspective which includes as subjects of Right all those who because they cannot avoid occupying a place on the earth, claim a right to such a place. Chapter 4 emphasised Kant's image of the earth's spherical surface as that unavoidable constraint of nature within the limits of which finite rational beings must resolve conflicts of external freedom and justice. The postulate's special authorisation of unilateral acts of acquisition leads to agents' reflective acknowledgement of the fact that any exercise of external freedom is obligation entailing. Unilateral acts count as provisionally rightful so long as they are committed 'in anticipation of and in preparation for'[1] a condition of peremptory Right. The postulate as *lex permissiva* thus stands to the general united will as a preliminary judgement stands to a determinate judgement. The legitimacy of its provisional authorisation depends on the possibility of a general united will.

Chapter 5 considered and rejected contractarian readings as well as natural law interpretations of the general united will. Contractarian interpretations usually treat the general united will as the product of a contractual agreement to its establishment among affected subjects. Natural law accounts tend to view the general united will as an antecedently given source of legislation whose authority subjects come to acknowledge in the course of their reflections on human nature. I argued that, in fixing on legitimation strategies familiar from the history of political thought, both approaches miss what is most distinctive about Kant's cosmopolitan perspective, i.e. the function of original possession in common as an idea of reason. On both of the two traditional views, the move is from primitive possession in common to the individuation of property and, relatedly, from the pre-civil condition to the division of the earth's spherical surface into distinct, territorially defined, and politically sovereign units. But Kant explicitly emphasises that *original* possession in common should not be confused with *innate* common possession, 'which is temporal and dependent on empirical conditions'.[2] On Kant's account, the move is from unilateral acquisition to *the idea* of original possession in common, and to the obligation to establish relations of Right with all peoples and individuals, wherever they happen to be on the earth's spherical surface. As an idea of reason, original possession in common of the earth's spherical surface – more specifically, *disjunctive* possession in common – represents a condition of cosmopolitan Right we ought to approach, not a pre-civil condition we decide to leave behind.

This inversion of traditional thinking about property rights and political obligation is a reflection of Kant's distinctive metaphysical perspective. In this concluding chapter, I want to return to the issue of metaphysics in political thinking. In so doing, I shall touch again on a number of themes raised in previous chapters – especially the relation between human finitude and practical freedom discussed in chapter 2, and the possibility of moral economic desiring considered

---

[1] *RL*, 6: 257.   [2] *RL*, 6: 262.

in chapter 3. But it is the image of the earth's spherical surface that I want to make the focal point of this concluding chapter. It is a striking and recurring image in the *Rechtslehre* which is yet easily overlooked. This may seem counter-intuitive: if it is striking, it should not be easily overlooked. Much depends, however, on how one interprets the image. It is possible to read it as nothing more than a correct, if banal, statement of the fact that the earth's shape is circular. On this literal interpretation of its meaning, the text's constant reminders about the earth's spherical surface tell us nothing of any great moment at all: they are easily overlooked. Yet what is arresting about the image is not its factual content, but what it manages to communicate beyond its factual content. Of course, such a claim is contentious. To point to 'that which the image communicates beyond its factual content' is not to say anything very precise. I conceded in chapter 1 that there is something irredeemably elusive about metaphysical meaning. This elusiveness reveals itself most markedly at the point of transition from immanent to transcendent metaphysics, i.e. when the task of justifying one's immanent perspective turns out to require commitment to a transcendent perspective. It is at this stage, when metaphysicians appeal to 'ultimate presuppositions', to 'ineffable knowledge', or to 'that which lies the other side of reality', that critics of metaphysics lose their patience and charge metaphysicians with committing something akin to intellectual fraud.

Critics' suspicions are not altogether unwarranted. In so far as a person's transcendent perspective goes beyond the limits of rational argument and general intelligibility requirements, it is difficult to see what its claim to general validity could justifiably be based on. However, it is not evident that every statement which lacks clear propositional content is *therefore* meaningless, or merely illusory. There are dimensions within human experience where the fact that the meaning of a judgement or proposition cannot be clearly expressed is precisely what makes it meaningful and, indeed, shareable.[3] Often it is through the elusiveness of a given image or proposition that its meaning and significance is communicated to us.

---

[3] A possible example may be aesthetic experience. Someone lacks aesthetic judgement, who cannot appreciate the non-propositional form of such a judgement, but who wants to be told exactly how and why, in so many words, a work of art does or does not succeed *as* a work of art. This is not to say, of course, that aesthetic judgements are unreasoned judgements, in the sense that no reasons can be offered for someone's judging a work of art successful. But there is a sense in which an aesthetic judgement exceeds the reasons proffered in its support. In contemplating a work of art, one either grasps its aesthetic qualities, or one does not. This

The elusive character of Kant's image of the earth's spherical surface is a case in point. One *need* not attribute any metaphysical significance to it. One can read it as an unremarkable factual statement about the shape of the earth. But, once one *does* credit the image with a metaphysical resonance that exceeds its factual content, Kant's property argument and his account of political obligation acquire a dimension whose significance remains, ultimately, difficult to express. The argument is no longer *simply* about the most fair or most efficient or most rational way of carving up available space and resources – the bread and butter of many current discussions of distributive justice. It points beyond such tangible distributive questions to something altogether more abstract and more general – to some conception of 'the human condition', for want of a better term, which those more tangible distributive questions and answers are framed by. In what follows, I shall suggest that the metaphysical significance of Kant's image of the earth's spherical surface lies in its articulation of the particular conception of subjects' historical and political responsibility towards the future which grows out of his account of freedom as a shared idea of pure practical reason. Before turning to this task, I want to say something about current receptions of Kant's cosmopolitanism.

2 KANT'S COSMOPOLITANISM TODAY

As I said at the beginning of this book, the last twenty years have witnessed an astonishing revival of interest in Kant as a political philosopher. This trend is overwhelmingly traced back to Rawls' and to Habermas' respective philosophical allegiances to Kant. There is more to Kant as a political philosopher, Rawls said in *A Theory of Justice*, than meets the eye. Since then Kant has become a household name in contemporary political philosophy. At the same time, it would not be correct to say that the return to Kant among liberal philosophers marks a return to Kant's *political* philosophy, strictly speaking. Both Rawls and Habermas initially focused on adapting Kant's ethics to their liberal theories of justice: Rawls in order to formulate his ideal conception of the liberal person, and Habermas

may make aesthetic judgements frustratingly elusive, but that does not render them meaningless in themselves. Something similar is true of Kant's metaphysical image of the earth's spherical surface, whose metaphysical resonances exceed the explanatory reasons one might offer in its behalf.

by reconceiving Kant's universalisability requirements in terms of the linguistic turn pioneered in his discourse ethics. The *Rechtslehre* did not figure in either of these early strategies of philosophical assimilation. Moreover, in contrast to Habermas, whose *Faktizität und Geltung* bears the imprint of its author's growing interest in Kant's late work, Rawls has shown a persistent lack of concern with Kant's political philosophy. This is so especially with regard to Kant's cosmopolitanism. In 'The Law of Peoples'[4] – his only direct contribution to problems of international justice – Rawls explicitly distances his position from that of Kant, and opts for a qualified endorsement of existing international law instead. Although this move has dismayed a number of his supporters,[5] it has meant that the interest in Kant, even among global Rawlsians, is indirect. On the whole, contemporary advocates of a liberal theory of global distributive justice concentrate their efforts on extending domestic liberal principles to the global context, be this in the form of an internationalised difference principle or by devising alternatives to it. It is the Rawlsian liberal conception of justice rather than Kant's that informs and shapes their endeavours in this regard.[6]

Even among those who *are* interested in Kant's cosmopolitanism, the focal text is not the *Rechtslehre* but the better-known essay, *On Perpetual Peace*. Consequently, the *Rechtslehre* has remained the preserve of Kant scholars. Given the many obscurities and distortions which afflict the text, this is hardly surprising. But it is also regrettable. Despite its obscurities, the *Rechtslehre* presents a more systematic exposition of Kant's position than do any of his earlier political essays, including *Perpetual Peace*. None the less, the current

---

[4] John Rawls, 'The Law of Peoples' in Stephen Shute and Susan Hurley, eds., *On Human Rights* (New York, Basic Books, 1993), 41–81.

[5] Most noticeably, Thomas Pogge in *Realising Rawls* (Ithaca, Cornell University Press, 1989), Part III; and more recently in his 'An Egalitarian Law of Peoples', *Philosophy and Public Affairs*, 23 (1994), 195–224. See also Barry, *Theories of Justice*, 183–212; and Thomas McCarthy, 'On the Idea of a Reasonable Law of Peoples' in Bohman and Lutz-Bachmann, eds., *Perpetual Peace*, 201–18. In contrast to Rawls, Habermas has begun to extend his discourse or ethical theory and philosophy of law more systematically into the global arena. See, for example, 'Staatsbürgerschaft und Nationale Identität' in *Faktizität und Geltung* (Appendix), 632–60; 'Kant's Idea of Perpetual Peace with the Benefit of Two Hundred Years' Hindsight' in Bohman and Lutz-Bachmann, eds., *Perpetual Peace*, 113–55; and *Die Postnationale Konstellation. Politische Essays* (Frankfurt, Suhrkamp, 1998). Habermas' approach to global justice remains, however, focused on issues of *European* integration.

[6] See, for example, Barry, *Justice as Impartiality*; Charles Beitz, *Political Theory and International Relations* (Princeton University Press, 1979), Part III; Thomas Pogge, 'Is Kant's *Rechtslehre* Comprehensive?', *The Southern Journal of Philosophy* (Supplement), 36 (1997), 161–88.

reception of Kant's cosmopolitanism is both more sympathetic and more systematic than it used to be. If theorists of international relations used to contrast what they perceived as Kant's 'political idealism' unfavourably with the then dominant creed of political realism, current assessments are decidedly in Kant's favour. This is partly due to changes in the practice of international relations, especially to the demise of the Cold War and the related acceleration of the process of globalisation, whose new problems and opportunities the state-centric perspective of political realism is ill equipped to deal with.[7] But it is also due to a more nuanced approach to Kant's cosmopolitanism. As indicated in the quote at the beginning of this chapter, Kant recognises three distinct though related levels of rightful relation: the 'Right of a state' specifies relations of Right between persons within a state; the 'Right of nations' pertains to relations of Right between states; and 'the Right for all nations' or 'cosmopolitan Right' concerns relations of Right between persons and foreign states. Traditionally, international relations theorists have tended to associate Kant's cosmopolitanism, i.e. his idea of 'world citizens' (*Weltbürger*), with a plea for a world state – a proposal which, as political realists, they were extremely wary of, not least because of the implied loss of state sovereignty.

It is true that in some of his essays Kant does entertain the idea of a world state or world republic. Indeed, Otfried Höffe has shown that even in *Perpetual Peace* Kant dithers between what he calls the 'positive idea of a world republic' and its 'negative surrogate', a free federation of republics.[8] If he finally settles for a federative association rather than a world state, he does so, according to Höffe, out of pragmatic considerations rather than for reasons of principle: states are simply not prepared to give up their sovereignty.[9] None the less, Kant's preferred option remains the idea of a world state.

Although Höffe's conclusion follows from a plausible analysis of the text, it does not rule out alternative readings. Höffe argues, for example, that Kant is mistaken in finding the concept of a world state self-contradictory. Since Kant draws an explicit analogy

---

[7] An informative overview of changing perspectives in current international relations theory was offered by Kenneth Booth in his Cambridge lecture, 'Dare Not to Know: International Relations Theory versus 2045' (University of Cambridge, Global Security Programme, March 1993).

[8] *Perpetual Peace*, 8: 357.

[9] Otfried Höffe, 'Völkerbund oder Weltrepublik?' in Höffe, ed., *Zum Ewigen Frieden*, 109–32.

between individuals and states as two kinds of moral person, the requirement that states cede (part of) their sovereignty in order to submit to a higher authority is no more self-contradictory than the demand that individuals give up their lawless freedom upon entrance into civil society. For Höffe, Kant's 'formal argument' does not succeed, and Kant resorts to pragmatic considerations regarding the non-feasibility of a world state. However, Kent's self-contradiction objection may not apply to states' loss of sovereign power so much as to the loss of their status as free republics. On this reading, the idea of a world state contradicts the reasons for its establishment in so far as a world state's coercive powers undercut the possibility of states *freely* associating with one another. Unification under a world state would be based on the threat of coercion, which is contrary to Kant's claim that a *lasting* global peace must be premised on the rejection in principle of the threat or use of force among states.[10]

Whether Kant rejects the idea of the world state as a matter of principle, or whether he merely postpones its realisation for pragmatic reasons, will no doubt remain a point of some debate.[11] In either case, the fluidity of current global politics, with the break-up of individual states, the semi-federative, regional associations

---

[10] A possible rejoinder to this line of argument is that the threat of coercion at state level also undercuts the possibility of individuals' freely given consent. There is then an inconsistency in what Kant is prepared to countenance at the intrastate level and what he rejects at the interstate level. There are two possible replies to this rejoinder. One is to say that a federation of free republics does not rule out the establishment of a legal and institutional structure with the capacity of exerting *some* pressure in the form of sanctions on recalcitrant members, even though that structure would not amount to the fully coercive state powers. The argument against a world state is that it leaves individual states no option but to be subsumed under it, given that a world state would encompass the spherical surface of the earth. By contrast, a state can abstain from joining a federation of free republics, or can forfeit its membership. The same holds for individuals, who can refuse to join civil society or can forfeit their citizenship as a result of some wrong-doing. The second line of reply would suggest that, while there is an analogy between individuals and states as moral persons, there is also a disanalogy. Free republics are more mature in their freedom than are individuals in the pre-civil condition. Hence, free republics are capable of non-coercive association to an extent to which individuals are not *yet* capable. According to this line of interpretation, the three levels of Right present ever higher or more sophisticated levels of free association. Cosmopolitan Right – the free association among individual citizens of different states – then constitutes the most mature form of rightful relation.

[11] Some global thinkers are critical of Kant's abandoning the idea of a world state. See, for example, David Held, *Democracy and the Global Order: From the Modern State to Cosmopolitan Government* (Cambridge, Polity Press, 1995). Habermas makes a similar case for transcending what he regards as the historically contingent connection between national identity and democracy in 'Staatsbürgerschaft und Nationale Identität'. For a defence of Kant's arguments against a world government, see Thomas Mertens, 'Cosmopolitanism and Citizenship: Kant Against Habermas', *The European Journal of Philosophy*, 4 (1996), 328–47.

between some states, and the vastly increased number of non-state
global agents has meant that Kant's three levels of Right are
attracting considerable practical interest today. Of particular
concern in the present context is the status of cosmopolitan Right.
Once Kant is no longer read as unambiguously endorsing the idea of
a world state, the status of the world citizen must change as well.
Within a world state, global citizenship would presumably replace
the current function of citizenship within individual states. The
world state would constitute a vastly enlarged version of our current
conception of individual statehood. But, in the absence of a world
state, world citizenship cannot fulfil the role conventionally assigned
to citizens of states. Instead, global citizens are citizens without a
world state who retain their citizenship in relation to the individual
states of which they are members. The idea of the world citizen as a
citizen *without* a world state has gained increasing currency among
discussants of global justice, be this in the context of a European
federation, of the international human rights debate, or that of
international law in general.[12] This has encouraged the extension of
Kant's own more restricted view of the content of cosmopolitan
Right. The *Rechtslehre* defines cosmopolitan Right, i.e. the rights of
individuals against a foreign state, as 'the right of hospitality'.[13]
Individuals have a right not to be maltreated or disturbed in their
possessions when on foreign territory. More generally, they have the
right to 'offer to engage in commerce with one another', and the
right 'to *try* to establish community with all, and to this end, to visit
all regions of the earth'.[14] However, the right to hospitality is not the
right of a guest to stay as long as they please, nor is it a right to
citizenship of that state. The right to hospitality is strictly limited to
a right to temporary abode and the right to being dealt with justly
for the duration of one's stay.

Despite its restricted content and economic orientation, Kant's
concept of cosmopolitan Right should not be interpreted as an

---

[12] Cf. Habermas, 'Staatsbürgerschaft und Nationale Identität'; Axel Honneth, 'Is Univers-
alism a Moral Trap? The Presuppositions and Limits of a Politics of Human Rights', and
James Bohman, 'The Public Spheres of the World Citizen', both in Bohmann and Lutz-
Bachmann, eds., *Perpetual Peace*, 155–78 and 179–200. A good discussion of the impact of
Kant's conception of cosmopolitan Right on traditional international law can be found in
Daniele Archibugi, 'Models of International Organization in Perpetual Peace Projects',
Review of International Studies, 18 (1992), 295–317. See also Reinhard Brandt, 'Vom
Weltbürgerrecht' in Höffe, ed., *Zum Ewigen Frieden*, 133–49.
[13] *RL*, 6: 352.   [14] *RL*, 6: 353.

apology for the free market ambitions of an emerging entrepre-
neurial class.[15] This would be to miss the status of cosmopolitan
Right as a 'strict right', i.e. as externally enforceable, hence as
subject to institutionalisation and as entailing obligations on the part
of the rights holder. The corollary of the right to try to establish
commercial relations with others is that the formal conditions for
choice of others must not be violated: no one has a right to *force*
commercial relations on others where they are not willing to enter
into such relations. Likewise, the right not to be maltreated by the
subjects or government of a foreign state entails the corresponding
obligation to respect the laws of the land and not to attack subjects
or the government of the state or community in question. Kant's
condemnation of colonialism,[16] for example, is a consequence of his
affirmation of cosmopolitan Right: the right to hospitality is not a
right to invasion and domination of foreign lands and peoples under
the pretext of spreading civilisation. If one does accept individuals'
cosmopolitan rights to hospitality as a strict right, its corresponding
obligations and requirements for institutionalised law enforcement
impose constraints on international agency that are more stringent
than the meagre content of cosmopolitan Right may initially
suggest.[17]

This is not to deny that Kant's conception of cosmopolitan Right
requires *some* extension under current conditions of globalisation. As
already indicated, this is now often done by means of linking Kant's
cosmopolitan Right to current human rights provisions. None the
less, overburdening cosmopolitan Right in terms of its content will
affect the structure of global justice as envisaged by Kant. Here it
does make a difference whether one conceives of cosmopolitan
Right in relation to the idea of a world state, or in relation to a
federation of free republics. If cosmopolitan Right constitutes the
rights of individuals against foreign states, fewer of the current list of
human rights will fall under the category of cosmopolitan Right than
if one thinks of the latter as specifying the rights of world citizens
within a world state. On the federal interpretation, refugee rights,

---

[15] This is a line of criticism developed by Richard Saage in 'Besitzindividualistische
Perspektiven der Politischen Theorie Kants', *Neue Politische Literatur*, 2 (1972), 168–93.
[16] *RL*, 6: 354.
[17] For an elaboration of Kant's cosmopolitan Right in terms of the corresponding perfect
obligations of non-deceit and non-coercion see Onora O'Neill, 'Transnational Justice' in
David Held, ed., *Political Theory Today* (Cambridge, Polity Press, 1991), 276–304.

including asylum rights and the right not to be imprisoned and/or tortured by the host state, would fall under cosmopolitan Right. On the other hand, the federal interpretation could not countenance the intervention by one state into the internal affairs of another on behalf of citizens' human rights, say, to political and religious freedom. Instead, peaceful negotiations among states with regard to what one might call intrastate human rights would have to be conducted at the level of the Right of nations. On the world state reading, there would obviously be no need to distinguish between human rights that apply at the intrastate level and those that apply at the cosmopolitan level. How one interprets the implications of Kant's cosmopolitanism for current global politics thus depends on how one interprets the structure of rightful relations as envisaged by Kant.[18]

There are two general observations that I want to make regarding the return to Kant in current discussions of global justice. The first pertains to the overwhelmingly empirical orientation of these discussions. By this I mean the tendency to treat Kant's articles of peace in *Perpetual Peace*, for example, as straightforward policy recommendations that compare favourably or unfavourably (as the case may be) with provisions in current international law. To a large extent, such an approach is justified. After all, the style of *Perpetual Peace* imitates the form of a legal document that sets out proposals for the progressive reform of actual relations between states. One test for assessing the current relevance of Kant's cosmopolitanism is to compare his recommendations with provisions in existing international law and practice. The question is whether Kant should be read *exclusively* at the level of policy recommendation. In many respects, the most interesting sections of *Perpetual Peace* are the two supplements, appended to the main text, on the relation between nature and morality in political agency. Since Kant's teleology of nature strikes many readers as obtuse, these sections are often dismissed as inaccessible or as historically outdated, and as irrelevant from a practitioner's point of view. Yet it is in the supplements that Kant sets out the philosophical perspective that informs his proposal for political reform. Since he deems his own approach a major departure from the views of the 'sorry comforters' of traditional

---

[18] Compare, for example, Charles Covell, *Kant and the Law of Peace*, 168–87; Otfried Höffe,'Die Vereinten Nationen im Lichte Kants' in Höffe, ed., *Zum Ewigen Frieden*, 245–72; Mulholland, *Kant's System of Rights*, 348–72.

international law,[19] neglect of Kant's distinctive philosophical outlook can encourage the conflation of his cosmopolitan aims and intentions with superficially similar but differently grounded policy proposals in traditional international law or in current proposals for international reform.

My second point concerns the content of cosmopolitan Right. Curiously, the aspect of cosmopolitan Right which one does not find much discussed is its economic content – i.e. individuals' right to try to establish commercial relations with others. Again, this omission may be due to the fact that it seems so evidently restricted – contemporary problems of globalisation encompass much more than economic relations between individuals. Moreover, the focus on economic relations may seem morally suspect to modern liberal sentiments: there seems to be something morally reprehensible about fixing the content of cosmopolitan Right exclusively in terms of *economic* rights and opportunities. On the other hand, such reservations encourage one to overlook systematic connections between Kant's three forms of Right. One answer to the question, 'why focus on economic rights in relation to cosmopolitan Right?' is that they are consisted with mine–thine relations between individuals *within* states. We saw in earlier chapters that the concept of Right is concerned only with the form of external relations between agents with regard to the choice of each: relations of external mine and yours are restricted to the category of *acquired* rights. This means that the restriction of cosmopolitan Right to global mine–thine relations mirrors parallel restrictions at the level of mine–thine relations between individuals within states. In expanding on these two general comments, the next section examines Kant's metaphysics of freedom in the context of cosmopolitan Right. Section 4 considers some of the practical implications of these metaphysical presuppositions, especially with regard to the problem of global economic agency.

3 FREEDOM AND FINITUDE IN KANT'S COSMOPOLITANISM

According to Kant, 'if the principle of outer freedom limited by law is lacking in any of [the] three possible forms of rightful condition, the framework of all the others is unavoidably undermined and must

---

[19] *Perpetual Peace*, 8: 355 (Kant mentions by name Grotius, Pufendorf, and Vattel).

finally collapse'.[20] In uniting all the places on its surface, the earth's spherical shape ensures that the effects of the choices and actions of one person are felt by all others, no matter where on earth nature has placed them. Now, just as it is possible to read over Kant's image of the earth's spherical surface as a true but banal statement of fact, so it is possible to interpret in purely literal terms the reference to agent responsibility contained in that image. The implications of a literal interpretation in this case are, however, rather more dramatic. Taken literally, the claim that each and every one of our choices and actions affects the possible choices and actions even of remote others is a blatant exaggeration. It amounts to a claim of agent responsibility that far exceeds any individual's actual moral capacities. A literal reading of the supposed moral implications of the earth's spherical surface invites the sort of complaint advanced by Ralph Walker in connection with Kant's metaphysics of freedom. Walker thinks that Kant's conception of noumenal causality (i.e. causality of action which is independent of the causality of nature) entails that, 'I can be blamed for the First World War, and for the Lisbon earthquake that so appalled Voltaire. Gandhi is no less guilty than Amin of the atrocities of the Ugandan dictator.'[21] This objection equates Kant's account of noumenal causality with the thesis' conception in the third antinomy of an uncaused first cause. It depicts the free agent as someone with the (noumenal) capacity to stand *outside* the conditions of time and space from where they can initiate any chain of causality of their choice *in* time and space. In so far as such an uncaused first cause is capable of initiating any spatio-temporal chain of causality of its choice, and in so far as all the subsequent chains of cause and effect can be traced back to the initiating cause, noumenal causality entails responsibility for all the effects generated in time and space as a consequence of that initial, timeless choice. On Walker's construal, my noumenal freedom entails my responsibility for the whole history of human actions.

One might suspect something similar to be going on in Kant's remark about the global effects of subjects' choices and actions. If my choices and actions really do affect the possible choices and actions of everyone else on the globe, this implies that I can be held responsible for all the consequences of my actions – intended as well

[20] *RL*, 6: 311.
[21] Ralph Walker, *Kant. The Arguments of the Philosophers* (London, Routledge, 1979), 149.

as unintended, foreseeable as well as unforeseeable. But it is doubtful whether a literal interpretation either of noumenal causality or of agent responsibility offers useful insight into Kant's metaphysics of freedom. I argued in chapter 2 that Kant's concern is to *reconcile* the causality of nature with the idea of freedom, not to set the one up above the other, as Walker's interpretation of noumenal causality implies. Moreover, although the third antinomy conceives of noumenal causality *in analogy with* the thesis' idea of an uncaused first cause outside the conditions of space and time, Kant does not equate the two: in fact, he rejects the position of the thesis in this regard. Finite rational agents' capacity to begin a causal chain *in* time and space is grounded in their capacity for deliberative spontaneity and reflective judgement. Noumenal causality refers to the deliberative spontaneity of the will, not to a free being's supersensible causal powers. A literal interpretation of noumenal causality, which equates it with the rationalist conception of an uncaused first cause, does not contribute to an understanding of freedom as an idea of *reason*. Similarly, it would not be illuminating merely to point out that the idea of our global responsibility for all the effects of our choices and actions is so absurd that Kant could not possibly have meant what he said. Of course a literal interpretation leads to absurd conclusions. But, if he cannot mean what he says literally, what does he mean?

One clue lies in Kant's conception of freedom as a shared idea of practical reason – indeed, of freedom as a *task* of practical reason.[22] In a metaphorical sense, Kant does mean what he says when he claims that as the 'initiating causes' (*in* time and space) of our actions we are responsible for each of their many and disparate effects, including those we cannot immediately foresee and those we never come to know of at all. In so far as they can be traced back to ourselves as the initiators of these actions, we are indirectly the initiators of all the effects they cause.[23] To this extent, Walker is right to point to the close connection in Kant between the idea of freedom and the notion of historical responsibility. None the less, the fact that as initiator of my actions I am responsible for all the effects they produce does not itself entail that there is anything I can do to prevent or manipulate all of these effects. I may be responsible for

---

[22] Cf. chapter 2.
[23] By 'all the effects' I here mean to include not only the *immediate* effects of one's actions, but also the effects of those effects, and so on.

having initiated all of the effects of my actions together with my actions. But this need not mean that I could, if I so chose, control or prevent the occurrence of all those effects. Nor, therefore, am I necessarily culpable with regard to all those effects. The seeming absurdity of Kant's proposal that we are responsible for all the effects of our actions lies in a tendency to leap from responsibility for action immediately to culpability with regard to effect. Yet there often are intermediate steps that intervene between responsibility for action and culpability for effect. One such intervening step is the actions of others and the effects *they* produce. Where the effects of my actions intertwine with the effects of others' actions, it is not only myself who is responsible for the outcomes and for the further effects they produce. Instead, we are each of us responsible for some part of these outcomes. However, who of us is responsible for precisely which part of a given outcome will be difficult if not impossible to ascertain.

A second intervening variable between agent responsibility and agent culpability are the constraints of nature. It may well be that, in so far as I am responsible for my actions, I am also responsible for the effects they produce. But I am not necessarily responsible for the conditions and circumstances within which I initiate my actions and which play a contributory role to their effects. The circumstances of my actions may be beyond my control; they may be brute givens within which I am constrained to act as best I can. The problem of unilateral acquisition discussed in chapter 4 illustrates this. I may be aware of the fact that, given unavoidable empirical constraints, my unilateral choices affect the possible choices of others. But this does not mean that I can avoid these consequences by ceasing to act altogether. Nor does it mean that I can change all the circumstances within which I am constrained to choose and act. I am not, for example, responsible for the earth's circular shape, nor can I do anything to change it.

Still, it would be a mistake to conclude that, because I can do nothing about all the effects of my actions, I need not acknowledge the general principle of agent responsibility that accompanies all my actions. Nothing in recognising that I can do nothing about it by myself prevents me from considering whether *we* might not be able to do something about it together. Walker's complaint about nou-menal causality fails to consider Kant's conception of freedom as a *shared* idea of practical reason. According to Walker, not only am *I* responsible for the whole of human history, but so is Voltaire, so is

Gandhi, and so are you, and you, and you. We are each of us individually responsible for the whole course of human history. That *is* absurd. Yet it never occurs to Walker that we might share responsibility for the course of human history. This is why he finds it more difficult than Kant to entertain the thought of our historical responsibility. Walker would be more justified in his suspicions if Kant's account of freedom as a shared idea of reason amounted to a collectivist conception of freedom such as Rousseau's *volonté générale*, for example, or if he did think of the notion of historical responsibility as amounting to individuals' personal responsibility for others' past actions. However, I emphasised in chapter 5 that Kant conceives our historical responsibility in terms of our contribution to the *future*. This orientation towards the future is especially evident in a number of his earlier essays, which link the notion of historical responsibility to the hope for moral progress.[24] But it is implicit also in the *Rechtslehre*'s explication of the three forms of Right as the *progressive* institutionalisation of global relations of Right. Again, shared responsibility need not mean collective responsibility, and shared historical responsibility need not consist in the collective execution of a particular political program, or in the charting of humanity's imagined or postulated historical destiny. In many ways, Kant's account of our shared historical responsibility renders *less* daunting and *more* tangible the notion of individual responsibility than do collectivist conceptions of freedom and responsibility. Kant's well-known preference for political reform over revolution suggests that he conceives of humanity's possible historical progress as an ongoing and relatively open-ended process consisting of individual contributions made over time by generations of people who set an example that others can follow.[25] This is why the Kantian notion of shared historical responsibility is probably best exemplified in figures like Martin Luther King, or Mother Theresa, or the individual contributor to Amnesty International, all of whom acknowledge their duty to humanity, but whose individual contributions to historical progress take different forms as well as different levels and degrees of engagement.

---

[24] In this regard, see especially, 'An Answer to the Question: What is Enlightenment?', and 'On the Common Saying, "This may be true in Theory but it does not apply in Practice"', both in Hans Reiss, ed., *Kant's Political Writings* (Cambridge University Press, 1970).

[25] Kant's defence of individuals' possible contributions to humanity's moral progress is especially eloquent in his reply to Moses Mendelssohn in *Theory and Practice*, 8: 307–13.

But, if Kant's understanding of shared responsibility remains individualist rather than collectivist, and if his idea of historical progress is open-ended rather than predetermined, what assurance is there that individual contributors *will* regard their individual contributions as part of a shared task or enterprise? This is where Kant's image of the earth's spherical surface becomes important. Earlier on I suggested that the image of the earth's spherical surface, which unites all the places on its surface, expresses a metaphysical insight into the human condition. A less elusive way of putting it is to say that the image constitutes a formal representation of Kant's categorial framework in relation to the problem of Right. Recall some of the features of Körner's general notion of a categorial framework outlined in chapter 1. In addition to experiential relevance and intersubjective validity, a categorial framework requires the integration of a person's theoretically supreme principles with their practically supreme principles. Chapter 2 applied this general scheme to Kant's metaphysics of freedom, casting the concept of causality as his theoretically supreme principle and the idea of freedom as his practically supreme principle. The task of the third antinomy was to integrate the two principles by way of reconciling the practical and the theoretical perspectives with one another. The principle of causality and the idea of freedom taken together form the building blocks of what Körner would call Kant's immanent metaphysics. But any proposed categorial framework is itself subject to the demand for justification: immanent metaphysics pushes towards transcendent metaphysics.

I said that Kant restricts the idea of the noumenal realm to a negative idea – it affords us a metaphysical perspective, reflection on which is unavoidable for us, but with regard to which we are not entitled to raise any knowledge claims. As a negative idea, the transcendent perspective both denies that truth claims made at the immanent level can be treated as absolute, and abstains from issuing such absolute truth claims itself. Kant's transcendent perspective thus constitutes an acknowledgement of human finitude. The transcendent perspective marks the limits of human knowledge: it 'denies knowledge in order to make room for faith'.[26]

References to human finitude are common in transcendent metaphysical thinking. Historically, they tend to carry negative connota-

[26] *CPR*, bxxx.

tions, especially where they are contrasted with the notion of a perfectly rational, supreme being. Human finitude is understood as a privation the overwhelming experience of which is of something disabling: our fate is ultimately in the hands of some higher, more powerful king.[27] Interestingly, Kant depicts human finitude not as a privation but as enabling. In *CPR*, recognition and acknowledgement of the limits of human knowledge lead to his thesis of the primacy of practical reason: the reference to faith is not to acquiescence in religious beliefs or to other-worldly contemplation, but to practical faith as a requirement of possible agency.[28] This is especially evident in Kant's admission in the third antinomy that we can have no theoretical proof of transcendental freedom. Given the limits of human knowledge, we cannot *know* whether or not we are free. But this is no cause for dismay. Our lack of knowledge of freedom at the theoretical level warrants our faith in practical freedom. If we knew that we are not free, there would be no point in acting at all, i.e. there would be no point in deliberating about action, in deciding on a particular cause of action, or in taking necessary steps towards achieving the end of the action, and so on. Instead, we should simply let the causality of nature proceed through us on its inevitable path. Whatever happened would have been bound to happen, and whatever we did we would have been bound to do. If, on the other hand, we knew that we are free, our actions would seem arbitrary to us. We would be able to undo our actions just as easily as we initially committed them. Since they could be undone as easily as they were done, our actions would require no commitment to their consequences on our part – in fact, none of our actions would be of much

---

[27] For a recent treatment of finitude as a metaphysical concept see Adrian Moore, *Points of View* (Oxford University Press, 1997), 253–79. Moore lists what he calls his 'three [metaphysical] principles' as (i) 'we are finite'; (ii) 'we are conscious of being finite'; and (iii) 'we aspire to be infinite'. The aspiration to be infinite implies the judgement of finitude as a privation. Moore goes on to distinguish between the craving for infinitude, and the aspiration to be infinite. The *craving* for infinitude is natural and ineliminable, i.e. it is part of the human condition. The *aspiration* to be infinite, by contrast, is 'bad', even 'evil': it gives rise to the attempt to say something about which we cannot say anything. The aspiration to be infinite amounts to a form of intellectual hubris and leads to talking nonsense. Moore attributes to Kant's transcendental idealism the *aspiration* to be infinite. For reasons I cannot go into here, I think this mistaken, though Moore may have been led to this conclusion because of his neglect of Kant's thesis of the primacy of practical reason. Moore is right in characterising his first two metaphysical principles as broadly Kantian. But the third principle should be replaced with (iii) 'we are capable of acknowledging our finitude'.

[28] A good account of the connection between hope and finitude in Kant can be found in Philip Stratton-Lake, 'Reason, Appropriateness and Hope: Sketch of a Kantian Account of Finite Rationality', *International Journal of Philosophical Studies*, 1 (1993), 61–80.

consequence to us. If we knew either that we were free, or that we were not free, there would be no room for practical faith. We would either be confronted with the certainty that everything we do we were bound to do, or would have to contend with the arbitrariness of actions which we are equally free to do as to undo, and the doing or not doing of which would not bind us in any way whatsoever. Yet to act is to commit oneself, and it is to commit oneself of one's own accord. Such freely willed commitment would not be possible in the knowledge either of our freedom or of our unfreedom. Faith in practical freedom is not a second best to theoretical knowledge of transcendental freedom. Our lack of knowledge at the theoretical level makes possible the idea of freedom at the practical level; i.e. it makes it possible for us to commit ourselves to a chosen course of action of whose consequences we cannot be certain, but commitment to which enables us to take responsibility for them.

In preceding chapters, I interpreted Kant's construction of the concept of Right in the *Rechtslehre* as an illustration of the capacity of pure practical reason to 'frame an order of ideas of its own'. The antinomy of Right initially presented us with a situation that admitted of no theoretical solution. We cannot say why the earth happens to be round, or why beings with a claim to freedom happen to coexist on its surface: 'theoretical principles of Right get lost in the intelligible [*verlieren sich im Intelligiblen*]'.[29] In the face of such ignorance, the *lex permissiva*, as a postulate of pure *practical* reason, resolved the conflict by taking a radical step into the dark: it authorised acts of unilateral acquisition that patently amount to a violation of the universal principle of Right. But taking this preliminary step committed us to taking a further step towards a possible permanent solution. The special authorisation of the postulate together with the effects of this authorisation enabled us to form the idea of a general united will, and to proceed from there to the establishment of public relations of Right. In the end, we still do not know why the earth is round and inhabited by beings with a claim to freedom. None the less, we have discovered a practical solution to the problem of Right and have passed from a state of lawless freedom to a condition of Right. It is the systematic unity of his thinking that gives Kant's political outlook its normative appeal. The image of the earth's spherical surface is construed with reference to

[29] *RL*, 6: 252.

two highly abstract metaphysical categories – the concept of causality and the idea of freedom – whose reconciliation with each other
is made possible through the notion of human finitude as a
practically enabling condition of human existence. This highly
abstract and highly evocative metaphysical framework accounts for
the normative appeal of Kant's cosmopolitan thought today.

   Still, one might detect an inconsistency in my claim that the
normative appeal of Kant's cosmopolitanism lies in its underlying
metaphysical framework, and my conflicting observation in section 2
that current theories of global justice adopt an overwhelmingly
empirical approach to Kant's political philosophy. Contrary to my
present contention, the trend seems to be to avoid the metaphysics
of Kant's cosmopolitanism and to focus on the more tangible
implications of his thought for global policy-making instead. None
the less, I believe that my claim can be upheld. One source of the
appeal of Kant's image of the earth's spherical surface is the
apparent simplicity of its conception. As such, it provides a basic
framework for thinking about global justice that is instantly recognisable and that remains flexible in the face of complex empirical
detail. Three features in particular are worth emphasising. The first
concerns the immediate visual impact of the image of the earth's
spherical surface. Everyone is capable of representing to themselves
the earth's spherical shape and the world population's spread across
it. Even if the details of individual representations differ, the image
itself possesses general credibility: its experiential relevance makes it
widely accessible. The second feature has to do with Kant's forward-
looking and open-ended conception of human history. With its two
principal components – the constraints of nature and the claims to
freedom – the image of the earth's spherical surface provides a guide
to thinking about the prospects for global justice that is not over-
determined with regard to particular content. It sets parameters for
theoretical exploration without directly prescribing any particular
practical solution. The framework's flexibility is attested, for
example, by the different possible interpretations of the relation
between the three forms of Right briefly discussed in section 2
above. Closely related is the third feature, i.e. the notion of a shared
but non-collectivist historical and political responsibility. The
abstract but widely accessible image of the earth's spherical surface
provides a theoretical context which enables different contributors to
explore and discuss issues of globalisation and of global justice from

a common perspective without in so doing fixing a predetermined policy-making agenda. General accessibility, flexibility, and discursiveness thus constitute three aspects of Kant's image of the earth's spherical surface which render it attractive even to those who are not necessarily acquainted with the details of Kant's metaphysical framework, and who approach his writings from a predominantly empirical and practice-oriented perspective.

4 COSMOPOLITANISM AND ECONOMIC AGENCY

I have just suggested that a principal appeal of Kant's metaphysical framework for global thinking today lies in the general parameters it identifies for thought and action within the constraints of which the integration is possible of otherwise disparate aspects of global justice. The importance of such parameters should not be underestimated: in contrast to domestic political theory, the absence of a shared conceptual and normative framework is frequently noted as an obstacle to cohesive global theorising.[30] None the less, critics may object that, whatever its possible value as a general guide to global thinking, Kant's image of the earth's spherical surface and his notion of individuals' shared historical responsibility remain far too abstract to provide real practical advice with respect to particular global policy concerns. Whatever its metaphysical connotations, today's global context is simply too complex for any notion of shared individual responsibility to have much purchase on actual global practices.

Current cosmopolitans usually favour an institutional approach over an agent-centred approach. In his 'Cosmopolitanism and Sovereignty', for example, Thomas Pogge distinguishes between what he calls 'institutional cosmopolitanism' and 'moral cosmopolitanism'. While Pogge does not think the agent-centred perspective of moral cosmopolitanism incompatible with the institutional approach, he none the less believes that the latter must be given priority over the former if one is to avoid overburdening individuals with unrealistic global obligations.[31] Like Walker, so Pogge tends to

---

[30] John Dunn, 'The Future of Political Philosophy in the West' in *Rethinking Modern Political Theory* (Cambridge University Press, 1985), 171–90; see also Dunn, 'Reconceiving the Content and Character of Modern Political Community' in *Interpreting Political Responsibility* (Cambridge University Press, 1990), 193–215.

[31] Thomas Pogge, 'Cosmopolitanism and Sovereignty', *Ethics*, 103 (1992), 48–75.

interpret the notion of individuals' global responsibility in a literal sense, i.e. as demanding individuals' direct and personal involvement in solving a host of given global problems. Conversely, Pogge expects that just global institutions can regulate and constrain individuals' actions in the desired manner: the justness of institutional design ensures the justness of individuals' actions. Pogge thus follows Rawls in characterising justice as a 'virtue of social institutions'.[32]

The institutional approach recommends itself most obviously in relation to global *economic* institutions. Global economic relations constitute a paradigm example of the powerlessness of individuals' action intentions in the face of their actions' unintended systemic effects. It is not surprising that many of those concerned about the deep inequalities that characterise the current structure of global economic relations turn to Rawls' difference principle as a possible model for institutionalised global distributive justice. Not only is the difference principle institutional in design, it also combines considerations of social justice with considerations of economic efficiency. Instead of a radical egalitarianism, Rawls advocates a scheme of moderate economic inequalities designed to benefit worse-off and better-off members of society alike. The principle that no (further) economic gains are to accrue to the better-off unless such gains work to the advantage of the worse-off ensures the provision of a social safety net to the worse-off without jeopardising the economic incentive structure necessary for encouraging increased economic productivity among the more talented and better-off. Instead of appealing to agent responsibility directly, Rawls' difference principle thus seeks to manipulate the *structure* of economic relations and their effects on individuals. Subsequent global adaptations of the Rawlsian difference principle have ranged from relatively straightforward extensions of its rationale to the global context, to modified versions of it in terms of a global income tax, or a global resource tax.[33]

At the level of implementation, any practically feasible theory of global distributive justice no doubt must include a theory of political and economic institutions. At that level, institutional cosmopolitanism may well have priority over moral cosmopolitanism. However, this does not mean that the agent-centred approach has

---

[32] This now widely accepted characterisation of liberal justice as concerned with the basic structure of society and therefore as a virtue of social institutions was originally advanced by Rawls in *A Theory of Justice*.
[33] For relevant sources, see some of the works listed under footnotes 5 and 6, above.

no contribution to make at the level of theoretical conception and institutional design. Social institutions do regulate and co-ordinate political and economic relations between individuals. But the very individuals whose actions are to be regulated and constrained by them set up these institutions. Social institutions thus tend to reflect the normative assumptions and expectations of those who set them up. Just as it is true, therefore, that institutions can regulate and constrain the actions of those who acknowledge their authority and legitimacy, so it is also the case that institutions – even just ones – can be abused by agents who for some reason or other do not acknowledge their authority and/or legitimacy. It is not the case, then, that individual agents' intentions and expectations, or their actual behaviour, do not impact upon the structure of global economic and political relations. The complexities of the global context, and the undoubted need for global institutions, should not detract from the related and equally important consideration of agent responsibility.

Agents' appreciation of their responsibilities as agents assumes special importance in the economic context, where the well-known dictum that the market follows its own laws all but invites the abnegation of agent responsibility. From the agent-centred perspective, the appropriateness of economic institutions can be assessed both with regard to the normative assumptions and expectations about individual agency they reflect, and with reference to the empirical context within which they operate. To put the same point differently, how one conceives the morality of individual economic agency, on the one hand, and the empirical context of such agency, on the other, makes a difference to what one regards as appropriate economic institutions and distributive schemes. If, for example, one were to assess the difference principle from an agent-centred perspective, one would focus on its explicit reliance on the motivational assumptions of 'standard [liberal] economic theory'.[34] On these assumptions, individuals are rationally self-interested maximisers of their own advantage who prefer more primary social goods rather than less, and whose willingness to co-operate with one another in the social venture depends on how much they expect to

---

[34] Rawls, *A Theory of Justice*, 142–60. Although the later Rawls has, as we have seen, substantially modified his erstwhile conception of the moral person, the initial description appears to have stuck with regard to the difference principle. Indeed Rawls has commented very little on the difference principle since its elaboration in *A Theory of Justice*.

get out of it.[35] What is more, the difference principle reflects standard economic assumptions not only about individuals' motivational incentives, but also about the context of economic agency. Thus, it is difficult to avoid the suspicion that a distributive scheme of well-ordered economic inequalities from which everyone is meant to benefit depends, at least implicitly, on the assumption of potentially unlimited economic growth. Rationally self-interested maximisers of their own advantage will participate in the co-operative scheme only for as long as they *continue* to get something out of it, and what they want to get out of it, according to Rawls, are more primary social goods rather than less. This implies that the social product must continue to increase over time.[36] The difference principle assumes an empirical context most evocatively captured in Locke's famous image of 'all the world as America',[37] where vast and uncultivated tracts of land, that are mostly unpopulated, leave 'as much and as good' for everyone, no matter how much each acquires for himself.

From an agent-centred perspective, the difference principle's underlying motivational assumptions and empirical presuppositions are contentious when applied to the current global context. There are plenty of regions in the world where the prospects of even

[35] It is a moot point whether 'standard liberal economic theory' is the same as 'classical liberal theory'. The classic defence of the latter remains Lionel Robbins' 'The Nature and Significance of Economic Science' (an abridged version is reprinted in Daniel Hausman, ed., *The Philosophy of Economics*, Cambridge University Press, second edition 1994, 83–110). According to Robbins, the psychologistic assumptions that attach to the characterisation of economic agents as self-interested maximisers of their desires are not a feature of classical economics but of welfare economics. Such psychologistic assumptions have no place in Robbins' account of economics as a science, where economic rationality consists simply in the most efficient choice between alternative uses of the same means under conditions of limited time and moderate scarcity.

[36] This claim is controversial: the difference principle need not require conditions of unlimited economic growth. Although Rawls conceives of the difference principle as a Pareto improvement which ensures that everyone will be made better-off, he also suggest that a well-ordered society is perfectly just when further improvements of the position of the worst-off are impossible, implying that the limits of economic growth will then have been reached. However, I am not sure how persuasive this is either in terms of the logic of Rawls' motivational assumptions or in terms of empirical evidence. If individuals are rational maximisers of their own advantage who want more rather than fewer social primary goods, economic stagnation is likely to have destabilising social and political effects. It is precisely for this reason that Western liberal democracies find themselves under pressure to keep their domestic economies on a stable growth curve, often at the expense of those who live beyond their territorial borders. For a sustained and persuasive critique of Rawls' motivational assumptions in relation to the difference principle see Brian Barry, *Theories of Justice*, 213–54.

[37] John Locke, *Second Treatise of Government*, chapter 5.

moderate economic growth are doubtful if not non-existent, be this
for ecological reasons, or social and political reasons, or both.
Moreover, the problem of uneven global economic prospects and its
implications for standard economic theory are recognised by an
increasing minority of economists and non-economists alike. From
the present perspective, proposed revisions regarding the standard
conceptions of economic rationality and of economic desiring are
the most interesting. Critics wary of the celebrated parsimony of
standard economic models of individual agency have long expressed
reservations about the morally impoverished conception of 'rational
economic man' encouraged by such theoretical parsimony.[38] It is a
common move among these critics to urge a broadening of the
motivational bases of agent rationality and of economic agency by
taking into account agents' other-regarding interests as well as their
non-economic self-regarding interests in economic computations.
Such proposals usually accept, at least in part, standard economic
theory's view of economic desire-formation and desire-pursuit: they
recommend the inclusion of *additional* moral considerations and
incentives, which function as extraneous constraints on economic
desiring.[39] More recently, the economic conception of desire-formation itself has come under scrutiny, most notably in Thomas
Scanlon's book, *What We Owe to Each Other*.[40] In his book, Scanlon
repudiates his former attachment to a psychologistic account of
desire-formation in favour of an account that emphasises the
cognitive components of desire-formation. According to Scanlon,
'desires are commonly understood in philosophical discussions to be
psychological states which play two fundamental roles: on the one
hand they are supposed to be motivationally efficacious, on the other

---

[38] See, for example, James Griffin, 'Against the Taste Model' in Jon Elster and John Roemer,
   eds., *Interpersonal Comparisons of Well-Being* (Cambridge University Press, 1991), 45–69; Albert
   Hirschman, 'Against Parsimony', *Economics and Philosophy*, 1 (1985), 7–21; Jennifer Roback
   Morse, 'Who is Rational Economic Man?' in Ellen Frankel Paul, Fred Miller Jr., and Jeffrey
   Paul, eds., *Self-Interest* (Cambridge University Press, 1997), 179–206; Amartya Sen, *On Ethics
   and Economics* (Oxford, Basil Blackwell, 1987); Hamish Stuart, 'A Critique of Instrumental
   Reason in Economics', *Economics and Philosophy*, 11 (1995), 57–83.
[39] Extraneous, that is, to desire-formation and desire-pursuit, though not extraneous to agents
   themselves. The plea for a more inclusive conception of agents' motivational incentives is
   reminiscent of the Humian model of the countervailing passions. According to the latter, an
   agent's calm passions counterbalance their hot passions, thus maintaining an equilibrium
   between the two. Similarly, the inclusion of additional moral and non-economic incentives
   within agents' motivational sets is meant to function as a break on the otherwise unbridled
   pursuit of economic desires.
[40] Thomas Scanlon, *What We Owe to Each Other*, especially Part I, 17–146.

hand they are supposed to be normatively significant'.[41] Against this view Scanlon counters that desires are not *sources* of motivation, but *consequences* of reasons for action: 'having what is generally called a desire involves a tendency to see something as a reason [for action]'.[42] This is because 'our practical thinking takes place within a framework of maxims, and is concerned with adopting, inter-preting, and modifying these principles, as well as with deciding, within the framework they provide, whether we have sufficient reasons for acting in particular ways'.[43]

I mention Scanlon's revised account because of its partial overlap with the conception of reasoned economic desiring I attributed to Kant in chapter 3. I there emphasised two aspects of Kant's cognitive account of desire-formation and desire-pursuit. The first was a rational being's imaginative capacities in relation to desire-for-mation, including not only its capacity to create new desires where none existed before, but also its capacity to think up solutions to, or at any rate strategies around, problems of economic scarcity and the constraints of economic choice. The second, and, in the present context, more relevant aspect concerned the morality of economic desiring. A rational being's reflective awareness of itself as a desiring subject presupposes, according to Kant, the subject's cognitive and evaluative capacities with regard to desire-formation. Reasoned economic desires are desires whose content takes into account the possible effects on others of the agent's pursuit of those desires. To that extent, the notion of moral constraint is built into the account of self-legislated economic desire-formation and desire-pursuit.

What makes the Kantian conception of self-legislated economic desiring of relevance to current global economic conditions is its conjunction of individual freedom of choice and unavoidable em-pirical constraints. On the one hand, economic desiring, i.e. indi-viduals' desires for and pursuit of material objects of their choice, has prima facie legitimacy, if only because it is unavoidable for existential reasons. On the other hand, this does not licence unconstrained maximisation of desires and choices. Cognitively desiring agents ought to take cognisance of the fact that their choices and actions unavoidably impose costs on others, and they ought to constrain the formation and pursuit of their desires accordingly. In so far as they *ought* to take cognisance of these constraints, individual

[41] Ibid., 37.   [42] Ibid., 39.   [43] Ibid., 52.

agents are presumed capable of doing so, and capable of adjusting their actions accordingly.

The implications for [economic] agency of a metaphysical framework that starts from the image of the earth's spherical surface and of the unity of all the places on its surface thus differ significantly from those which begin with a view of all the world as America, and as providing virtually unlimited space and opportunity for individuals to choose and act independently of each other, unconstrained by shared empirical conditions for choice. This is not to deny that the Kantian account of economic desiring, and of global political agency more generally cannot be transported from the *Rechtslehre* to the current global context without further exploration and modifications. The *Rechtslehre* does function at a very high level of abstraction and generality, and Kant's remarks about (economic) agency remain sketchy and suggestive rather than conclusive. None the less, the growing recognition of the inadequacy of conventional assumptions about economic and political agency under rapidly changing global circumstances suggests that the *Rechtslehre* may not be the worst place from which to begin exploring alternative approaches to these problems.

5 CONCLUSION

There is a widespread presumption against metaphysics among contemporary political philosophers, according to whom the practical relevance of political thinking depends on remaining on the surface, philosophically. Throughout this book I have tried to argue against this presumption. In this concluding chapter, I have indicated two levels at which metaphysical thinking can contribute to our understanding of global politics and the problems of global justice. At a more abstract and general level, metaphysics can provide a conceptual and normative framework – call it a categorial framework – that offers a guiding idea of what it is one is trying to think oneself towards, whether this takes form in the idea of a world state, or a federation of states, or some other alternative still. A metaphysical framework orders and integrates seemingly disparate aspects of globalisation and global justice into a cohesive moral and political project. Apart from this abstract function, metaphysics also informs our thinking at a more directly practical level. I have used economic agency as an example, partly because it seems to me one of the most urgent philosophical issues in global thinking today, and partly because Kant's insights in this regard are perhaps the least expected. Kant's account of economic desiring and agency is tentative and exploratory, requiring theoretical development and refinement. Even so, it is evident that the metaphysical presuppositions which inform Kant's account differ significantly from the assumptions of classical and contemporary liberal thinking. To the extent to which this is the case, it is difficult to deny metaphysics its legitimate place in political thinking.

More generally, this book has pursued two aims. First, I have tried to show that, its many textual difficulties and philosophical obscurities notwithstanding, the *Rechtslehre* offers a sustained political argument which is exciting in itself and which repays patient scrutiny and interpretation. Second, I have tried to show that the practical relevance of the *Rechtslehre* to political thinking today may lie less in its proximity to the basic assumptions and expectations of contemporary liberalism than in its distance from them. If I do not think this regrettable, this is not because the achievements of contemporary liberalism are negligible. But the liberal tradition today is at a historical juncture at which it can either turn inward and continue along settled ideas and convictions, or it can turn outward and re-examine the continued adequacy of some of these convictions under rapidly changing global conditions. The latter approach does require that one *cease* to remain on the surface philosophically. Kant's willingness to do this explains, I think, much of his distance from contemporary liberal thinking.

Select bibliography

Allison, Henry, *Kant's Transcendental Idealism*, New Haven, Yale University Press, 1983.
Kant's Theory of Freedom, Cambridge University Press, 1990.
Idealism and Freedom, Cambridge University Press, 1996.
Arendt, Hannah, *Lectures on Kant's Political Philosophy*, Ronald Beiner, ed., University of Chicago Press, 1982.
Ayer, A. J., *Language, Truth, and Logic*, Harmondsworth, Penguin Books, 1971.
Baron, Marcia, 'Freedom, Frailty, and Impurity', *Inquiry*, 36 (1993), 431–41.
Barry, Brian, *Theories of Justice*, volume 1, London, Harvester and Wheatsheaf, 1989.
Justice as Impartiality, Oxford University Press, 1995.
Baumgarten, Peter, 'Zwei Seiten der Kantschen Begründung von Eigentum und Staat', *Kantstudien*, 85 (1994), 147–59.
Baynes, Kenneth, 'Kant on Property Rights and the Social Contract', *The Monist*, 72 (1989), 433–53.
The Normative Grounds of Social Criticism: Kant, Rawls, and Habermas, New York, State University of New York Press, 1992.
Baynes, Kenneth, James Bohman, and Thomas McCarthy, eds., *Philosophy: End or Transformation?*, Chicago, MIT Press, 1987.
Beck, Lewis White, *Studies in the Philosophy of Kant*, New York, Bobbs Merrill, 1965.
Kant Studies Today, Illinois, La Salle, 1969.
Essays on Kant and Hume, New Haven, Yale University Press, 1978.
Beitz, Charles, *Political Theory and International Relations*, Princeton University Press, 1979.
Bennett, Jonathan, *Kant's Dialectic*, Cambridge University Press, 1974.
Blum, Lawrence, *Friendship, Altruism, and Morality*, London, Routledge & Kegan Paul, 1980.
Böckerstette, Heinrich, *Aporien der Freiheit und ihre Aufklärung durch Kant*, Stuttgart, Frommann-Holzboog, 1984.
Bohman, James and Matthias Lutz-Bachmann, eds., *Perpetual Peace. Essays on Kant's Cosmopolitan Ideal*, Cambridge, MA, MIT Press, 1997.
Booth, Kenneth, 'Dare Not to Know: International Relations Theory

versus 2045', Public Lecture, Global Security Programme, University of Cambridge, UK, March 1993.

Brandt, R. B., *A Theory of the Right and the Good*, Oxford, Clarendon Press, 1979.

Brandt, Reinhardt, *Eigentumstheorien von Grotius bis Kant*, Stuttgart, Frommann-Holzboog, 1974.

'Das Erlaubnisgesetz, oder: Vernunft und Geschichte in Kants Rechtslehre' in Brandt, ed., *Rechtsphilosophie der Aufklärung*, Berlin, de Gruyter, 1982, 233–75.

'Die Politische Institution bei Kant' in Gerhard Göhler, ed., *Politische Institutionen im Gesellschaftlichem Umbruch*, Opladen, Westdeutscher Verlag, 1990, 335–57.

'Zum Weltbürgerrecht' in Otfried Höffe, ed., *Zum Ewigen Frieden*, Berlin, Akademie Verlag, 1995, 133–49.

Bubner, Rüdiger, 'Metaphysik und Erfahrung' in *Antike Themen und Ihre Verwandlung*, Frankfurt, Suhrkamp, 1992, 134–51.

Buchda, Gerhard, 'Das Privatrecht Immanuel Kants. Ein Beitrag zur Geschichte und zum System des Naturrechts.' Unpublished dissertation, Jena, 1929.

Buchdahl, Gerd, 'The Kantian "Dynamic of Reason" with Special Reference to the Place of Causality in Kant's System' in Lewis White Beck, ed., *Kant Studies Today*, Illinois, La Salle, 1969.

Buckle, Steven, *Natural Law and the Theory of Property: Grotius to Hume*, Oxford, Clarendon Press, 1991.

Carnap, Rudolf, 'The Elimination of Metaphysics through Logical Analysis of Language' in A. J. Ayer, ed., *Logical Positivism*, New York, Free Press, 1959, 60–80.

Christman, John, *The Myth of Property: Towards an Egalitarian Theory of Ownership*, Oxford University Press, 1994.

Collingwood, R. G., *An Essay on Metaphysics*, Oxford, 1940.

Covell, Charles, *Kant and the Law of Peace*, London, Macmillan, 1998.

Davidson, Donald, *Essays on Truth and Interpretation*, Oxford, Clarendon Press, 1984.

Deggau, Hans-Georg, *Die Aporien der Rechtslehre Kants*, Stuttgart, Frommann-Holzboog, 1983.

Dews, Peter, 'Modernity, Self-Consciousness, and the Scope of Philosophy: Jürgen Habermas and Dieter Henrich in Debate' in *The Limits of Disenchantment*, London, Verso Press, 1996, 169–93.

Dodson, Kevin, 'Autonomy and Authority in Kants Rechtslehre', *Political Theory*, 25 (1997), 93–111.

Dreier, Ralf, 'Zur Einheit der Praktischen Philosophie Kants', *Perspektiven der Philosophie*, 5 (1979), 5–37.

Dunn, John, *Rethinking Modern Political Theory*, Cambridge University Press, 1985.

Interpreting Political Responsibility, Cambridge University Press, 1990.

Dunn, John, ed., *The Economics Limits to Modern Politics*, Cambridge University Press, 1992.
Dworkin, Ronald, 'The Original Position' in Norman Daniels, ed., *Reading Rawls*, Oxford, Basil Blackwell, 1975, 16–52.
Engstrom, Stephen, 'Allison on Rational Agency', *Inquiry*, 36 (1993), 410–18.
'Kant's Conception of Practical Wisdom', *Kantstudien*, 88 (1997), 16–43.
Feinberg, Joel, 'Rawls and Intuitionism' in Norman Daniels, ed., *Reading Rawls*, Oxford, Basil Blackwell, 1975, 108–23.
Flikschuh, Katrin, 'On Kant's Rechtslehre', *The European Journal of Philosophy*, 5 (1997), 50–73.
'Freedom and Constraint in Kant's Metaphysical Elements of Justice', *History of Political Thought*, 20 (1999), 250–71.
'Kantian Desires: Freedom of Choice and Action in Kant's *Rechtslehre*' in Mark Timmons, ed., *New Essays on Kant's Metaphysics of Morals*, Oxford University Press, forthcoming.
Forster, Michael, 'On the Very Idea of Denying the Existence of Radically Different Conceptual Schemes', *Inquiry*, 41 (1998), 133–86.
Friedman, Michael, 'Causal Laws and the Foundations of Natural Science' in Paul Guyer, ed., *The Cambridge Companion to Kant*, Cambridge University Press, 1992, 161–99.
Gaus, Gerald, *Justificatory Liberalism*, Oxford University Press, 1996.
Gauthier, David, *Morals by Agreement*, Oxford, Clarendon Press, 1986.
Gregor, Mary, *The Laws of Freedom*, Oxford, Basil Blackwell, 1963.
'Kant's Theory of Property', *The Review of Metaphysics*, 41 (1988), 757–87.
'Kant on "Natural Rights"' in Ronald Beiner and William James Booth, eds., *Kant and Political Philosophy: The Contemporary Legacy*, New Haven, Yale University Press, 1993, 50–75.
Griffin, James, 'Against the Taste Model' in Jon Elster and John Roemer, eds., *Interpersonal Comparisons of Well-Being*, Cambridge University Press, 1991, 45–69.
Grotius, Hugo, *The Rights of War and Peace* trans. Francis Kelsey, Oxford, Clarendon Press, 1925.
Guyer, Paul, *Kant and the Claims of Knowledge*, Cambridge University Press, 1987.
'Justice and Morality', *The Southern Journal of Philosophy* (Supplement), 36 (1997), 21–8.
Habermas, Jürgen, *Faktizität und Geltung*, Frankfurt, Suhrkamp, 1992.
Nachmetaphysisches Denken, Frankfurt, Suhrkamp, 1992.
'Kant's Idea of Perpetual Peace with the Benefit of Two Hundred Years' Hindsight' in James Bohman and Matthias Lutz-Bachmann, eds., *Perpetual Peace. Essays on Kant's Cosmopolitan Ideal*, Cambridge, MA, MIT Press, 1997, 113–55.
Die Postnationale Konstellation. Politische Essays, Frankfurt, Suhrkamp, 1998.
Hampton, Jean, 'Should Political Philosophy be done without Metaphysics?', *Ethics*, 99 (1989), 794–814.

Harper, William and Ralph Meerbote, eds., *Kant on Causality, Freedom and Objectivity*, Minnesota University Press, 1984.

Hausman, Daniel, ed., *The Philosophy of Economics*, Cambridge University Press, 1994.

Heimsoeth, Heinz, 'Zum Kosmologischen Ursprung der Kantischen Freiheitsantinomie', *Kantstudien*, 57 (1966), 206–29.

Held, David, *Democracy and the Global Order: From the Modern State to Cosmopolitan Government*, Cambridge, Polity Press, 1995.

Henrich, Dieter, 'Die Grundstruktur der Modernen Philosophie' in *Selbstverhältnisse*, Stuttgart, Reclam, 1982.

'Was ist Metaphysik – was Moderne? Zwölf Thesen Gegen Habermas' in *Konzepte*, Frankfurt, Suhrkamp, 1987, 11–39.

'The Origins of the Theory of the Subject' in Axel Honneth, ed., *Philosophical Interventions in the Unfinished Project of Modernity*, Cambridge, MA, MIT Press, 1992.

Henrich, Dieter and Rolf-Peter Horstmann, eds., *Metaphysik nach Kant?*, Stuttgart, Klett, 1987.

Herb, Karlfriedrich and Bernd Ludwig, 'Naturzustand, Eigentum und Staat', *Kantstudien*, 83 (1994), 283–316.

Herman, Barbara, *The Practice of Moral Judgment*, Cambridge, MA, Harvard University Press, 1993.

Hill, Thomas, 'Kant's Argument for the Rationality of Moral Conduct', *Pacific Philosophical Quarterly*, 66 (1985), 3–23.

Dignity and Practical Reason in Kant's Moral Theory, Ithaca, Cornell University Press, 1992.

Hirschman, Albert, *The Passions and the Interests*, Princeton University Press, 1977.

'Against Parsimony', *Economics and Philosophy*, 1 (1985), 7–21.

Hobbes, Thomas, *Leviathan* (1651), the Penguin English Library, Harmondsworth, 1982.

Höffe, Otfried, 'Kant's Principle of Justice as Categorical Imperative of Law' in Y. Yovel, ed., *Kant's Practical Philosophy Reconsidered*, Amsterdam, Kluwer Academic Publishers, 1989, 149–67.

'"Even a Nation of Devils Needs a State": The Dilemma of Natural Justice' in Howard Williams, ed., *Kant's Political Philosophy*, Cardiff, University of Wales Press, 1992, 120–42.

Kategorische Rechtsprinzipien, Frankfurt, Suhrkamp, 1994.

Höffe, Otfried, ed., *Zum Ewigen Frieden*, Berlin, Akademie Verlag, 1995.

Honneth, Axel, 'Is Universalism a Moral Trap?' in James Bohman and Matthias Lutz-Bachmann, eds., *Perpetual Peace. Essays on Kant's Cosmopolitan Ideal*, Cambridge, MA, MIT Press, 1997, 155–78.

Hont, Istvan, 'Free trade and the economomic limits to national politics: neo-Machiavellian political economy reconsidered' in John Dunn, ed., *The Economic Limits to Modern Politics*, Cambride University Press, 1992, 14–120.

Hume, David, *An Enquiry Concerning Human Understanding*, ed. L. A. Selby Bigge, 3rd revised edition, Oxford, Clarendon Press, 1975.

Kersting, Wolfgang, 'Freiheit und Intelligibler Besitz: Kants Lehre vom Synthetischen Rechtssatz a priori', *Zeitschrift für Philosophie*, 6 (1981), 31–51. *Wohlgeordnete Freiheit* (revised paperback edition), Frankfurt, Suhrkamp, 1993. Originally published in hardback in 1984.

Körner, Stephan, *Metaphysics. Its Structure and Function*, Cambridge University Press, 1984.

Korsgaard, Christine, *Creating the Kingdom of Ends*, Cambridge University Press, 1996. 'Taking the Law into Our Own Hands: Kant on the Right to Revolution' in Andrews Reath, Barbara Herman and Christine Korsgaard, eds., *Reclaiming the History of Ethics. Essays for John Rawls*, Cambridge University Press, 1997, 297–328.

Küsters, Gerd-Walter, *Kants Rechtsphilosophie. Erträge der Forschung*, Darmstadt, Wissenschaftliche Buchgesellschaft Darmstadt, 1988.

Langton, Rae, *Kantian Humility. Our Ignorance of Things in Themselves*, Oxford University Press, 1998.

Larmore, Charles, *Patterns of Moral Complexity*, Cambridge University Press, 1987.

Loux, Michael, *Metaphysics: A Contemporary Introduction*, London, Routledge, 1998.

Ludwig, Bernd, 'Der Platz des rechtlichen Postulats der praktischen Vernunft innerhalb der Paragraphen 1–6 der Kantischen Rechtslehre' in Reinhard Brandt, ed., *Rechtsphilosophie der Aufklärung*, Berlin, de Gruyter, 1982, 218–32. *Kants Rechtslehre. Ein Analytischer Kommentar*, Hamburg, Felix Meiner Verlag, 1988. 'Will die Nature unwiderstehlich die Republik?', *Kantstudien*, 88 (1997), 218–36.

Ludwig, Bernd and Karlfriedrich Herb, 'Naturzustand, Eigentum und Staat', *Kantstudien*, 83 (1994), 283–316.

MacIntyre, Alasdair, *After Virtue*, London, Duckworth, 1981.

Mandt, Hella, 'Historisch–politische Traditionselemente im politischen Denken Kants' in Zwi Batscha, ed., *Materialien zu Kants Rechtsphilosophie*, Frankfurt, Suhrkamp, 1976, 292–330.

Mauss, Ingeborg, 'Zur Theorie der Institutionalisierung bei Kant' in Gerhard Göhler, ed., *Politische Institutionen im Gesellschaftlichem Umbruch*, Opladen, Westdeutscher Verlag, 1990, 358–85.

Mautner, Thomas, 'Kant's Metaphysics of Morals: A Note on the Text', *Kantstudien*, 73 (1981), 356–9.

McCarthy, Thomas, 'On the Idea of a Reasonable Law of Peoples' in James Bohman and Matthias Lutz-Bachmann, eds., *Perpetual Peace. Essays on Kant's Cosmopolitan Ideal*, Cambridge, MA, MIT Press, 1997, 201–18.

Meerbote, Ralf, 'Kant on the Nondeterminate Character of Human Actions' in William Harper and Ralf Meerbote, eds., *Kant on Causality, Freedom and Objectivity*, Minnesota University Press, 1984, 138–63.

Mendus, Susan, 'The Practical and the Pathological', *The Journal of Value Inquiry*, 19 (1985), 235–43.

Mertens, Thomas, 'Cosmopolitanism and Citizenship: Kant Against Habermas', *The European Journal of Philosophy*, 4 (1996), 328–47.

Moore, Adrian, *Points of View*, Oxford University Press, 1997.

Mulhall, Stephen and Adam Swift, *Liberals and Communitarians*, Oxford, Basil Blackwell, 1992.

Mulholland, Leslie, *Kant's System of Rights*, New York, Columbia University Press, 1990.

Münzer, Stephen, *A Theory of Property*, Cambridge University Press, 1990.

Murphy, Jeffrie, *Kant: The Philosophy of Right*, London, Macmillan, 1970.

Nagel, Thomas, 'Rawls on Justice' in Norman Daniels, ed., *Reading Rawls*, Oxford, Basil Blackwell, 1975, 1–15.

The View from Nowhere, Oxford University Press, 1986.

'Moral Conflict and Political Legitimacy', *Philosophy and Public Affairs*, 16 (1987), 215–40.

Nozick, Robert, *Anarchy, State and Utopia*, Oxford, Basil Blackwell, 1974.

Nussbaum, Martha, 'Kant and Cosmopolitanism' in James Bohman and Matthias Lutz-Bachmann, eds., *Perpetual Peace. Essays on Kant's Cosmopolitan Ideal*, Cambridge, MA, MIT Press, 1997, 25–58.

Oberer, Hariolf, 'Zur Frühgeschichte der Kantischen Rechtslehre', *Kantstudien*, 64 (1973), 88–101.

O'Neill, Onora, 'Abstraction, Idealization, and Ideology' in J. D. G. Evans, ed., *Moral Philosophy and Contemporary Problems*, Cambridge University Press, 1988, 55–69.

Constructions of Reason, Cambridge University Press, 1989.

'Transnational Justice' in David Held, ed., *Political Theory Today*, Cambridge, Polity Press, 1991, 276–304.

'Vindicating Reason' in Paul Guyer, ed., *The Cambridge Companion to Kant*, Cambridge University Press, 1992, 280–308.

Towards Justice and Virtue, Cambridge University Press, 1996.

'Political Liberalism and Public Reason: A Critical Notice of John Rawls, *Political Liberalism*', *The Philosophical Review*, 106 (1997), 411–28.

Bounds of Justice (forthcoming) Cambridge University Press.

Pocock, J. G. A., *The Machiavellian Moment*, Princeton University Press, 1975.

Pogge, Thomas, *Realising Rawls*, Ithaca, Cornell University Press, 1989.

'Cosmopolitanism and Sovereignty', *Ethics*, 103 (1992), 48–75.

'An Egalitarian Law of Peoples', *Philosophy and Public Affairs*, 23 (1994), 195–224.

'Is Kant's *Rechtslehre* Comprehensive?', *The Southern Journal of Philosophy* (Supplement), 36 (1997), 161–88.

Potter, Nelson, 'Does Kant have two Concepts of Freedom?' in G. Funke and I. Kopper, eds., *Akten des Vierten Internationalen Kant Kongresses*, Berlin, de Gruyter, 1974, 590–6.

Prauss, Gerald, *Kant über Freiheit als Autonomie*, Frankfurt, Vittorio Klostermann, 1983.

Rawls, John, *A Theory of Justice*, Oxford University Press, 1973.

'Kantian Constructivism in Moral Theory', *The Journal of Philosophy*, 77 (1980), 515–72.

'Justice as Fairness, Political not Metaphysical', *Philosophy and Public Affairs*, 14 (1985), 223–51.

'The Idea of an Overlapping Consensus', *Oxford Journal of Legal Studies*, 7 (1987), 1–25.

Political Liberalism, New York, Columbia University Press, 1993.

'The Law of Peoples' in Stephen Shute and Susan Hurley, eds., *On Human Rights*, New York, Basic Books, 1993, 41–81.

Raz, Joseph, *The Morality of Freedom*, Oxford, Clarendon Press, 1986.

'Facing Diversity: The Idea of Epistemic Abstinence', *Philosophy and Public Affairs*, 19 (1990), 3–46.

Reath, Andrews, 'Intelligible Character and the Reciprocity Thesis', *Inquiry*, 36 (1993), 419–31.

'Hedonism, Heteronomy, and Kant's Principle of Happiness', *Pacific Philosophical Quarterly*, 70 (1989), 42–72.

'Kant's Theory of Moral Sensibility', *Kantstudien*, 80 (1989), 284–301.

Riley, Patrick, 'On Kant as the Most Adequate of the Social Contract Theorists', *Political Theory*, 1 (1973), 450–71.

Ritter, Christian, *Der Rechtsgedanke Kants nach den frühen Quellen*, Frankfurt, 1971.

Roback Morse, Jennifer, 'Who is Rational Economic Man?' in Ellen Frankel, Fred Miller Jr., and Jeffrey Paul, eds., *Self-Interest*, Cambridge University Press, 1997, 179–206.

Rosen, Allen, *Kant's Theory of Justice*, Ithaca, Cornell University Press, 1993.

Rosen, Michael, 'Kant's Anti-Determinism', *Proceedings of the Aristotelian Society*, 89 (1989), 125–41.

Röttges, Heinz, 'Kants Auflösung der Freiheitsantinomie', *Kantstudien*, 65 (1974), 33–49.

Saage, Richard, 'Besitzindividualistische Perspektiven der Politischen Theorie Kants', *Neue Politische Literatur*, 2 (1972), 168–93.

Sandel, Michael, *Liberalism and the Limits of Justice*, Cambridge University Press, 1982.

Scanlon, Thomas, *What We Owe to Each Other*, Cambridge, MA, Belknap Press of Harvard University Press, 1998.

Seidler, Victor, *Kant, Respect, and Injustice. The Limits of Liberal Moral Theory*, London, Routledge & Kegan Paul, 1986.

Sen, Amartya, *On Ethics and Economics*, Oxford, Basil Blackwell, 1987.

Shell, Susan, 'Kant's Theory of Property', *Political Theory*, 6 (1978), 75–90.

Sprigge, T. L. S., 'Has Speculative Metaphysics a Future?', *The Monist*, 81 (1998), 513–33.

Steiner, Hillel, *An Essay on Rights*, Oxford, Basil Blackwell, 1994.

Stekeler-Weithofer, Pirmin, 'Wille und Willkür bei Kant', *Kantstudien*, 81 (1990), 304–19.

Stratton-Lake, Philip, 'Reason, Appropriateness, and Hope: Sketch of a

Kantian Account of Finite Rationality', *International Journal of Philosophical Studies*, 1 (1993), 61–80.

Strawson, P. F., *Individuals*, London, Routledge, 1959.

The Bounds of Sense, London, Routledge, 1966.

Freedom and Resentment and Other Essays, London, Methuen Publishers, 1974.

Stuart, Hamish, 'A Critique of Instrumental Reason in Economics', *Economics and Philosophy*, 11 (1995), 57–83.

Sullivan, Roger, 'The Influence of Kant's Anthropology on his Moral Theory', *Review of Metaphysics*, 49 (1995), 77–94.

Taylor, Charles, *Philosophy and the Human Sciences. Philosophical Papers*, vol. 2, Cambridge University Press, 1985.

Sources of the Self, Cambridge, MA, Harvard University Press, 1989.

Tenbruck, Friedrich, 'Über eine notwendige Textkorrektur in Kant's "Metaphysik der Sitten" ', *Archiv für Philosophie*, 3 (1949), 216–20.

Tuck, Richard, *Natural Rights Theories*, Cambridge University Press, 1979.

Vossenkuhl, Wilhelm, 'Von der aüßersten Grenze aller praktischen Philosophie' in Otfried Höffe, ed., *Grundlegung zur Metaphysik der Sitten. Ein Kooperativer Kommentar*, Frankfurt, Vittorio Klostermann, 1993, 299–313.

Waldron, Jeremy, *The Right to Private Property*, Oxford, Clarendon Press, 1988.

Walker, Ralph, *Kant. The Arguments of Philosophers*, London, Routledge, 1979.

Walsh, W. H., *Metaphysics*, New York, Harbinger Books, 1963.

Kant's Criticism of Metaphysics, Edinburgh University Press, 1975.

Walzer, Michael, *Spheres of Justice. A Defence of Pluralism and Equality*, Oxford, Basil Blackwell, 1983.

Thick and Thin. Moral Argument at Home and Abroad, Notre Dame, Indiana, University of Notre Dame Press, 1994.

Weinstock, Daniel, 'Natural Law and Public Reason in Kant's Political Philosophy', *Canadian Journal of Philosophy*, 26 (1996), 389–411.

Westphal, 'Do Kant's Principles of Justice Justify Property or Usufruct?', *Jahrbuch für Recht und Ethik*, 5 (1997), 142–94.

Wheeler, Samuel, 'Natural Body Rights as Property Rights, *Noûs*, 14 (1980), 171–93.

Williams, Howard, *Kant's Political Philosophy*, Oxford University Press, 1983.

Wood, Allen, 'Kant's Compatibilism' in Wood, ed., *Self and Nature in the Philosophy of Kant*, Ithaca, Cornell University Press, 1984, 73–101.

'The Final Form of Kant's Practical Philosophy', *The Southern Journal of Philosophy* (Supplement), 36 (1997), 1–20.

Yaffe, Gideon, 'Freedom, Natural Necessity and the Categorical Imperative', *Kantstudien*, 86 (1995), 446–58.

Index

Lightning Source UK Ltd.
Milton Keynes UK
UKOW031622230113

9 780521 073028